A View From The West

A VIEW FROM THE WEST
THE NEOLITHIC OF THE IRISH SEA ZONE

Vicki Cummings

OXBOW BOOKS
Oxford and Oakville

Published by
Oxbow Books, Oxford, UK

© Oxbow Books and Vicki Cummings, 2009

ISBN 978-1-84217-362-6

This book is available direct from:

Oxbow Books, Oxford, UK
(Phone: 01865-241249; Fax: 01865-794449)

and

The David Brown Book Company
PO Box 511, Oakville, CT 06779, USA
(Phone: 860-945-9329; Fax: 860-945-9468)

or from our website

www.oxbowbooks.com

A CIP record of this book is available from the British Library

Library of Congress Cataloging-in-Publication Data

Cummings, Vicki, Ph. D.
  A view from the west : the neolithic of the Irish Sea zone / Vicki Cummings.
      p. cm.
  Includes bibliographical references and index.
  ISBN 978-1-84217-362-6
  1. Neolithic Period--Irish Sea. 2. Megalithic monuments--Irish Sea. 3. Irish
Sea--Antiquities. I. Title.
  GN774.22.I73C86 2009
  916.3'37--dc22
                                        2009034116

Printed and bound in Great Britain by
Hobbs the Printers Ltd, Totton, Hampshire

Contents

List of figures

Acknowledgements

This book has been a long time in the writing. The very beginnings of this project really started with my doctoral research which I began back in 1997, and which considered the chambered tombs of west Wales and south-west Scotland. Once that was complete, I then embarked on a one year project which looked at all of the chambered tombs in Wales: a volume resulted, co-authored with Alasdair Whittle, my PhD supervisor and collaborator on the Welsh megaliths project (Cummings and Whittle 2004). The British Academy then kindly funded further fieldwork, this time enabling me to look at all the Clyde cairns in western Scotland, and to get a start at visiting the eastern Irish sequence. Subsequently, I was supported through a Leverhulme Early Career Fellowship at the University of Central Lancashire, where I completed the eastern Irish fieldwork and did most of the research presented here. Finally, the volume was written up in between lecturing at UCLan. So my first thanks are to everyone who has supported this research: Cardiff University, the Board of Celtic Studies, the British Academy, the Leverhulme Trust and the University of Central Lancashire.

I have received an enormous amount of help from lots of people during the fieldwork conducted for this volume, which was extremely time-consuming but also really good fun. Meli Pannett read the maps, supplied tea and biscuits and braved the rain around the western Scottish islands. Steve Trick kindly accompanied me around many of the sites in both northern and southern Ireland, and offered accommodation in Belfast. Bob Johnston helped with a preliminary visit to northern Ireland and also kindly helped with accommodation in Belfast. All the B&B owners who looked after me on various trips around the Irish Sea zone are also thanked, as are the farmers who kindly let me visit sites on their land.

A big thank you must go to the University of Central Lancashire, in particular my colleagues Rick Peterson, Dave Robinson, Jennie Robinson and Mick Wysocki, but also to Nigel Simmons who started archaeology at UCLan and helped arrange my Leverhulme fellowship. A particular thanks must go to Rick and Julia, for their kindness, patience and especially fine buns. I have benefited enormously from discussions on various aspects of this work with Richard Bradley, Hannah Cobb, Chris Fowler, Bob Johnston, Lesley McFadyen, Meli Pannett, Rick Peterson, Bronwen Price, Dave Robinson, Gary Robinson, Alison Sheridan, Julian Thomas and Steve Trick and I must make a particular note of thanks to Alasdair Whittle for his ongoing help and support. Claire Litt at Oxbow books showed unwavering patience, and draft chapters were kindly read by Hannah Cobb, Chris Fowler, Oli Harris and Rick Peterson. Finally, this book is for Richard, my husband, with all my love.

1

An introduction

Introduction

In this first chapter I introduce the study area, the Irish Sea zone, and detail how I have defined this area in this volume. This is not the first study to consider the Irish Sea zone and as such I also summarise previous studies of this area. I outline what this volume hopes to achieve with a consideration of the Neolithic of the Irish Sea zone, in particular a study of the landscape settings of the chambered tombs of this area, which is the focus of the volume.

Introducing the study area

To start off with, I would like to discuss why I have chosen the Irish Sea zone as a study area and then describe how I defined this study area. I should state from the start that the aim of this volume is not to suggest that the Irish Sea zone is, or ever was, a bounded entity. I am also not trying to claim that there was such a thing as a shared Irish Sea cultural identity. However, all archaeological studies require boundaries of some kind, this study being no exception and there are a number of justifications for choosing the Irish Sea zone as an area of study. Firstly, apart from early culture-historical approaches (e.g. Piggott 1954), there has been a tendency in the past (although with some key exceptions: see below) to study either side of Irish Sea separately. Scholars have tended to study either one side or the other of the Irish Sea zone. This is in part due to long-standing and excellent traditions of the study of prehistoric remains in Ireland, England, Scotland and Wales, which reflect modern political administrative boundaries (e.g. the survey work done by the Royal Commissions). However, the Irish Sea area has clearly been important for many thousands of years. From more recent periods, there is clear evidence of interaction (see various papers in Bowen 1970).

In this study I have used a number of criteria to help define the Irish Sea zone. Partly, the Irish Sea zone is simply those parts of the landscape which border onto the sea. There is of course an issue here: how 'close' does one have to be in order to be considered in the study? I did not want to use a simple cut-off distance (e.g. sites must be a maximum of 10km from the sea in order to be included) as sometimes this approach is too rigid and does not take into account the evidence. A good example of how such an approach is inappropriate is in relation to the setting of chambered tombs. There are examples where a site is located on the coastline, but the sea is not visible. At such a site you could argue that the main focus is not the sea, although quite clearly this site should be included in the study. However, sites located much further away from the sea often have spectacular views with wide vistas of the sea. At these sites you could suggest that the sea was a major focus of the landscape setting of the site, but if they fell outside a random cut-off distance then they would not be included. A more contextual definition was therefore required.

However, the precise definition of the study area was ultimately defined by the chambered tombs themselves. The focus of this volume is, after all, on the early Neolithic chambered tombs, and there is a clear and distinctive distribution of these sites in the Irish Sea zone. There is a clear distribution of monuments on the eastern seaboard of Britain, with a 'blank' area beyond: this blank area has been used to mark the boundary of the Irish Sea zone in this study. On the eastern side, I have taken the Irish Sea zone to comprise west Wales (as defined by the distribution of chambered tombs), the west coast of northern Britain (essentially Merseyside, Lancashire and Cumbria, none of which have any early Neolithic chambered tombs), and coastal south and western Scotland (as defined by the distribution of Clyde cairns). This eastern side of the Irish Sea incorporates a number of islands with chambered tomb architecture: Arran, Islay and Jura all have chambered tombs, as does Anglesey. The Isle of Man sits at the very heart of the Irish Sea zone (see Fig. 1.1).

The western side of the Irish Sea zone was initially harder to define. In Ireland, the distribution of chambered tombs alone does not define the study area. This is because there is no clear and obvious break in the distribution of monuments, particularly in the north where court cairns are found across the northern part of Ireland (from Antrim and Down to Mayo and Sligo). Yet by taking into consideration the classification of the sites and their overall topographic setting, it was possible to define the edge of the study area. There are differences between the central court cairns of western Ireland and the single façade court cairns of eastern Ireland, which made it obvious that there were real differences between east and west in the broadest sense. In the north, the final decision was informed by the topography: Lough Neagh acts as a good cut off point in the centre of northern Ireland and there are less monuments to the west of it. All of the monuments in counties Antrim, Down and Louth

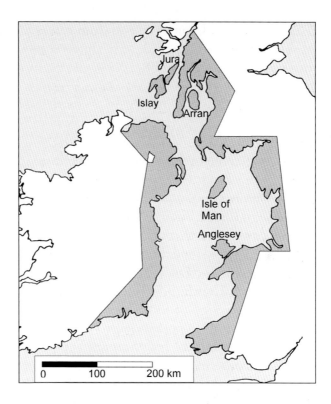

Figure 1.1. The Irish Sea zone: the areas included in this study

were therefore included, as were most of those in Armagh and Derry, with a couple in Tyrone. Only one court cairn is to be found south of Louth all the way down in County Waterford, which was also included. Ultimately, then, a combination of topography and the distribution of different styles of court cairns defined the Irish Sea zone in the north. Portal and passage graves within this area were also visited, although there are only a few of these sites.

In the southern half of Ireland there are two different dominant styles of monument: dolmens and passage graves. The passage graves were easy to deal with here: the larger passage graves are almost certainly later in date than the earlier traditions of dolmens and court cairns. Therefore, I removed the large middle Neolithic passage graves from the distribution. This left just dolmens which cluster quite clearly in the south-east of Ireland anyway. So, in the southern part of Ireland, this creates a very clear distribution of sites, incorporating the modern day county boundaries of Dublin, Wicklow, Carlow, Wexford, Kilkenny and Waterford (see Fig. 1.1).

So while the case study area presented in this volume is based around the distribution of megalithic architecture, as we will see other similarities either side of the Irish Sea also suggest that this zone is a worthy study area (see chapters

3 and 4). The selection of this study area was further justified once the results of the study were completed (see chapters 6 and 7) and I will discuss the entire area once again in chapter 8.

The significance of the Irish Sea zone

This is not the first piece to examine the Irish Sea zone as a case study. In fact, there is a long history of research into the area which suggests that this was an area of considerable significance in the past. An early reference to the Irish Sea is by Mackinder 1902 (in Bowen 1970) who referred to it as the 'British Mediterranean'. The Mediterranean of course has been an important waterway for thousands of years, enabling trade and the movements of people from all the adjacent landmasses as well as being the focus of settlement. This idea was subsequently picked up by others (e.g. Crawford 1912; Fleure 1915), and in 1932 Fox's *The Personality of Britain* suggested considerable interactions across the Irish Sea in the past (Fox 1932). In an important paper, Davis (1945) discussed the distribution of monuments around the Irish Sea zone and possible movements around this area by sea. This paper really marks the heyday of considerations of the Irish Sea zone within a culture-historical framework, an issue discussed and debated by many in the 1950s and 1960s (e.g. Daniel 1941; de Valera 1960; Piggott 1954). At this stage, the search was on for pinpointing the origins of various culture groups in Britain which were thought to originate in the Mediterranean. The Irish Sea was considered one of the areas which saw primary colonisation which then spread to other parts of the British and Irish Isles, an idea which culminated with the publication of *The Irish Sea Province in Archaeology and History* (Moore 1970).

The edited volume by Moore (1970) was already rather outmoded when published as the late 1960s saw an increased emphasis on regional variation and less explicit discussion of the movements of people across the Irish Sea. Regional sequences were investigated in detail at this time, divided up along modern political boundaries: de Valera's work in Ireland (de Valera 1960; de Valera and Ó Nualláin 1961; 1964; 1972), Henshall and Scott's work in Scotland (Henshall 1963; 1972; J. Scott 1969) and Lynch's work in Wales (Lynch 1969b; 1972). These pioneering studies have led the way for later scholars to consider regional sequences in ever increasing detail, and an understanding that things were not the same throughout this area (see subsequent chapters for details). This is not to suggest, however, that the Irish Sea zone has fallen completely out of favour. Two papers in the late 1980s/early 1990s again highlighted the importance of the Irish Sea zone as an area of interaction and exchange in prehistory (Lynch 1989; Waddell 1991) and a subsequent edited volume has further considered these issues (Cummings and Fowler 2004c). Throughout the volume I return to the issue of interactions across the Irish Sea, again in more detail in the final chapter.

Overall aims of the volume

At one level, the volume is designed to give a broad and simple introduction to the Mesolithic and Neolithic of the Irish Sea zone. It is aimed to provide a summary of previous work for students who are less familiar with this area than the Neolithic archaeology of, say, Wessex or Orkney. It also offers a starting point for those wishing to read more extensively about the Irish Sea zone. The main focus of the volume is on the early Neolithic chambered tombs of the region and that an understanding of these monuments cannot be gained without a broader consideration of their landscape settings. I look in detail at the landscape setting of the chambered tombs of the Irish Sea zone, both overall and in more detail through a number of specific case studies. My consideration of landscape has been inspired by recent archaeological and anthropological literature on the significance of landscape (see chapter 6), yet the scale of analysis incorporates a much wider area than has been previously considered by these approaches. One aim is therefore to try and incorporate my landscape analysis into a broader understanding of the Neolithic sequence in this area and beyond.

Other key themes are considered and addressed throughout the volume:

– What was the late Mesolithic background against which the Neolithic began in the Irish Sea zone? Were there already hints of a worldview or mindset that might have been amenable to adoption of Neolithic things, including the construction of monuments?
– Following on from that, how does a consideration of chambered tombs and landscape articulate with our understanding of the Mesolithic-Neolithic transition?
– How does studying the landscape setting of sites enable us to see regional differences or long term trajectories for the development of the Neolithic in different parts of the Irish Sea zone?
– What might have been the nature of contact across the Irish Sea zone in the Neolithic? Were people regularly in contact, or just occasionally? Furthermore, how might people on one side of the Irish Sea have conceived of people on the other side?
– What does a study of the chambered tombs of the Irish Sea zone in their landscape setting tell us about the Neolithic, but also what are the

shortcomings of looking at this type of evidence only? What are the future research questions we should be addressing in this area if we are to further our understanding of the sequence here?

All of these issues are raised at various points in the volume, and then returned to at the end of the book in chapter 8.

Dates and dating

One of the great frustrations with the data sets considered in this volume is the lack of a good series of dates (see chapter 4). Radiocarbon dates exist, but not in the quantity that one would wish for. Many dates have large deviations which mean they are not particularly useful, and others come from potentially contaminated sources. This is a frustrating situation, but of course one that is paralleled in other parts of the country.

Throughout the volume I refer to different periods in general terms. The bulk of the volume considers evidence from the early Neolithic, defined here are 4000BC–3400 BC. It is this period that sees the construction of what I describe here as the early Neolithic chambered tombs of the Irish Sea zone.

Late Mesolithic c6500 BC–4000 BC
Early Neolithic c4000 BC–3400 BC
(Within this the **Earliest Neolithic** is c4000 BC–3800)
Middle Neolithic 3400 BC–2900/2800 BC
Late Neolithic 2900/2800 BC–2400 BC

Conclusion

In this first chapter I have introduced the Irish Sea zone and discussed how this study area was defined in relation to the chambered tomb architecture of the area. I summarised earlier work on the Irish Sea zone which highlighted this area as one which saw considerable prehistoric interaction. I went on to suggest why studies of such broad areas have gone out of fashion in recent years, but are still worthy of consideration. I have also detailed the key aims of the volume, issues which will be addressed individually in the chapters and again as a whole in the concluding chapter. I have also created a very rough chronology which I use throughout. We now turn our attention to the start of the sequence, with a consideration of the late Mesolithic sequence of the area.

2

A late Mesolithic background

Introduction

In this chapter I will consider the nature of the late Mesolithic of the Irish Sea zone. This period dates from about 6500 BC to the start of the Neolithic around 4000 BC. This chapter is not designed as a summary of the British and Irish Mesolithic sequences, of which there are excellent examples already published (e.g. David and Walker 2004; McCartan 2004; Mithen 1994; Warren 2005; Woodman 2004) but as a specific introduction to the archaeology of the Irish Sea zone. This late Mesolithic background specifically provides a context against which the Neolithic must be understood. The mobile nature of late Mesolithic settlement in the Irish Sea area, the absence of formalised cemeteries and a lack of enduring architecture means that the evidence is primarily from lithic scatters. However, western Scotland in particular has also produced late Mesolithic evidence in the form of shell middens. We will see that there seem to be differences either side of the Irish Sea which may well have had an impact on the start of the Neolithic, and on how the Neolithic progressed. It also highlights some of the key themes that will be explored throughout the remainder of the book, in particular regarding people's interactions with landscape. I will start by briefly considering the evidence for the late Mesolithic in the Irish Sea zone, in order to paint a general picture of life at this time. In particular, I will highlight the types of material culture found in the late Mesolithic, and suggest ways in which people may have engaged with the landscape. Contrary to lots of discussions of the Mesolithic, I am not going to discuss evidence from Scandinavia as a parallel for the British and Irish evidence, nor am I going to discuss ethnographic examples. Instead, I wish to focus only on the evidence from the Irish Sea zone.

The late Mesolithic of the Irish Sea zone

By the late Mesolithic, many of the coastal areas which had been previously been land were now submerged, as the sea levels continued to rise after the last Ice

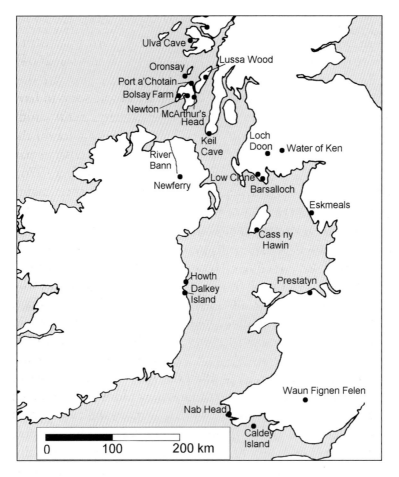

Figure 2.1. Map of Mesolithic sites mentioned in the text

Age. Ireland was separate from Britain and Europe by the start of the Mesolithic as was the Isle of Man, but in the late Mesolithic, Britain also became isolated from the continent. However, due to isostatic lift (land rising after being released from the pressure of the ice sheets) in western Scotland and eastern Ireland sea levels would actually have been a little higher than they are currently. This means that coastal sites frequently survive in these areas, often on or near raised beaches. In contrast, in north-west England, west Wales and south-east Ireland (the lower part of the Irish Sea zone) areas that now lie under water were still above sea level in the late Mesolithic (see Bradley 2007b, 11). This means that much of the ancient coast in these areas lies underwater (e.g. Heyworth and Kidson 1982), potentially destroying much of the archaeology.

The landscape of late Mesolithic Britain would have been quite striking, and very different from today: much of the study area would have been wooded (see Tipping 2004). In such a heavily forested landscape, it is perhaps not surprising that people chose to live predominately along the coasts and river valleys. Throughout the Irish Sea zone there is clear evidence for a riverine, lacustrine and coastal focus of settlement (e.g. David and Walker 2004; Woodman 2004). This is not to say that the inland and upland areas were ignored: there are sites known from these areas too. Nevertheless, late Mesolithic people seem to have had some kind of affinity with the sea and rivers, particularly in this study area. While much of the landscape was wooded, there is some evidence for the manipulation of the landscape through fire, and we could perhaps envisage small scale clearances actively maintained in upland and inland areas (Mellars 1976). These clearances may have been useful for attracting animals or encouraging the growth of specific plant species, but they may also have acted as locations for settlement or possibly more ritualised activity (cf. Jordan 2003).

Late Mesolithic sites almost always consist of lithics, with only limited quantities of structural evidence surviving in the archaeological record (Wickham Jones 2004). Considering the fact that we are dealing with hunter-gatherers, who were almost certainly predominately mobile (cf. Whittle 1997), it is perhaps unsurprising that there are few structural remains. People probably lived in tents (or something similar like tepees, yurts and so forth) which would leave only very ephemeral traces in the archaeological record (remains of hearths and stakeholes primarily or very occasionally, postholes). There is some evidence of this kind of temporary occupation: scoops were found Low Clone and Barsalloch in south-west Scotland for example (Cormack 1970; Cormack and Coles 1968) which may have been the bases for structures of some kind. Other possible structural remains have been found in the Irish Sea zone, such as the remains of the base for a structure at Newton on Islay, Eskmeals in Cumbria and Cass ny Hawin on the Isle of Man (Wickham-Jones 2004, 231–5). The evidence from the middens in western Scotland has also produced occupation evidence including hearths, depressions and levelled areas (Wickham-Jones 2004, 229). This evidence has also prompted discussions of more permanent settlement at these locations (e.g. Mithen 2000b and see below).

Our search for a more sedentary existence (and its associated architecture) comes, I think, from our desire to have definitive evidence of 'complex' hunter-gatherers in the late Mesolithic. Complex hunter-gatherers exist in the ethnographic record and those such as the north-west coast groups of America lived in permanent settlements and had complex social relations, burial practices and material culture sets. I think the desire to find complex hunter-gatherers in Britain relates to a number of factors. Firstly, Scandinavian evidence in particular hints at the possible presence of complex groups in the late Mesolithic: evidence comprises settlements which were clearly occupied for a long period of time, cemeteries and complex social interactions with neighbouring farmers (e.g. Tilley 1996a). If it was happening there, why not here? In the past there was the tendency to use the Scandinavian evidence to 'plug the gaps' in our own sequence and as such I think we have also acquired, inadvertently perhaps, the desire for complexity. A presence of complex groups in the late Mesolithic is also the desire to find some kind of precursor to the subsequent Neolithic period. For a long time now, British archaeologists have been enamoured with the idea that the transition to the Neolithic was firmly in the hands of the native, hunter-gatherer population, a backlash against the culture-historical and processual models of invasion, migration and acculturation (e.g. Thomas 1988). There is very much a theoretical desire to show that late Mesolithic people were already in possession of some of the key elements that would make the adoption of the Neolithic a smooth transition (complex social relations ideal for the introduction of exchangeable material culture, for example, or tethered mobility patterns suitable for the adoption of cattle herding; and see Rowley Conwy 2004). I myself argued that middens may well conceptually be some kind of precursor to monumental architecture (Cummings 2003, and see Pollard 2000a), although I have since moved away from this idea (Cummings 2007a). There is therefore very much the sense that the late Mesolithic *should* be fairly similar to the subsequent early Neolithic period. We have perhaps borrowed a few too many ideas from the early Neolithic and placed them onto the late Mesolithic sequence where-ever possible. However, theoretically-informed Mesolithic studies are now becoming much more commonplace, and a flow of critical papers and volumes have appeared as a result of this (see for example the excellent range of papers in Conneller and Warren 2006). These papers suggest that Mesolithic people were much more complex than perhaps they had previously been given credit for (but without borrowing the Scandinavian sequence to illustrate this) and that the Mesolithic is just as rich as subsequent periods (Warren 2005).

There is also an issue here relating to preservation. We have already noted how much of the late Mesolithic coastline is submerged, particularly in the southern part of the Irish Sea zone. This is also the area that lacks the archaeologically richer sites such as the shell middens, found instead in western Scotland. Yet even when we have well-preserved landscapes that have not suffered from coastal degradation or erosion, is it perhaps surprising that we are not finding settlements? If we move forward into the subsequent Neolithic period, there is still a notable lack of settlement evidence. You do get Neolithic houses but the large timber halls in Scotland from the early Neolithic for example are just as likely to be specialised ritual structures as they are 'houses' in any traditional sense (cf. Cross 2003). It is likely that the vast majority of people were still dwelling in impermanent structures. Indeed if we look beyond the exceptional timber halls, Neolithic settlement is, for the most part, just as lacking as it is in the preceding Mesolithic period. Perhaps we are searching for something that simply rarely exists in the archaeological record, whether that is from the Mesolithic or Neolithic. I would argue that it is clear that people in the late Mesolithic were mobile, perhaps staying in some locations longer than others, but moving on nevertheless. Quite clearly, people were not investing time in creating permanent domestic architecture.

What we *do* have surviving in abundance from the late Mesolithic are a large numbers of lithic scatters, which have been found along the coasts of the Irish Sea. These scatters are not usually *in situ* or associated with any features (Saville 2004), and are often found in coastal locations. The scatters have frequently been found as part of targeted fieldwork usually involving fieldwalking and test pitting, or they have been found through coastal erosion or chance finding. This undoubtedly skews the picture of settlement in favour of the coastal zone. Where work has been conducted, however, there are scatters from inland areas. One good example of this is in inland Dumfries and Galloway where a series of scatters have been found around Loch Doon and the Water of Ken in particular (Edwards 1996). Unfortunately, not all areas of the Irish Sea zone have seen comparable histories of research: in Ireland, the north-east has a long tradition of research (Woodman 2004), while the south-east has only seen any fieldwork in the last few decades (e.g. Green and Zvelebil 1990). Surprisingly few sites are known from west Wales (David and Walker 2004), while western Scotland has a better set of sites, primarily due to detailed surveys there in recent years (e.g. the work of Mithen (2000a) in the southern Hebrides). Most scatters are flint, but other sources of stone were utilised in the Mesolithic. Of particular note to the Irish Sea zone, Arran pitchstone was in use in the late Mesolithic, as were a range of other types of stone including chert, chalcedony, Rum bloodstone, quartz and quartzite. There is a sense that for the most part people did not travel long distances in order to acquire stone. Instead people utilised what was available locally (Saville 2004, 185, but also see Cobb 2008). Most of the Irish Sea zone does not have flint occurring in the local geology (a notable exception being county Antrim where flint outcrops on the coast). Within these other areas, flint would have been available as beach pebbles only, and this may be why other types of stone were used.

These late Mesolithic assemblages are frequently characterised by the presence of large quantities of debitage. Bolsay Farm, Islay, was excavated by Steve Mithen (2000a) and produced nearly 330,000 lithics, still only an estimated 20% of

Figure 2.2. Nab Head, west Wales

the overall assemblage (Mithen *et al.* 2007). This is an extraordinary quantity of material. In west Wales, Nab Head Site II is a particularly important site, and one of the few known and explored late Mesolithic sites from Wales as a whole (Fig. 2.2). The site itself has produced a large lithic assemblage even though it has not been fully excavated (David 1990). Many of the lithics date to the early Mesolithic but the site was also visited a number of times in the late Mesolithic (David and Walker 2004, 319), with date evidence spanning 3000 years into the Neolithic. Therefore, it seems to represent a place in the landscape that was returned to time and time again. The assemblage seemed to fall into three discrete zones surrounding an empty area about 5m across (a possible location for a structure). Another possible hearth was also identified (Aldhouse-Green 2000, 32). For the most part, the assemblage consists of flint tools and debitage, with all parts of the reduction sequence present (i.e. people were making tools on site from the raw material: Aldhouse-Green 2000, 33). This stone tool assemblage is fairly typical for a late Mesolithic site, however, Nab Head has also produced ground stone tools, including three pecked and ground stone axes and a perforated stone disc (David 1990; David and Walker 2004, 325, fig. 17.7). These axeheads were made from local rock, and remain rather unusual in a British context, although axes are found more commonly in Ireland.

In Ireland, late Mesolithic occupation was again concentrated along rivers and the sea, and it seems that fishing played a key role in the subsistence economy (Woodman 2004). The absence of some of the larger animals that are found in the British sequence here and in the Isle of Man have led to suggestions that people relied more on wild pig and riverine fish. A series of sites have been found along the River Bann at Newferry, for example, where the excavator suggested that people fished for eels (Woodman 1977, 193). At Newferry people clearly returned to this location on a number of occasions, not only in the late Mesolithic, but also into the early Neolithic (Woodman 1977, 183). Although this was clearly a location that was revisited on a number of occasions, there was nothing to suggest anything but temporary and ephemeral occupation (Woodman 1977, 194). Intriguingly, Irish late Mesolithic assemblages vary from British ones not only in their use of broad blades (see below) but they also contain axes. The presence of axes in British assemblages is fairly unusual, Nab Head, mentioned above, being exceptional. However, during Woodman's excavations at Newferry he found at least 35 complete axes and numerous fragments (Woodman 1977). These were clearly part of a different repertoire of material culture found in Ireland (and see below).

Although not all late Mesolithic sites produce massive quantities of lithics (there are plenty of examples of sites which produce small assemblages), it is intriguing that large lithic assemblages are frequently found in the late Mesolithic, particularly when contrasted with later, Neolithic assemblages. There is an argument here I think that people were producing large quantities of debitage due to the nature of the raw material they were using (for most the Irish Sea zone this was beach flint): beach pebbles were so poor quality that large amounts of debitage would be produced in order to get just a few workable flakes or blades. While there is almost certainly an element of truth here, I would suggest that the production of large quantities of debitage may also have been quite deliberate. Graeme Warren (2006, 28–32) argues quite convincingly that material culture, in this case lithics, articulated wider meanings, identities and relationships within society (also see Cobb 2007). I suggest that reducing flint beach pebbles (and quartz and other workable materials) was a key metaphor in the late Mesolithic. It may relate in part to the powerful metaphor of fragmentation (cf. Chapman 2000; Chapman and Gaydarska 2006): a number of material things in the late Mesolithic seem to have been fragmented (including bodies) before being deposited. Stone, just like other partible bodies (cf. Fowler 2004, 66–71), may have dictated to people how it should be treated prior to discard, as well as becoming vehicles for memory (of places, of people, of events and so on). There may be an argument here that the reduction of lithics down into smaller pieces was also in part about performance. It may have been appropriate to knap flint into fragments, and, just as bodies were reduced to fragments, then potentially turned into objects which travelled round with people (see Bradley 1998a, 27; Whittle 1996, 202) prior to being deposited. Lithics too, may have required people to reduce the larger pebbles or nodules into fragments, with token pieces moving on with people. The remainder stayed behind, a material expression of a community who had now moved. Finlay describes this as the 'deliberate choices of discard strategies' (Finlay 2006, 53), an idea I like very much. I would argue that there was a clear need amongst late Mesolithic groups to return to specific locations and leave behind material, fragmented and then discarded in specific ways (see also Cobb 2008, chapter 6). This was the deliberate articulation of connections with particular things in particular places, relationships, however, that were temporary in nature, and which needed to be concluded prior to people moving on. This argument, I think, is also relevant when we think about some of the most obvious examples of accumulation and deliberate discard in the late Mesolithic, the shell middens of western Scotland. I want to move on now to consider these sites. In some ways, these sites seem to represent something rather different to the evidence we have so far considered, but I will argue they are simply a regional development on some of the broader themes we have discussed: affinity with place and specific and deliberate discard strategies. In western Scotland, though, this involved shell as well as stone.

Of shell and stone: durable locales in the late Mesolithic

How does a place endure? Does it endure purely through the construction of architecture, built in stone to survive the ages? Or do places exist in much more ephemeral ways? If places are where events occurred, where people hold onto memories, then places do not require permanent markers to exist. Nevertheless, there is a tendency to think about the shell midden sites of western Scotland as something rather different from the rest of the late Mesolithic evidence. Certainly, this is because shell middens have produced 'exceptional' remains: human remains along with a wealth of data on subsistence strategies and seasonal occupations (Mellars 1987). However, there is also the temptation to see these things as something they are not (precursors to architecture: see Cummings 2003 for example). These sites have been key in our understanding of the late Mesolithic sequence in the Irish Sea zone. I want here, not to go into the details of the sites and finds as there are good summaries elsewhere, but to consider what these sites may have represented.

The western Scottish midden sites were found around Oban, Skye and the Inner Sound. Some are open-air sites and some are in caves (Fig. 2.3). Many, although not all, of these sites were initially used in the later Mesolithic (Mithen *et al.* 2007) and they are characterised by the presence of large accumulations of marine shells, with a distinctive associated assemblage, comprising wild animal remains (from the land, the sea and the air), antler and bone tools, and stone tools. One of the key differences between these sites and the assemblages found throughout western Scotland in this period are that these 'Obanian' sites consist almost entirely of bipolar debitage, with no retouched tools: this contrasts with the microlithic assemblages from western Scotland which are blade platform

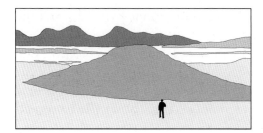

Figure 2.3. The shell midden of Casitel nan Gillean, Oronsay (after a photograph by W. Galloway published in Mellars 1987)

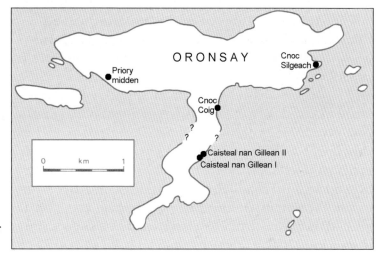

Figure 2.4. The island of Oronsay, indicating the location of sites in relation to Mesolithic sea levels

debitage with microliths, scrapers and retouched tools (Bonsall 1997, 25). It is clear, however, that these sites are not representative of different cultures as was once suggested, as these sites overlap both chronologically and spatially with microlithic sites. Furthermore, microliths *have* been found in small numbers at some sites (Mithen *et al.* 2007) as have blades and this suggests that middens were simply special purpose camps, associated with a different range of practices (Bonsall 1997, 32). These sites are also well-known for having produced human remains, which are rare in the late Mesolithic (see below). The human remains have been subjected to stable isotope analysis and have demonstrated that these people had a high marine diet (Schulting and Richards 2002b but see Milner *et al.* 2004). It is also significant that these shell middens seem to have remained in use until about 3500 BC, well into the Neolithic (Bonsall 1997, 27; Mithen *et al.* 2007).

The small island of Oronsay to the south of Colonsay in the Inner Hebrides is perhaps the best known site and it has the remains of five large shell middens (Fig. 2.4), which have been the focus of archaeological investigation in both the nineteenth century and more recently (Mellars 1987). Although all the sites have been examined, Cnoc Coig has received the most attention, revealing three main occupation phases. The main phase dates to around 4300 BC and produced the remains of over 50 hearths, two structures, an animal bone assemblage and a shell midden containing human remains (Mellars 1987, 238). Evidence from fish otoliths indicate that Oronsay was inhabited in virtually every season of the year (Mellars and Wilkinson 1980), although the question of whether people lived permanently on the island remains a point of speculation (Richards and Mellars 1998; Mithen 2000b).

The sites around Oban are the best known shell middens from the study area, but others have been found in western Scotland such as those at Keil Cave, Kintyre, McArthur's Head and Port a'Chotain Cave, Islay (Tolan-Smith 2001), which suggest that this practice may have been more widespread than just around Oban. Indeed, middens are also found elsewhere in the Irish Sea zone, for example, in Ireland there are middens on Dalkey Island and Howth Co. Dublin., Rough Island, Co. Down and Rathlin Island, Co. Antrim: (McCartan 2000), with other possible examples identified (Cobb 2008, 220). In Wales only two shell midden sites are known, one on Caldey Island, the other near Prestatyn (David and Walker 2004, 331): this might be a reflection of the fact that much of the coastline in Wales is now submerged, but we might also want to consider the possibility of regional variation at this time. It is the sites around Oban, however, which have produced the wealth of evidence I will now go on to discuss.

Middens offer us a unique insight into life in the late Mesolithic. Yet it is fair to say that these sites are not typical of the entire Irish Sea zone. They must be considered within their own context, which in the case of western Scotland seems to be a very specific historical trajectory which resulted in the long term use of these middens and landscapes. As we have seen, the vast majority of occupation evidence from the Mesolithic is in the form of lithic scatters. Middens clearly do represent long occupations: the repeated return to place of groups of people who deliberately chose to reuse a location which had been used before. Perhaps the big difference between these sites and other sites in the late Mesolithic is not the fact that people chose to return to a specific place time and time again: this was clearly happening at other sites where the only remains are lithics. The difference with these sites is that people chose to deliberately discard shells in the same place time and time again, and that these places were repeatedly used as places for settlement. One wonders what made shells particularly appropriate at these times and these places that people felt that they needed to accumulate them. Certainly, it is not the case that these were about making large visible statements in the landscape: many of these middens were in caves (not the best place to put something you wish to be seen from miles around), and others would not have been highly visible if approached from the sea (see Warren 2007). In this way, middens are quite different from monuments which appear in the Neolithic.

What is significant here is the act of deposition, taking shells and placing them in a particular location, which, after the first deposit, was somewhere redolent with meaning and history. Perhaps there was something about life in western Scotland in the few hundred years prior to the Neolithic that made people react in this way. It may, quite simply, have been about the expression of social identity, a day to day practice which left these remarkable remains. It may also have been about a connection to place, one that may well have existed in other parts of the Irish Sea zone but here was expressed slightly differently. It may be the communities who made them, so reliant as they were on the sea and boats, chose shells as their favoured object for deposition. Elsewhere, the material may have varied: stone, wood, bone or flesh. I do not think middens are about marking place the way that monuments did in the Neolithic, but about *connections* to specific parts of the landscape, and particular ways of doing things in those places.

Burial practices

One aspect of these middens which has received considerable attention in recent years is the presence of human bone on these sites. This has led to discussions on the treatment of the dead in the late Mesolithic (Conneller 2006). There are no formal cemeteries from this period in Britain and Ireland, a direct contrast to the Scandinavian evidence (e.g. Bradley 1998a, 25–8). The sites around Oban in particular, however, have produced human remains. Cnoc Coig, for example, on Oronsay had the remains of at least seven individuals with both children and adults being represented: the bones were primarily from the hands, feet and cranium (Mellars 1987, 290). One of the shell middens from Ireland has also produced human remains: a femur was found at Rockmarshall in County Louth (Conneller 2006, 144). It is tempting to see the remains of the dead at middens as somehow analogous to the presence of the dead in chambered tombs, but I think this may be rather misguided. Firstly, human bone is also found in cave sites in the late Mesolithic (Conneller 2006, 142). For example, bone was found in some of the caves on Caldey Island off the Pembrokeshire coast. Potter's Cave and Ogof-yr-Ychen both produced mixed deposits which contained late Mesolithic human bone (Burrow 2003, 25). It is unclear precisely how these deposits were formed: at Ogof-yr-Ychen it seems that bones were dropped down a vertical shaft on the

surface which led to the cave (Conneller 2006, 155), although in some cases it may
be the case that they were washed in from deposits outside the cave (see Schulting
and Richards 2002a, 1017). Other examples, such as Pontnewydd Cave in north
Wales, suggests some at least were deliberate. It is of interest that there are actually
very few late Mesolithic human deposits in caves, especially when compared with
the preceding and subsequent periods (Chatterton 2006, 116), so it seems that
while cave deposition occurred, it was rather 'out of vogue' at this time, or only
reserved for a small number of individuals.

   We have already seen how bodies in the late Mesolithic were found in
smaller pieces (see above), potentially token parts of the skeleton turned into
artefacts. There is clear evidence for the deposition of disarticulated human
bone throughout the Mesolithic of Europe (Conneller 2006, 158). I think the
reason we are seeing the pieces within the shell midden assemblages and caves
is due to preservational factors: small fragments of human bone simply would
not survive in most settings where we have found late Mesolithic material.
We might actually be looking at standard practice in the late Mesolithic: the
disarticulation of bodies down into smaller parts to be curated or deposited
where appropriate. Conneller (2006) has written some wonderfully evocative
ideas on the deposition of human and animal bodies (bones) and I think we
should envisage people depositing not only lithics but all forms of material
culture in very specific ways and in specific places. There are further possibilities
for Mesolithic mortuary practices. We must accept the possibility that there
was a strong cremation rite, which again would not be easily visible in the
archaeological record. There are hints, however, that cremation was practiced
in the Mesolithic (British Archaeology 2007). There have also been suggestions
that bodies were deposited in watery places (Conneller 2006; Cummings 2003),
in particular in the sea and rivers, and again, this would of course be virtually
undetectable archaeologically (although there are a few known examples: see
Chatterton 2006, 107–8). I think I would argue very strongly for the careful
and deliberate deposition of human remains in the late Mesolithic, which clearly
involved disarticulation in some cases and deposition in specific locales.

Ritualised activity

We struggle in the late Mesolithic to identify ritual or ritualised behaviour.
As I have already argued above, we tend to see evidence such as lithic scatters
as the remains of purely 'domestic' activity: debitage was quite simply waste
and unwanted material, not the deliberate creation and deposition of material

culture at specific points in the landscape. Some might argue: how are we to tell the difference between material left after making an object (debitage) and material left behind as part of a ritualised act? The answer is: we cannot, but we must not jump to the assumption that everything we see is purely 'domestic' and 'functional' in character. It has convincingly been argued that people in the past did not have strict divisions between 'ritual' and 'domestic', instead most activities involved both, perhaps with emphases on one or the other (Bradley 2005; Tilley 1996a, 62). If we look carefully, there are some good examples of ritualised behaviour in the Irish Sea zone.

Chatterton (2006, 104–5) has argued that objects may have been deliberately deposited in water. He cites the Lydstep Haven boar, found with two microliths in its neck and weighed down by a tree trunk: shells were also found in the silts nearby (Chatterton 2006, 105–6). We have already noted the possibility of human bodies being deposited in water (above), and there seems to be good evidence for the deposition of stone tools in water too (Chatterton 2006, 109–111). Nyree Finlay (2003) lists 14 known late Mesolithic caches of stone tools in the north-east of Ireland alone, again representing the careful disposal of objects. Late Mesolithic pits are also known which again contain deliberate deposits of flint, bone and other organic material (Chatterton 2006, 117–9). Pits are an area which clearly require more research. There are also hints of other ritualised practices. Fragments of worked whale bone were found directly under the hearth at Caisteal nan Gillean I, Oronsay (Mellars 1987, 187), a similar phenomenon noted at other late Mesolithic structures/locales. At Lussa Wood on the Isle of Jura a very unusual stone structure was found. It comprised a line of three interconnecting stone rings. Each ring had an internal diameter of just over a metre, and intriguingly, they seem to have been filled with gravels containing lithic artefacts, charcoal, burnt hazelnut shells and tiny fragments of bone (Wickham Jones 2004, 231). Although this could be the remains of domestic occupation, the construction of stone rings is not consistent with the simple discard of material. The composition of material also sounds very reminiscent of the type of deposit found in Neolithic chambered tombs (see chapter 5), which we would, of course, describe as ceremonial.

Clearly, then, late Mesolithic people were involved in a range of practices, some of which may have overlapped considerably with everyday activities, but which indicate a careful and considered treatment of all forms of material culture. There seems to have been some locales associated closely with deposition: water seems to be one of these, interestingly, a theme we will return to when considering the early Neolithic evidence. Places used for settlement also seem to have resonated with people: not only were specific spots returned to time and again, but carefully selected deposits were also chosen for deposition. We are missing from our view the role of organics, and I think wood would have been a particularly potent metaphor in the late Mesolithic, with people living in such a heavily forested world. There is also considerable evidence that people in the late Mesolithic had a considerable affinity with islands. We have already considered the middens in western Scotland. It seems that virtually all of the islands in Western Scotland were utilised by Mesolithic people, and the same is true all around the Irish Sea coasts.

I would also like to suggest that myths and stories would have been an absolutely crucial part of Mesolithic people's lives. Myths are a way of understanding many elements of society including history, religion and how to act within particular social contexts (e.g. Basso 1984; 1996). Some myths must have been associated with events. Graeme Warren's discussion of the Støregga tsunami is striking (Warren 2005, 44): this event occurred somewhere around 6000 BC and 5750 BC and would have had a massive impact on eastern Scotland. One wonders what kinds of stories would have been told about this event in subsequent years? Furthermore, how did communities understand the loss of coastal environments and the rise in sea levels? It is quite clear that coastal zones in the Mesolithic were quite dynamic places, and it is likely that the loss of land was often not a slow and gradual process, but one that happened quickly and suddenly. Myths must also have been associated with places and landscapes.

Origin mythology elsewhere in the world is almost always tied up with landscape (e.g. Taçon 1991), and one can envisage a similar relationship between people and places in the Mesolithic. How we get at this archaeologically, however, is a different matter, and one with which we seem to struggle. However, there are indications and hints. The small island of Oronsay was clearly the focus of settlement and associated ritualised activity in the late Mesolithic, even though the island itself can never have provided all resources required for the community (not just in terms of food but other resources too). Yet this small island saw repeated occupation over hundreds of years, and an obvious interpretation of this evidence is that Oronsay played some key role in landscape mythology. There were reasons why people returned here which had nothing to do with food.

An Irish Sea connection?

For many years now it has been noted that there were different technologies either side of the Irish Sea in the late Mesolithic. This has been used to suggest that people were not in contact across the Irish Sea, with Britain and Ireland essentially having separate trajectories (McCartan 2004; Saville 2004; Woodman 2004). These differences are manifested most clearly in lithic styles: as we have already discussed, western Britain is characterised by the presence of microlithic technologies whereas in Ireland the lithics are rather different, consisting primarily of retouched and unretouched broad blades and flakes. Butt-trimmed forms are found ubiquitously in the late Mesolithic (Kimball 2000, 37), with Bann flakes (leaf-shaped flakes trimmed and retouched at the butt) being of particular interest here since they are found in large numbers near the River Bann in north-east Ireland (Woodman 1986, 13). Polished stone axes are also found, frequently in association with large picks and borers: this contrasts with the British sequence, due to the lack of microliths or transverse arrowheads: end scrapers and burins are also rare in Ireland (Woodman 2004, 287). Quite clearly, people were using different sets of stone tools either side of the Irish Sea.

Raw materials add another dimension to this discussion. For the most part, people in the late Mesolithic of the Irish Sea zone were utilising beach flint, supplemented by a range of predominately local materials such as chert, quartz, Arran pitchstone and so on (David and Walker 2004, 321). One exception to this in the study area is north-east Ireland, where flint outcrops along the Antrim coast. This source of flint was undoubtedly of significance in north-east Ireland (and has also resulted in a research bias in this area: Woodman 2004, 293), yet there is little evidence at present for raw materials moving a long way *across* the Irish Sea. There is evidence of some material moving around (e.g. Aldhouse-Green 2000, 36–7; Barton *et al.* 1995; Cobb 2008; Kador 2007; Woodman 2004, 295), with a possible connection between Ireland and the Isle of Man, but at present little evidence for connections between Ireland and Scotland (but see Cobb 2007).

The Isle of Man has a further role to play in this discussion. Lithic technology in the late Mesolithic of the Isle of Man is very similar to that found in Ireland, and is suggestive of 'significant' levels of social contact between people here and in Ireland (Woodman and McCarthy 2003, 36). This is because the assemblages on the Isle of Man include Bann-style flakes, the broad blades typical of the Irish assemblages. For example, at the site of Rhendhoo, a late Mesolithic assemblage was found which includes some Bann flakes, probably with a late fifth millennium BC date (Burrow 1997, 9). However, although there are some small differences between Irish and Manx assemblages (McCartan 2004), it is clear that people were more than capable of crossing the Irish Sea and were clearly doing so in this case. On the one hand, then, there seems to be different histories either side of the Irish Sea, yet the evidence from the Isle of Man suggests contact (Fig. 2.5).

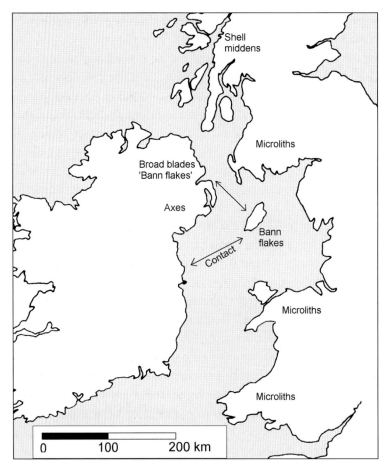

Figure 2.5. The traditional view of cultural traditions and contact in the late Mesolithic

There were other differences either side of the Irish Sea. Large ungulates found in Britain (aurochs, elk, red and roe deer) were absent in Ireland (Woodman 2004, 287; Woodman and McCarthy 2003, 32). This means that people in Ireland may well have been much more reliant on marine resources (Woodman 2004, 287), which in turn would almost certainly have had an impact on mobility. The lack of large ungulates also has implications for the production of material culture: antler and bone were used for making tools in Britain. Wild pig in Ireland would provide bone, but there would be no ready supply of antler. Then of course there would be differences in belief systems. It has been suggested that animals such as aurochs and red deer would have been potent symbols in the Mesolithic (Bradley 1998a, 32), tied up in myths, worldviews and belief systems. One wonders how the absence of these animals would have enabled different understandings of the world to become prevalent.

People certainly had the ability to cross the Irish Sea in the late Mesolithic.

People in the Mesolithic were skilled fishers and there is evidence that people even caught deep-sea fish (oft-cited is Morton, Fife: Coles 1971). There is limited direct evidence in the form of boats: a fragmentary boat of oak was found on the shores of Lough Neagh in Ireland dating to the late Mesolithic (McCartan 2004, 280) and of course there is the wooden paddle from the early Mesolithic site of Star Carr (Clark 1954). However, skin boats (curragh) would have been very well suited to sea crossings, even across the stormiest parts of the Irish Sea. Late Mesolithic connections between Ireland and Isle of Man are entirely feasible with this simple technology. If people did not cross the Irish Sea in the Mesolithic, it was because they chose not to, not because they were incapable of doing so.

I would argue that it is too simplistic to suggest that there was no contact across Irish Sea. We have known for years that distinctive types of material culture do not necessarily equal different cultural groups (Hodder 1982). People may well have chosen to express their identities through different material culture sets, things that undoubtedly had a functional role to play in subsistence strategies, yet were intimately tied to local identities. If people did not cross between Britain and Ireland, it was for social reasons, not because they could not do so. We must bear in mind that if people genuinely were not crossing the Irish Sea in the late Mesolithic, then something changed radically between then and start of the Neolithic, when people were most certainly moving around and across the Irish Sea extensively. This is an issue discussed in more depth in chapter 8.

A late Mesolithic worldview

Before we end this chapter by considering the Mesolithic Neolithic transition, I want to very briefly summarise the late Mesolithic period.

- People were mobile to a greater or lesser extent. In most areas, people probably moved around the landscape quite frequently. This would have given them a considerable knowledge of the topography and associated resources. I would argue that these landscapes were embedded within people's belief systems, mythologies and worldviews.
- Some places, especially in the island systems of western Scotland, became particularly potent locales, and people returned to these on numerous occasions. These large and repeatedly occupied shell midden sites seem to have been a localised phenomenon which so far has not been found in all parts of the Irish Sea zone. This could either suggest a fragmented and localised regional sequence in the late Mesolithic, where people were fairly

oblivious to communities in the wider world and therefore followed their own regional trajectories. Alternatively, people maintained wide networks of contacts, but chose to express difference through differing depositional practices and material culture sets. I would argue this is one of the biggest questions facing late Mesolithic scholars, and one we should investigate in the future.

- Water seems to have been a particularly important natural feature in the late Mesolithic, also receiving deposits. The water and seaways were also the focus for movements around this area.
- Ritualised activity was actually prevalent in the late Mesolithic but we struggle to separate this from what we call 'domestic' activity. The two were clearly intertwined, and much of what we see in the record needs to be interpreted in this way.

The Mesolithic Neolithic transition

The Mesolithic Neolithic transition remains, I would argue, one of the most contested periods in prehistory. A recent summary of the state of knowledge (Whittle and Cummings 2007) indicated that opinion is still seriously divided about how and why people became 'Neolithic', with us still having no clear consensus about what being 'Neolithic' actually meant to people. There is a massive literature which has proposed a whole range of different scenarios for this transition period, and I do not have the space here to summarise it. What I do want to do is consider the evidence, with a particular focus on landscape. When I talk about the transition period, I am considering the transition to cover the period 4200–3800 BC. We know that by 4200 BC people seem to be in some sort of contact with mainland Europe, evidenced by domesticated cattle remains at sites like Ferriter's Cove (Woodman et al. 1999). This is not to say that people prior to this date were not in contact with mainland Europe, but there is no direct evidence at present for the exchange of material culture or ideas. We could envisage a period of 'availability' (Zvelebil and Rowley Conwy 1986) where Neolithic 'things' became available to people in Britain and Ireland, although I am never quite clear how this would actually work on the ground. Did people in Europe suddenly decide to leave their shores with cows in tow and explore new ones? If so, what was this driven by? The desire to find new lands, new peoples or new resources? Were people already in contact across the English Channel, and it was social relations that changed in this period? Quite simply, we struggle to answer the question of why, a few hundred years prior to the start of the Neolithic proper, a few things (animals especially) seem to start arriving on our shores. Are we looking at a similar situation to that in Denmark where the Ertebølle seem to have actively resisted 'becoming Neolithic' for hundreds of years? Did the hunter-gatherer groups in Britain and Ireland actively resist all the new forms of material culture found just across the English Channel? Were people in France/Belgium/Holland not willing to share their knowledge? Were there taboos in place, perhaps, preventing people from travelling, or using these new things? Were the exchange systems not in place? Were there ideological reasons why people did not wish to use Neolithic things?

We struggle further to understand why, around about 4000 BC, it seems that *lots* of Neolithic things (and people??) arrived in Britain. What had suddenly changed at this particular point compared to what had come before? Again, we do not have an answer for this, but it is now quite clear that more or less throughout Ireland and Britain at around about 4000 BC certain new 'Neolithic' things were available, specifically Carinated Bowl pottery and domesticated animals (especially cattle). Other elements of the Neolithic 'package' seem to have been present, but not adopted consistently throughout Britain and Ireland (for example, cereal cultivation certainly occurred in some areas, but does not seem to have been adopted everywhere: see various papers in Whittle and Cummings 2007). Other elements of the Neolithic package do not really seem to have been particularly important in this earliest Neolithic phase: monuments were not typically constructed until after 3800 BC (Bayliss and Whittle 2007) and large numbers of polished stone axes were not produced until after 3600 BC (Bradley and Edmonds 1993). In its earliest phase, then, the Neolithic involved a new technology (pottery) and a new animal species (although only sheep/goat would have been completely new to people, since there were wild counterparts of cows and pigs in Britain at least). The big question is, what impact did this have on people? Did they stop hunting and gathering to become pastoralists? Did these new forms of material culture have a massive impact on people's lives and belief systems or were they simply assimilated into pre-existing modes of thought? At present the evidence, sadly, cannot answer all these questions: we still lack adequate sites and suites of dates to answer these, especially in the Irish Sea zone. But I do want to consider the range of evidence we have got and see what picture this paints.

Continuity

There is quite clearly some good evidence for elements of continuity in the period 4200–3800 BC. As we have seen above, the late Mesolithic is associated with distinctive styles of stone tool: microliths throughout much of Britain, and Bann Flakes in Ireland and the Isle of Man. The early Neolithic, on the other hand, is associated with new forms of stone tool, most specifically the leaf-shaped arrowhead, along with axes. This would appear to mark a clear distinction between the two periods. Typically for the transition period, however, a simple change from one to the other is not present. In western Scotland, microlithic technology already seems to have been on the decline in the late Mesolithic (Burrow 2003, 25). Elsewhere, microliths continue to be found into the Neolithic period. We have already seen how in Ireland (and in one example in Wales) stone axes were already part of the late Mesolithic stone tool suite. A further problem that must be considered is that the vast majority of lithic scatters are from undated contexts (found through fieldwalking for example), so this makes it very hard for us to pinpoint precisely, and chart changes in, lithic styles in this critical 400 year period. We have also noted above that many places that were used in the late Mesolithic, including the western Scottish shell middens, continue to be used in the early Neolithic. As far as it is possible to ascertain, areas of the landscape that were used in the late Mesolithic for settlement and occupation continue to be used in the early Neolithic (and see Cobb 2008 for specifics). Lithic scatters continue to be found in coastal and riverine locations, suggestive of short-term occupations. This supports the idea of considerable overlap in the occupation of the landscape.

Special places in the landscape also saw continued use: caves, for example, saw the deposition of human remains in the early Neolithic. In Little Hoyle cave in Pembrokeshire, four early Neolithic individuals were deposited in a chimney connecting the cave to the surface (Burrow 2003, 41) and the caves on Caldey Island also contained Neolithic human remains. Certainly, prior to the construction of chambered tombs around about 3800 BC the treatment of the dead seems to have considerable elements of continuity with the preceding period (in the sense that there is only very limited evidence). Everyday life, then, may well have followed older patterns, with cattle incorporated into pre-existing movements through the landscape. The same places in the landscape seem to have been used and there seems to have been considerable continuity in the more ritualised elements of people's lives. The fragmentation of material culture and deposition in specific ways also seems to have continued, this time incorporating small quantities of pottery into assemblages (e.g. see Sheridan 2007b).

Or change?

The start of the Neolithic clearly sees the introduction of new things: this is most obvious when we think about material culture. Not only did people start making pottery (for which they would have needed to have a good knowledge of the various stages of pottery production) but people in Britain and Ireland also came into possession of imported jadeite axes, brought over from the continent (Sheridan 2007a). This in turn may have inspired people to start making axes from particular stone sources in Britain and Ireland: we know that some axe sources were in use from the very beginning of the Neolithic (Clough and Cummins 1988), although large-scale production did not really take off for a few hundred years. Pottery in particular would have had an effect on people in terms of mobility, although this depends of course whether people used it as an everyday item or whether its production and use was reserved for special occasions. The other big change at the start of the Neolithic is the appearance and seemingly widespread adoption of domesticated animals, especially cattle (Schulting and Richards 2002b). We should also note the presence, if not widespread adoption of cereals, and also the clearance of woodland, although traditionally, the elm decline, thought to be part of the clearing of trees for agriculture, does not appear until 3800 BC (Edwards and Whittington 1997), so a few hundred years into the Neolithic.

The big question of course is did these new things create a big change? Pottery and axes may well have had an effect on exchange networks which in turn could have had a big impact on social relations. Likewise, domesticated crops and animals may well have had their greatest impact on social dynamics in terms of possession, exchange and consumption. Domesticated cattle in particular require looking after in specific ways (Edmonds 1999) and the movements around the landscape which had previously been dictated by hunting, fishing, gathering or social reasons (cf. Kelly 1995) may now have been more structured by the herding of cattle. It is unclear at this stage whether these changes happened in the long-term or short-term: it is entirely feasible that looking after cattle did not have an immediate impact on people, instead being fitted into movements around the landscape that were already in place (cf. Kent 1989). It is clear that these things must have *eventually* changed the structure of society, but whether in the first 200 years is unclear.

One of the biggest arguments in recent years concerning the changes at the start of the Neolithic in Britain and Ireland comes from the stable isotope evidence (Milner *et al.* 2004; Schulting and Richards 2002a; 2002b; 2006). This evidence suggests that people stopped eating marine foods, and started utilising terrestrial (presumably domesticated) resources instead. Schulting (2000; 2004) in particular is keen on there being a swift change to the Neolithic around about 4000 BC, with people adopting domesticates throughout the British Isles. Quite clearly, there was a shift in people's diets from marine to terrestrial foodstuffs, but again, the question is whether this occurs at 4000 BC, or later in the sequence. Since the majority of bones sampled for isotopes date to after 3800 BC (for example, those from chambered tombs and causewayed enclosures), we must not assume a sudden shift in diet at 4000 BC, especially when we take into account the continued accumulation of shells at the midden sites and apparent use of fish at other sites (e.g. the Orcadian sites). I would advocate the approach that the Neolithic did indeed involve some big changes: changes to subsistence practice, changes to material culture sets, changes to exchange systems, and changes in beliefs and the organisation of society. I would be cautious of placing all of these changes at 4000 BC, preferring a much longer, drawn-out sequence, lasting hundreds of years.

Conclusions

The late Mesolithic of the Irish Sea zone has a number of characteristics which help us define this period. I have argued very strongly for a series of close connections between people and certain parts of the landscape. We are able to identify these associations with place if we consider the types of deposition happening at this time. I have suggested that in the Irish Sea zone, stone and shell were powerful metaphors and as such were deposited in very specific ways. The fragmentation of objects and their subsequent deposition was also an important element of late Mesolithic life, and seems to have involved human and animal bodies as well as other forms of material culture such as stone. When we consider the transition period, and the start of the Neolithic, I have argued that we are still struggling to understand this due to a lack of archaeological sites. What we do know is that some Neolithic things were adopted by people from about 4000 BC, but I have argued that their impact took several hundred years to be felt. Only after about 3800 BC did the real changes begin to occur and this is when people started to construct chambered tombs in the landscape. In the next chapter we go to consider the evidence from the Neolithic in general in this area, before moving on in chapter 4 to look at the chambered tombs themselves.

3

The Neolithic of the Irish Sea zone: background

Introduction

The Neolithic of the Irish Sea zone is characterised by the presence of all elements of the 'Neolithic package': pottery, polished stone tools, domesticated animals and crops, settlements and monuments. This chapter is designed as a summary of current knowledge of all aspects of the Neolithic of this region, bar monuments which are dealt with separately in the next chapter. We begin by considering the evidence of pottery and axes, before considering the range of evidence for settlements, domesticates and diet.

Pottery

The study of pottery has always been a crucial part of understanding the Neolithic of the Irish Sea and in Britain as a whole. Early pioneering work on pottery attempted to classify different styles so that the different cultures of the Neolithic could be identified (e.g. Piggott 1931). This was part of a broader culture-historical approach where changes in pot style were due to external influences (mostly incoming peoples). But early and relatively simple schemes became much more complicated as more and more material was uncovered, until by the 1970s there was a confusing array of names for different pottery styles around the Irish Sea. Over the last 10 years, however, important summaries of pottery from the Irish Sea zone have been published (Burrow 1997; Gibson 2002; Peterson 2003; Sheridan 1995) which have clarified and simplified the pottery sequence. This section aims to summarise the different pot styles from the Irish Sea zone.

Early Neolithic Carinated Bowls
The earliest Neolithic (4000–3800 BC) saw the production of Carinated Bowls throughout Britain and Ireland (formerly known as 'Western Neolithic' wares or Grimston-Lyles Hill Ware). Carinated Bowls are undecorated with marked

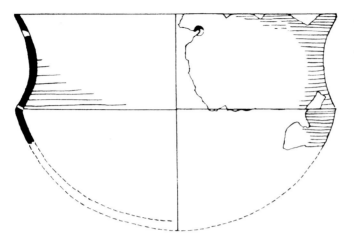

carinations and simple rims. These bowls were very finely made and show a great deal of uniformity across the Irish Sea area and in Britain as a whole (Fig. 3.1; Gibson 2002; Sheridan 1995). The high quality of these bowls has led to suggestions that the knowledge of pottery production arrived in Britain fully-formed from the Continent (Sheridan 2000; 2004). There are also some similarities between British pottery and contemporary bowls in northern France and the Low Countries (Gibson 2002, 69). However, despite claims that people arrived from the Continent with pottery, as has been suggested for the Irish Sea zone (see Sheridan 2004), it seems more likely that the knowledge of pot production was brought over to Britain. Furthermore, there is some evidence for people experimenting with ceramic technology (Rick Peterson *pers. comm.*), which supports the idea of native people learning to make new material culture. It also seems likely that 'the medium was the message' with these early bowls: the pottery itself was significant, not what it was used for (Cooney 2000, 184). This would explain the very restricted range of pot forms found in the earliest Neolithic.

Carinated Bowls are found throughout the study area, although no Carinated Bowls have yet been found on the Isle of Man (Burrow 1997, 9). These early Carinated Bowls are found from a variety of contexts in the Irish Sea zone, including in pit deposits (e.g. Newton, Islay: McCullagh 1988–9) and settlement sites (e.g. Lyles Hill: E. E. Evans 1953, and see below).

Developed bowls
From almost the beginning of the Neolithic, people modified the classic Carinated Bowl form. Initial modifications were followed by the production of a wide variety of decorated and undecorated pots, many with characteristic

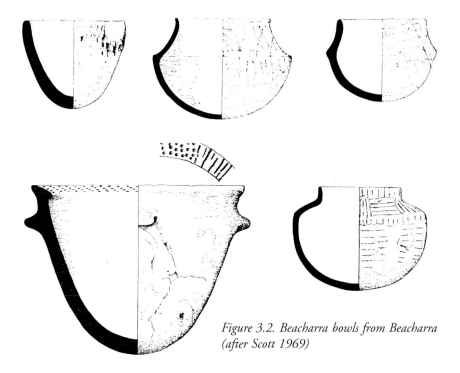

Figure 3.2. Beacharra bowls from Beacharra (after Scott 1969)

regional variations. In western Scotland, the Beacharra bowl (named after a chambered tomb in Kintyre which contained a series of pots) belongs to this group of developed bowls. Beacharra bowls have incised decoration above the carination (see Fig. 3.2). They are most commonly found in association with Clyde cairns (see chapter 4). While the Isle of Man has yet to produce any definite examples of Carinated Bowl, there are clearly examples of developed bowls. These shouldered bowls (also known as Mull Hill ware) have also been found in monumental contexts, from the chambered tombs of Ballaharra, Cashtal yn Ard and Mull Hill itself (Piggott 1932). Again, they share a number of similarities with developed bowls in western Scotland as well as north-east Ireland. In Wales, a wide range of developed bowls are found (Irish Sea Ware), again primarily from chambered tombs, such as Dyffryn Ardudwy in the north (Peterson 2003). In Ireland there is also a sequence of decorated 'bipartite bowls', which are developed Carinated Bowls. These pot forms are very similar to developed bowls in south-west Scotland although they have been given a different set of names. Drimnagh or Ballyalton bowls date to 3500–3300 BC and developed from simple Carinated Bowls in north-east Ireland (Fig. 3.3). They are very similar to Beacharra Ware from western Scotland and the shouldered bowls from the Isle of Man. Typically they are decorated with crescents and this

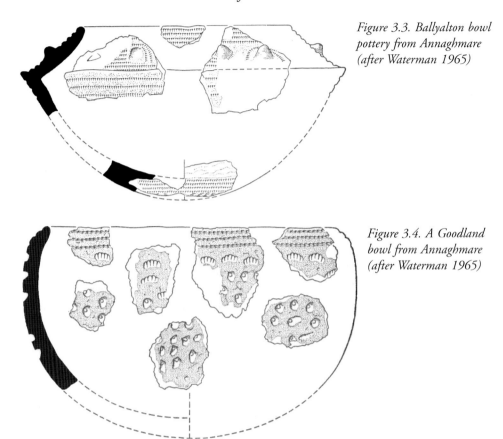

Figure 3.3. Ballyalton bowl pottery from Annaghmare (after Waterman 1965)

Figure 3.4. A Goodland bowl from Annaghmare (after Waterman 1965)

is a design found on pots in Ireland, Scotland as well as further afield in Brittany (Sheridan 1995, 11). Just like their Scottish counterparts, many of these bowls are found in mortuary contexts, in particular in court cairns.

Middle Neolithic diversity

By the middle Neolithic (c3400 BC) a wide variety of pot forms were in use in the Irish Sea zone. The modified carinated bowls found in western Scotland, Wales and Ireland continued in use, and another set of pot styles developed from these. In Ireland in particular there was an abundance of richly decorated impressed wares found with distinctive regional styles. These Irish bowls were more ornate than their British counterparts (Gibson 2002, 81). For example Goodland Bowls are found in Ulster and are decorated around the upper part of the pot (Sheridan 1995, 12; Fig. 3.4). Another Irish style of pottery, Carrowkeel Ware, are coarse bowls with heavy decoration, and share similarities with Peterborough Ware from England and Wales. They are found primarily

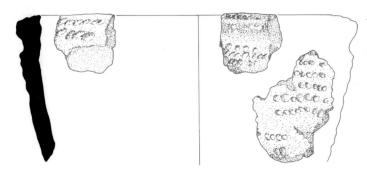

Figure 3.5. Peterborough Ware from Caldey Island (after Gibson 1995)

in passage graves but are also found from other contexts such as court cairns (Sheridan 1995, 11). It is also of interest to note that Hebridean Ware has been found at Portstewart in northern Ireland, showing the ongoing connections across, and beyond, the Irish Sea (Sheridan 1995, 18).

Peterborough Ware is one of the classic forms of middle Neolithic pottery (Fig. 3.5). It is a highly decorated form of thick-rimmed bowl pottery found throughout England and Wales and up into eastern Scotland. It appears from 3300 BC and continues to be used till the end of the Neolithic. In our study area Peterborough Ware is only really found in Wales. However, it is clear that some of the heavily decorated wares of the Irish Sea were at least in part influenced by Peterborough Ware, shown by clear similarities between the different types of pottery (Sheridan 1995, 15).

Later Neolithic traditions

Many of the impressed wares in Ireland continue to be used up until the end of the Neolithic (Gibson 2002), as do modified carinated bowls elsewhere around the Irish Sea. This period also saw the emergence of Grooved Ware across the whole of Britain and Ireland, followed at the end of the sequence with the arrival of Beakers.

Grooved Ware. Grooved Ware is one of the best known styles of late Neolithic pottery (formerly known as Rinyo-Clacton Ware with 'Woodland' and 'Durrington Walls' substyles) and is found throughout the British Isles (Fig. 3.6). It marks a considerable break in the ceramic sequence as Grooved Ware does not resemble the bowls which had been used in Britain for a thousand years. Instead they have flat bottoms and are covered in decoration. Probably originating in Orkney, Grooved Ware dates from about 3000 BC (Cleal and MacSween 1999, 6), possibly earlier, with the earliest dates being from vessels found in northern Scotland. In Orkney, this form of pottery is found primarily in settlement sites as well as in some chambered tombs and henges (Renfrew

Figure 3.6. Irish Grooved
Ware (after Cooney 2000)

1979). There is also a claimed connection between Grooved Ware and passage graves, as pot decoration shares similarities with passage grave art (Gibson and Woods 1990; but see Kinnes 1995). In southern Britain, Grooved Ware is often found in pit deposits as well as in association with the large late Neolithic henges such as Durrington Walls (see Thomas 1999, 114). The association of Grooved Ware and henges, and the possible connections with passage graves, has led to suggestions that this form of pottery was used primarily for feasting and ritual activity. This may have included brewing alcohol and serving food in ritual contexts (Richards and Thomas 1984).

While Grooved Ware is a relatively common find in northern Scotland and southern Britain, it is less common in the Irish Sea area. This is almost certainly to do with a paucity of excavated sites, but may also be a reflection of people's desires to make and use (or not) certain styles of pottery. In Ireland, Grooved Ware has only been found on 13 sites (Brindley 1999; Cooney 2000), primarily in ceremonial contexts. There is a particular connection in Ireland between Grooved Ware and passage graves, as this form of pottery has been found at some of the largest passage graves: Newgrange, Knowth, Fourknocks and Lough Crew (Brindley 1999; Eogan and Roche 1999). Grooved Ware was also found at Ballynahatty henge and Monknewtown henge (Eogan and Roche 1999; Hartwell 1998). However, Grooved Ware also occurs on settlement sites, such as Donegore in Co. Antrim, suggesting that it was not exclusively linked to monumental complexes. In western Scotland, Grooved Ware is also a rare find. Some material has been found as secondary deposits in the Clyde monuments (e.g. in Tormore on Arran: Cowie and MacSween 1999). Grooved Ware was also found at the stone circle complex at Machrie Moor (Cowie and MacSween 1999). It also occurs on settlement sites in western Scotland such as Luce Sands in Dumfries and Galloway and Townhead, Rothesay (Cowie and MacSween 1999). However, these are rare and isolated instances of this pottery form in the area. In Wales, Grooved Ware has been found at sites such as Upper Ninepence barrow in the Walton Basin, although it would be fair to say that late Neolithic evidence is fairly limited in Wales (Peterson 2004). Some possible examples of Grooved Ware also occur on the Isle of Man (Burrow 1997), although the late Neolithic here is characterised by the distinctive 'Ronaldsway jars' (Woodcock 2004).

It would appear, then, that communities along the Irish Sea were aware of the Grooved Ware tradition, and in some cases made and used Grooved Ware pottery. The relative absence of Grooved Ware from some parts of the Irish Sea suggests that while people in this area were still in contact with the wider British population, and did use Grooved Ware to a certain extent, it perhaps had less resonance in the Irish Sea zone. As we shall see this is manifest in a number of other ways, where the late Neolithic trajectory of the Irish Sea zone differs from that elsewhere in Britain (henges etc). Alternatively, Grooved Ware may have inherited *more* significance because it was rare.

Beaker. Grooved Ware, and other decorated wares were still in use when the final form of Neolithic pottery appeared around 2600 BC. Beaker is found throughout Britain in the very late Neolithic and into the early Bronze Age. Visually striking with a fine surface finish and elaborate decoration, Beakers were made in a number of sizes including bowls, jars and larger pots (Fig. 3.7). Originally thought to indicate the arrival of the Beaker People from the continent (e.g. Childe 1930), it seems more likely that the concept of Beakers only was imported into Britain and Ireland (and in fact Beaker was not widely adopted in Ireland: Gibson 2002, 87). Although the odd Beaker from Europe has been found, the vast majority were locally produced. They are found in henges and graves, and as secondary deposits in chambered tombs.

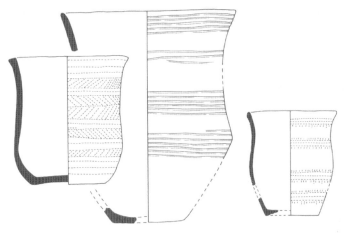

Figure 3.7. Beakers from Ireland (after Case 1995)

Pottery and the Irish Sea connection

The style of pottery demonstrates unequivocally that there were close contacts between people on different sides of the Irish Sea from the earliest Neolithic onwards. A number of traditions are found in all areas bordering the Irish Sea, from the earliest Carinated Bowls to later traditions of Grooved Ware and Beaker. Furthermore, seemingly regional pottery styles almost always share many characteristics with pot styles found elsewhere in the Irish Sea zone, such as the bipartite bowls from north-east Ireland and Beacharra bowls from western Scotland. While it would be problematic to suggest that regional styles are indicative of regional identities, these distinctive styles of material culture clearly demonstrate connections across this broader area.

It is also worth considering the contexts from which different pot styles occur in the Irish Sea region, and again this shows similarities across this broad area not only in the style and design of the pottery but also in the ways in which pots were actually used and deposited. It also highlights the fact that while there is no question that pottery had practical uses, it was also linked from an early stage with the dead, monumentality and a range of depositional practices.

Early Carinated Bowls, for example, are found from a variety of contexts in the Irish Sea zone, including in pit deposits, on settlement sites and sometimes in (or under) chambered tombs. This suggests that right from the onset of the use of these pots, they were an appropriate medium to be deposited in a specific range of locations. However, there is also increasing evidence to show that these early Carinated Bowls were often used for heating and storing food (Thomas 1999, 98), so there was also an association with food preparation and consumption. This may not seem particularly surprising, so it is interesting that there seems to be an increased connection between pottery and the dead a few centuries into the Neolithic. As we have already seen, developed early Neolithic bowls (Beacharra; Drimnagh; Ballyalton, etc) are frequently found in the primary phases of chambered tombs. The exceptional preservation afforded by the chambers as well as a focus of research on these monuments has perhaps partly biased our view of these developed bowls as primarily associated with the dead, as they are also found on 'settlement' sites (Sheridan 1995, 11). Nevertheless, it is interesting to consider the range of associations being created between pottery, monuments and the deposition of the dead (and see Fowler 2004).

Moving to the later Neolithic, the limited quantities of Grooved Ware from the regions around the Irish Sea occur in both 'monumental' and 'non-monumental' contexts. Monumental contexts include the complex at Machrie Moor on Arran (Cowie and MacSween 1999), the Ballynahatty henge in Co. Down and the Brú na Bóinne complex in Co. Meath (Eogan and Roche 1999). Grooved Ware is also found in non-monumental contexts: for example at the Donegore settlement site in Co. Antrim (Brindley 1999) and Luce Sands in Dumfries and Galloway (Cowie and MacSween 1999). From Wales, a quantity of Grooved Ware was recovered from pits underneath the Upper Ninepence barrow (Gibson 1999). The pottery had been used for cooking beef and was associated with flint tools used for cutting meat and working wood (Peterson 2004, 196). However, there is very much a sense of ambiguity with regards the context of much of this Grooved Ware, which almost certainly reflects the inadequacy of our terminology rather than the sets of ways in which it was used in the past. Eogan and Roche (1999, 105) note that it is difficult to ascertain whether the Grooved Ware from Newgrange was ritual or domestic: i.e. from the monumental or domestic phase of the site. This exemplifies the point that is relevant to discussions on all types of material culture and that was discussed in the previous chapter in relation to lithics: the division between ritual and domestic is unhelpful in considering the ways in which objects were used and subsequently deposited. There was almost certainly no real conceptual divide between the two in the Neolithic (and see Bradley 2005). Instead everyday 'domestic' life was embedded in ritual activity and *vice versa*.

The potential of pots

What did pottery mean to the people around the Irish Sea? Firstly, on a practical level, it enabled more complex sequences of food production. In the first instance pottery enables you to store food and some forms of pottery were probably used as part of a complex series of storing foods, such as salting, smoking and so on. Pottery also enables people to cook foods in distinctive ways, including over an open fire. It has also been suggested that pottery enabled the brewing

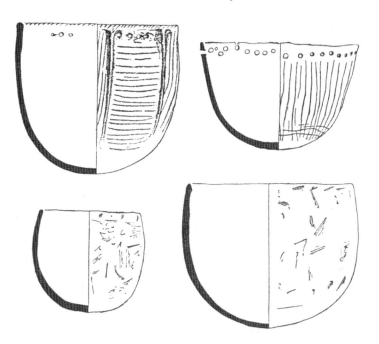

Figure 3.8. Pottery from Dooey's Cairn

of alcohol for the first time (Dineley and Dineley 2000), which has interesting implications for its presence as part of funerary rituals. While pottery may have made storage and cooking slightly easier, pre-pottery people nevertheless had a whole suite of methods and techniques at their disposal for achieving the same results. Furthermore, one clear disadvantage of pottery is that it is not easily transportable over long distances, a clear issue when considering the mobility of Neolithic groups (see below).

The significance of pottery may relate less to ways of cooking food, but more with ways of *serving* food. In many societies even today, food is a highly charged substance. The exchange, preparation and consumption of food is often a crucial part of belief systems. Certain foods can only be served in certain dishes, and particular foods eaten in a specific order. This frequently relates to everyday life but is even more pronounced in special, ritualised contexts (Counihan 1999; Lysaght 2002). Ethnographic examples also show how the throwing of feasts is a way of gaining social status. The preparation and serving of extravagant quantities of food was a key part of the potlatch ceremony (Kan 1989), for example, which would potentially enable individuals to gain status within a community. Pottery would potentially have been an important element of these events. Pottery, then, may have had a relatively minor impact on cooking techniques and storage, but fulfilled an important role in social relations and interactions.

The significance of pottery in the Neolithic is likely to have gone beyond the ways in which it was simply used for cooking and serving food. The production of pottery involves a long process which may have made all sorts of connections with people and places. Firstly, the source of materials in the Neolithic seems to have been significant to people, exemplified by the taking of particular stone from specific mountains and outcrops and turning them into stone axes (see below). The source of the clay used to make pots may have been equally as important (A. Jones 2002). One of the key themes of this book is the significance of place, and I have (Cummings and Whittle 2004) and will argue again here that places in the Neolithic world were imbued with significance in relation to local and more wide-reaching mythologies and cosmologies. Thus, the taking of clay from a particular place in the landscape may have been a potent act in itself, associating the finished pot with a specific location and set of myths. Equally, the making of the pot may have been an important event in people's lives. In the Neolithic there were no kilns. Instead, pots would have been fired in 'bonfire firings', which involved stacking up the unfired pots with wood and charcoal. A considerable amount of preparation would be required for a firing, involving not only the making of the pottery, but also the collection of wood and charcoal. A firing would also have been quite a visual spectacle. We could suggest that the investment of time may have meant that a community may only have made and fired pots once or twice a year, perhaps making it a seasonal event.

There are further aspects to consider when thinking about the manufacture of pottery. A considerable amount of knowledge is required to make pottery – not only with regards shaping and decorating the pot itself, but also how to prepare the clay properly and how to fire it successfully. It has been suggested that not everyone in each community knew how to make pots, instead this was knowledge restricted to a small group of people. Ethnographic examples show that women traditionally make pots in many societies (e.g. Crown and Wills 1995, 247), offering one possible parallel for Neolithic society. As already noted above, the earliest Neolithic pottery (Carinated Bowl) from Britain and Ireland was extremely well made right from the outset. The knowledge of how to make pots must have been carefully taught to people in Britain, or introduced by incoming Europeans (Sheridan 2004). Perhaps, then, from the beginning of the Neolithic pottery production was connected with only a specific group of people who had the knowledge (magic) to turn clay into pottery (cf. Gell 1998). Another interesting aspect of pottery that must be considered is the actual life history of the pot and how this affected people's understanding of this form of material culture. Questions such as what was kept in each pot, who owned them, and how did they get to the site must have been significant. Often societies make connections between the life of an object and the life of a person (e.g. Bloch 1995) while other studies suggest that pots may even have been a crucial part of a person's identity (Fowler 2004). In the previous chapter we considered how flint nodules or pebbles were fragmented through knapping and were then deposited in very specific ways. The fragmentation and deposition of material culture is also found in the Neolithic (in this case with pottery), hinting at elements of continuity from the previous period.

Once we begin to consider the different elements of pottery, both its construction and subsequent use, we can begin to see how this particular form of material culture would have resonated with people throughout the Irish Sea zone. Therefore, we can summarise that pottery was:

- Connected to specific places
- Connected to particular people
- Associated with the preparation and serving of food
- Frequently deposited at places used to house the dead
- A crucial part of social relations
- Connected to wider identities across a broader area
- Connected with the origins of the Neolithic in Europe

Pottery therefore may have operated at a variety of different scales; individual, community, local and even national. Each of these aspects would not always have been at the forefront of people's minds when engaging with these things, but would have been known about by people, and drawn on at relevant times.

Lithics

Another characteristic of the Neolithic is the distinctive range of stone tools found in assemblages around the Irish Sea. Polished stone axes and leaf-shaped arrowheads are the two best-known Neolithic stone tools, but the region also saw the use of many distinctive types of stone, including stone from axe 'factories' and the distinctive sources of Antrim flint and Arran pitchstone. This section begins by considering the axe factories of the Irish Sea region, before looking at all stone tools found in the area.

Axe factories

The areas around the Irish Sea have produced considerable quantities of polished stone axes as well as the vast majority of the large Neolithic axe factories being found in this area (Fig. 3.9). The best-known and most prolific axe factory was that at Langdale in Cumbria (Bradley and Edmonds 1993; Fig. 3.10). Axes from

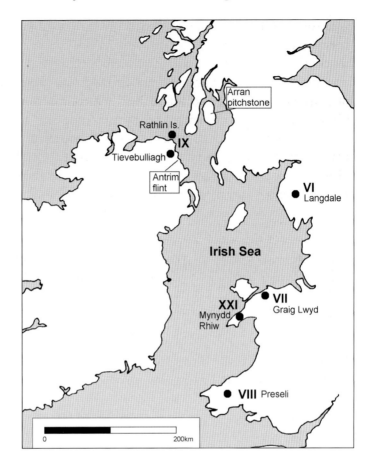

Figure 3.9. The location of the major early Neolithic axe factories in the Irish Sea zone, with the source of Antrim flint and Arran pitchstone also indicated

Figure 3.10. A roughout axe from Langdale

this group (Group VI) were quarried primarily from rock sources close to the summit of the Landgale Pikes, two visually distinctive peaks in Cumbria, as well as from Scafell Pike, the highest mountain in England. Langdale axes are found in virtually every part of Britain and Ireland (see Clough and Cummins 1988, map 6), although the precise date that these axes were exchanged and deposited is hard to define due to the difficulty in dating the extraction and movement of axes from the source. There is a general sense that the vast majority of axes were made and then moved after about 3300 BC (Bradley and Edmonds 1993, 201), although some axes were clearly made in the earlier Neolithic. One of the most intriguing aspects of the Langdale axe source is that the stone chosen to make into axes was frequently not the best quality stone in the area. Instead, people seem to have deliberately chosen the more inaccessible stone sources in order to get stone. In fact people would actually have had to pass the places with the best quality stone in order to get to the quarries they were using. This suggests that the stone source itself, as opposed to the quality of the stone, was important (Bradley and Edmonds 1993).

Other axe sources found in the Irish Sea area share similarities with Langdale. In Ireland, Group IX axes come from Tievebulliagh and Rathlin Island, the former another visually distinctive mountain in Co. Antrim (Fig. 3.11). Just as at Langdale, the remains of axe working debris can be seen running down the side of the mountain. And, just as at Langdale, it would have been a precarious and perilous place for people to visit. Considerable quantities of porcellanite (Group IX) axes have been found in Ireland: 1000 are known to be found in Co. Antrim alone, with another 1300 axes listed from north-east Ireland with no known locality (Sheridan 1986, 19). Furthermore, Knowles, the original investigator of Tievebulliagh reported over 4000 axes from the site itself, and 'abundant' specimens on Rathlin Island. It is clear, therefore, that Tievebulliagh and Rathlin Island produced considerable numbers of axes. It is interesting that Ulster, especially counties Antrim and Derry, has more axes than any other part of Ireland. This is not purely because of the presence of the axe factory in Co. Antrim, as non-porcellanite axes are also far more numerous in Ulster even though they did not originate from there (Cooney *et al.* 1999). This may be in part due to the long tradition of research in this area, but also hints at the possibility that there was a particular resonance between people and axes in this part of the Irish Sea zone. Porcellanite axes are also found across the Irish Sea and throughout Britain and Ireland, with a number in Kintyre, south-west Scotland and even Wales (Clough and Cummins 1988, 273). It is also worth noting that this stone source was used to make other tools as well as axes: adzes, chisels, knives, scrapers and leaf-shaped arrowheads have all been found in porcellanite (Sheridan 1986, 27).

Figure 3.11. The axe source of Tievebulliagh and Rathlin Island, Co. Antrim

Figure 3.12. The summit of Carn Meini, one of the sources of axes in south-west Wales

Other important axe factories in the Irish Sea zone include the Preseli source (Group VIII) in south-west Wales. Axes from this source came from St David's Head and Ramsey Island (Barker 1992, 71), as well as from the Preselis, including Carn Meini (Fig. 3.12). Just as at Tievebulliagh and Langdale, Carn Meini is a visually very striking mountain, and also famous for being the source of the Stonehenge bluestones (and see Bradley 2000a). Although little work has been done on the axe sources themselves, two axehead manufacturing sites have been found at the base of the Preselis, showing that roughout axes were being made here (David and Williams 1995). Finally, there were two important axe factories in north Wales, Graig Lwyd, Penmanmawr (Group VII) and Mynydd Rhiw (Group XXI). Graig Lwyd axes were made from a volcanic plug of rock found at the summit of the hill on the edge of the Snowdonia mountains. These axes date from the early Neolithic and have been found as far away as the Isle of Man (Clough and Cummins 1988). Mynydd Rhiw on the other hand produced shale axes and seems to have been used from the late Mesolithic into the early Neolithic (Lynch 1995, 26). However, very few Group XXI axes have been found, and all are from Wales, which suggests that this axe source was only used for local production. Other axe sources are located in the Irish Sea zone (see Clough and Cummins 1988, 265) but these are small-scale production sites which are almost certainly very late Neolithic or early Bronze Age in date.

The axe factories demonstrate that specific parts of the landscape were chosen to be turned into objects. As clearly shown with the Langdale example, people were not choosing sources solely because they produced high quality stone. Instead, people seem to have chosen the most visually striking mountains with inaccessible rock outcrops as the source of axes. These sources may have been desirable *because* they were dangerous to reach. It may have been a rite of passage to visit these sources and extract stone to be made into axes (Price 2007). It has also been suggested that the mountains from which the stone axes came were important places in their own right. As already described, the Langdale Pikes can be considered the most visually distinctive mountains in Cumbria. Their unique domed profile makes them easy to spot amongst the peaks of the Lake District. Likewise, Carn Meini in south-west Wales, Tievebulliagh in Co. Antrim, Graig Lwyd and Mynydd Rhiw are all visually distinctive mountains in their respective landscapes (Cummings and Whittle 2004). These may have been mountains already associated with a whole range of myths and stories, relating back to a Mesolithic worldview (see Cummings and Whittle 2004). To take stone from such cosmologically important locations may have been an extremely potent act (cf. Taçon 1991). Elsewhere I have drawn attention to the fact that the summit of one of the axe factories, that of Carn Meini in south-west Wales, consists of a number of rocks erupting out of the hill. On closer examination, many of these look like they have been built, resembling chambered tombs, standing stones and stone circles (Cummings 2002a; Cummings and Whittle 2004). Neolithic people may well have had a whole series of interpretations of such a place, and the extraction of stone from here to make axes may well have been imbued with the significance of this particular place. Therefore, making an axe was literally taking a bit of a special place and turning it into an artefact (Bradley 2000a, 88).

Axes
While the axe factories are able to tell us a great deal about axe manufacture in Neolithic society, the axes from these factories are in many ways quite problematic to study. It has already been mentioned that we have no way of knowing the series of interactions that took place in the life history of an axe. From its initial quarrying from the source to its final deposition it may have undergone many

transactions over many years. So although we can see the kinds of distances that objects such as axes travelled, we cannot be sure whether this was through a complex series of exchanges (like the Kula network: see Ray 2004) or the long distance movement of individuals, or a combination of both. Another problem with the study of axes is that, for the most part, they come from unknown or uncertain contexts. Large quantities of axes in museum collections were picked up from fields or during construction projects in the eighteenth, nineteenth and early twentieth centuries. Even now, many axes are found through fieldwalking as opposed to excavation. This makes it hard to understand the variety of ways in which axes were deposited. However, some axes do come from secure contexts. Axes have been found in causewayed enclosures (e.g. Windmill Hill: Whittle *et al.* 1999), although there are very few of these in the Irish Sea zone. In Britain, axes are relatively rare in chambered tombs, although there are exceptions. The fragment of a jadeite axe which originated in the Alps was found at Cairnholy in south-west Scotland (Piggott and Powell 1949), and four polished stone axes were found associated with Bryn yr Hen Bobl on Anglesey (Lynch 1969a, 166). In contrast, axes are more commonly found in Irish monuments, although still only 11 court tombs, two portal tombs and two passage graves have produced axes (Sheridan *et al.* 1992). In Ireland many axes are found in rivers and bogs (Cooney and Mandal 1998). In fact nearly 50% of Irish stone axes come from rivers: hundreds of examples come from the River Bann and over 700 have been dredged from the River Shannon (Sheridan *et al.* 1992, 392). This phenomenon may be partly explained by the drainage of a number of rivers there, as compared to Britain. However, the sheer number of axes from rivers and bogs suggests these were deliberate and special deposits in watery places.

So what can the study of the axes themselves tell us about the Neolithic? Firstly, since the deposition of an object represents its final resting place, it could have gone through many transactions before then, some at very small scales, others at much wider scales. The distribution of axes from known sources does show, however, that people were moving across the Irish Sea. Irish axes have been found in Britain and Langdale axes have been found in Ireland (Clough and Cummins 1988; Cooney and Mandel 1998). Therefore, this is another strand of evidence in support of the idea that people were in frequent contact across the Irish Sea in the Neolithic. The findspots of Neolithic stone axes also suggests that people were travelling by water in the Neolithic. Luce Sands in Dumfries and Galloway for example, has produced a large quantity of stone axes (c.200), including large numbers of Cumbrian axes and two jadeite axes (Williams 1970). A polishing stone has also been found near Luce Sands (Taylor 1996, 232) and this, combined with the sheer density of stone axes and axe debris found, has led to suggestions that Luce Bay was used for the importation by sea and working of axes from distant sources (Williams 1970, 112). Furthermore, water transport would have had to have been employed at the Rathlin Island axe factory. While we will never be able to say for certain that someone from Cumbria, say, travelled by boat to south-west Scotland, or even that someone from south-west Scotland went to Cumbria to get axes, it does show that some people at least were moving around the Irish Sea. The most likely scenario is that axes were transported in a complex series of ways, some perhaps making one long voyage, others being traded and exchanged between communities. Nevertheless, axes exemplify the interconnectedness of the Irish Sea zone in the Neolithic.

One key aspect of these polished stone axes is that it would have taken considerable effort to polish a rough-out axe. Many hours of labour would be required to make the finished object. It is interesting, therefore, that polishing an axe does not make it any more efficient at cutting or chopping. It is also relevant to note that the vast majority of axes found in Britain and Ireland had never been used. It would seem, therefore, that polished stone axes were not for the most part functional objects. Instead they may have been prestige objects, perhaps things that enabled people to gain social power or privilege. Although roughouts are sometimes found as hoards (see below) there is little evidence that polished stone axes were accumulated. They are, for the most, deposited singly, or in fragments, in the ground, in monuments, in pits or in watery places. In this way polished stone axes may have given people prestige but they were not things that could be accumulated. Perhaps they were designed more for display, but ultimately the object was destined to be exchanged or given away (Ray 2004), in some cases to other people, in others back to the earth itself (Whittle 1995). The complex set of processes required to make an axe (from quarrying it, working it, transporting it and polishing it) also meant that a number of people could have been involved in creating it (cf. Finlay 2000), creating complex social networks amongst and between communities.

Another important aspect of polished stone axes relates back to the idea that it was the source of the axe that was significant. It has been suggested that polishing an axe brings out the character of the raw material, showing where it originated (Bradley and Edmonds 1993, 49; Whittle 1995). So by polishing an axe from Langdale it would bring out the distinctive qualities of that particular stone, and people would know that the axe came from Cumbria. This may in turn link back to the significance of sources themselves, where the distant and exotic would have been source of respect and awe (cf. Gell 1998). It is also worth considering the possibility that axes, just like pots and people, had their own histories and biographies. This would relate not only to the source of the stone, but also processes of knapping, polishing and exchange. If axes were part of a complex exchange network, they may have then become associated with particular individuals or communities. Likewise, they may have acquired biographies which related to their role in particular events. This may have reinforced notions of interconnectedness between communities across the Irish Sea. There are also interesting implications for the role of axes with regards the origins of the Neolithic. As we have already seen, there are some antecedents of the stone axe in the Mesolithic, especially in Ireland (see chapter 2). However, axes were very rare in Mesolithic Britain. In Britain, polished stone axes may have been considered something rather new, while there may have been more of a sense of continuity in Ireland.

Flint and other stone tools
As we have already seen, microlithic technology was in decline in western Scotland in the late Mesolithic, and abandoned completely in Ireland in favour of the Bann flake. Microlithic technology persisted in other parts of the Irish Sea, but was finally abandoned in most areas from around 4000 BC (Burrow 2003, 48). In addition to the widespread appearance of polished stone axes, the Neolithic is also marked by the first use of elaborate retouched and polished forms such as leaf-shaped arrowheads (Fig. 3.13) as well as some other beautifully-made objects

Figure 3.13. A leaf-shaped arrowhead from Kintyre

such as plano-convex knives. These stone tools are regularly picked up during
fieldwalking and as stray finds. They are also commonly found in megalithic
contexts: leaf-shaped arrowheads are frequently found in the chambers of megaliths
throughout the Irish Sea region, as are knives and scrapers (and see chapter 4). This
means that these Neolithic tools, just like early Neolithic pottery, were associated
with monumental contexts from early on. The same range of tools are not found
consistently throughout the Irish Sea zone: serrated flakes are found in most parts
of Britain and Ireland, but are less common in Scotland (Edmonds 1995, 40).
Hollow scrapers, commonly found in Ireland in megalithic contexts as well as on
settlement sites (Nelis 2004, 164) also occur in Cumbria and north Wales, but
are not found in western Scotland or south Wales (Edmonds 1995, 40). The tools
used by people also changes throughout the Neolithic, so leaf-shaped arrowheads
were mostly replaced with laurel-leaf and 'javelin' style arrowheads in the later
Neolithic (Edmonds 1995, 101).

The vast majority of lithic assemblages from the Irish Sea zone are made of
flint, although chert and quartz were also used in some areas (Wickham-Jones
1986). It is significant, therefore, that many areas bordering on the Irish Sea
do not have plentiful supplies of flint. There are no sources of flint nodules
in western Scotland, Cumbria, the Isle of Man or Wales (Burrow 2003, 42;
Wickham-Jones 1986; Wickham-Jones and Collins 1978). In these areas, flint
could be acquired as beach pebbles, and in some areas flint nodules derived
from off-shore sources may also have been available (for example in south-west
Scotland). However, this means that high quality and large pieces of flint were
in limited supply in the local area. The nearest sources of flint for communities
in western Britain were the Yorkshire Wolds, south-west England and north-
eastern Ireland. It is not surprising, therefore, that Antrim flint is found in
western Scotland, demonstrating unequivocally another connection across the
Irish Sea. One example of Antrim flint in Scotland comes from the hoard of
stone axes and flakes near Campbeltown in Kintyre (Saville 1999). This cache
of 178 items, all made from Antrim flint, was found on the side of a grassy
knoll a few hundred metres from the sea. The cache included five axeheads
which were all final-stage roughouts, requiring only polishing to finish them
(Saville 1999). This cache of Antrim flint is not unique: two other caches have
been found in western Dumfries and Galloway (Saville 1999, 107). The large
flint tools found in the chambered tombs of Arran were also made from Antrim
flint (Saville 1999, 106) and all this hints at the widespread use of Antrim flint
in Scotland.

Just like in western Scotland, there are no *in situ* flint deposits in Wales
(Burrow 2003, 42). However, a considerable number of flint axes have been

recovered in Wales which shows that flint was also being imported into this part of the Irish Sea zone, probably from south-east England, and in some cases, from further afield. A late Neolithic hoard of flint was found at Penmachno where 36 large flint pieces were found eroding out of the peat. The nearest flint supplies to this area were either southern England (200km away over land) or Ireland (200km away over the Irish Sea).

Arran pitchstone is another distinctive stone found in the Irish Sea area, and again distributions of this material demonstrate contacts across this area. It was utilised from the late Mesolithic into the middle Bronze Age, and is a visually very distinctive shiny dark stone. Not surprisingly, it is found throughout the Isle of Arran itself, but it is also found further afield up to 300km from its source (Williams Thorpe and Thorpe 1984). Pitchstone has been recovered from sites on the Isle of Bute, Islay, Dumfries and Galloway, and as far away as Ireland where it was found at Lyles Hill and Ballygalley (Simpson 1995), both in Co. Antrim. It was not being exported across this area as other lithic sources were impoverished: firstly, Antrim has plentiful flint sources, and secondly, when pitchstone is found it is only ever a small part of larger assemblages (Wickham-Jones 1986, 7; Williams Thorpe and Williams 1984). This suggests that just like with stone axes, it was the source and appearance of the stone that was significant.

There is a wide range of different lithics from the Neolithic of the Irish Sea zone. However, they clearly paint a picture of interaction in the Neolithic. Therefore, we can summarise that lithics were:

- Connected to specific places, especially visually distinctive mountains
- Appropriate media for use as 'everyday' items as well objects more suited to deposition in monumental and other significant locales
- Associated with particular people and their biographies
- About the movement of both people and things
- A crucial part of social relations, quite possibly connected with prestige and status
- Part of wider connections across a broader area, especially the Irish Sea region, but also Britain as a whole as well as further afield to Europe

One of the most interesting aspects of the study of lithics in the Irish Sea zone is that it shows that people were obviously moving 'bits of places' across the Irish Sea. This is important for helping us to understand and further consider the nature of interactions in this area (see chapter 8).

Occupation and settlement

We have already considered the evidence for settlement in the form of lithic scatters (see above), which are the most prolific evidence we have for occupation in the Neolithic. Lithic scatters represent the remains of occupations of place: they can indicate everything from a quick knapping episode as part of a hunting trip (as has been suggested for the lithics from Waun Wignen Felen in Wales: Barton *et al.* 1995), to locales utilised for extended periods of time and returned to repeatedly (e.g. Luce Sands in Dumfries and Galloway and Donegore, Co. Antrim in Ireland). Lithic scatters are rarely associated with any structures, although the remains of stakeholes, hearths and scoops in the earth imply the presence of tents or temporary dwellings of some description. Lithic scatters are useful for demonstrating which parts of the landscape were being utilised by people, and also for modelling the types of activity that were occurring. In the Irish Sea zone it is clear that Neolithic people were utilising both upland and lowland zones, although at present there is limited evidence for the use of the very mountainous regions (e.g. the Cumbrian Fells: Bradley and Edmonds 1993, 139).

There is also some evidence of people creating or reusing shell middens in the Neolithic which are also likely to be indicative of occupation activity. Many of the shell middens of western Scotland were still in use in the early Neolithic up until about 3500 BC (Bonsall 1997, 27). Shell middens elsewhere in the Irish Sea zone also have Neolithic levels (e.g. Schulting and Richards 2002b). There is also some indication that caves were used in the Neolithic period (Tolan-Smith 2001), although in most cases this evidence does not suggest permanent occupation but either quick visits as part of a movement around the landscape or even the remains of funerary or ritualised activity (see next chapter).

In addition to the scatters indicative of settlement, there are also a number of structures which have been interpreted as houses. These remain rare in western Britain, but increasingly common in Ireland. In west Wales the site of Clegyr Boia, Pembrokeshire (Williams 1953; Vyner 2001) consisted of the remains of three huts as well as a midden. The site was reused in the Iron Age but it is possible that some of the ramparts at the site date to the Neolithic. However, it has been suggested that these remains are only from a short occupation phase which ended with the burning of the site (Vyner 2001, 88). Other structural remains are rare in Wales. However, at the site of Llandegai in north-west Wales, the original excavations uncovered the remains of two possible buildings (Houlder 1968, 219), which have been interpreted as houses. The association with the henge complex at Llandegai shed some doubt on this. However, a whole new series of structures have just recently been found close to the original Llandegai site, and on Holyhead, which suggest that Neolithic houses were indeed present at this site (Gary Robinson *pers. comm.*).

Elsewhere in the Irish Sea zone houses are equally uncommon. On the Isle of Man a house was uncovered at Ronaldsway, giving its name to a distinctive style of late Neolithic Manx pottery (see above). Although this structure had a central hearth and was associated with tools and pottery, it may not have been a 'domestic' dwelling, but rather a structure for ritualised activity (Burrow 1997, 20). In western Scotland, there are two sites on Cowal which have been interpreted as the remains of houses. At Ardnadam, a sequence of Neolithic houses were represented by postholes, cobbled areas and hearths (Ritchie 1997, 44). Another site, Auchategan, also consisted of a series of structures with postholes and hearths. Both sites produced pottery and lithics, however, the structures were not necessarily permanent: all may have been fairly insubstantial and not long-lived (Ritchie 1997, 45). Therefore, throughout western Britain there are very few examples of Neolithic houses. Those that have been found do not seem to suggest permanent dwellings and also may not even be associated with domestic life in its most traditional sense (and see below). A number of years ago it would have been argued that permanent settlements from the Neolithic were simply waiting to be unearthed in Britain, so it was a matter of doing more fieldwork to find them. It is fair to say that some areas of western Britain could certainly benefit from more intensive fieldwork programmes, as clearly shown with the recent finds north Wales. However, we must also accept the possibility that there were never large numbers of permanent houses in Neolithic Britain and that people remained, for the most part, mobile (see below).

The situation in Ireland, however, is quite different from that in Britain. Over the past decade a surprising number of houses have been found in Ireland (Armit *et al.* 2003; Grogan 1996). This new data compliments the settlements already known from the area. There seems to be a particular concentration of sites in Antrim, partly a result of developer-funded projects (see Armit *et al.* 2003). New sites include sites on Islandmagee, including the site at Ballyharry. This complex multi-phase site has evidence for houses, including House 1 which was a rectangular structure. There were a number of phases of activity in this structure before it was abandoned. At this site the main rectangular structure was burnt, in association with 34 projectile points: this evidence has been used to suggest that the site was attacked (Moore 2004, 143). The building was then reconstructed with stone tool deposits in the post-holes. The last phase of activity was a series of shallow pits containing large quantities of stone tools (including flakes of Langdale stone axes), cereal grains and pottery (Moore 2004, 144). This later phase is reminiscent of the activity on Lyles Hill (see below).

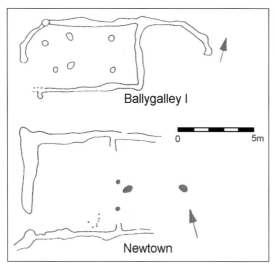

Figure 3.14. 'Houses' from Ireland: Ballygalley I, Co. Antrim and Newtown, Co. Meath (after Grogan 1996)

Another well-known site is that of Ballygalley, Co. Antrim (Fig. 3.14). Two structures were found here, one much better preserved than the other (Simpson 1996). House 1 cut through an earlier structure, suggesting continuity of place. However, at some point it was dismantled and the holes packed with beach stones and flint. The site produced a mass of artefacts: tens of thousands of struck flint flakes, 2000 flint artefacts, 150 axes (some from Langdale) and an Arran pitchstone assemblage (Simpson 1996, 129). Another important site, Lyles Hill, Co. Antrim, was excavated in the 1930s. This site produced tens of thousands of finds of pottery and flint and a series of pits. These are the remains of several hundred pots and the lithics included fragments of polished stone axes. This material spread also included cremated bone (some human and some animal), all of which was found under a burnt layer which was then covered with stones (E. E. Evans 1953). This material was found within a semi-circular stone built feature, very much like the façade of a court cairn. Although originally interpreted as a settlement site, the site also includes a circular cairn with a central cist burial, which has led to suggestions that this site is more 'ritual' in nature than domestic (Cooney 2000, 113). Another similar site to Lyle's Hill which has been claimed as a settlement site, Donegore Hill, may actually be a causewayed enclosure (Nelis 2004).

What do these different structures suggest about the nature of settlement on the shores of the Irish Sea? The contrast between western Britain and eastern Ireland is an interesting one, and may have implications for the origins and development of the Neolithic on the different sides of the Irish Sea zone (see chapter 8). It is also interesting that Ireland is not the only area that has started to produce evidence of timber structures. Along with the new houses in north Wales, sites have now been found in Scotland, including Balbridie and Claish Farm (Barclay *et al.* 2002), which were both large early Neolithic timber structures, both destroyed by fire. It is clear that some areas of Neolithic Britain and Ireland did have houses. However, we must consider the possibility that these sites were not simply 'houses' in the traditional domestic sense. It has been suggested that these structures may have been used more as gathering places for feasting (Cross 2003) or for preparing food stuffs such as beer (Dineley and Dineley 2000). This may explain the rather exceptional range of finds from sites such as Ballygalley and Lyles Hill. It may also explain why these structures were fragmented through fire at the end of their lives.

It therefore seems reasonable to suggest that for the most part people were fairly mobile in the Neolithic. In some areas people may have built houses, which may have been lived in for some of the year. However, these structures may equally have acted as gathering places for groups or communities and simply been another part of a ritualised landscape punctuated by built structures. In these areas, in Ireland for example, we could imagine people operating a form of 'tethered' mobility (Whittle 1997), with a stronger focus on structures than in other areas. Elsewhere we might want to consider circulating mobility, tied up with the movements of animals (especially domesticated cattle) around the landscape (and see Whittle 1997 for a discussion on different mobility models). We must also consider the possibility that different elements of each community had very different mobility patterns, with contrasts between young and old, male and female and so on. However, for the most part, people in western Britain seem to have been predominately mobile. Once again, we should be careful suggesting a single model of settlement: there may well have been considerable differences between areas, and also over time.

Therefore, we can summarise Neolithic settlement in the Irish Sea zone as:

- Variable, with some key differences between Ireland and western Britain
- People remained, for the most part, mobile
- Connected to the movement of both people and their animals
- What we identify as houses may have been more akin to other forms of permanent architecture found in the Neolithic such as monuments

Environmental background

In the last chapter we saw how the Mesolithic in Britain was a period of climatic warming, with rising sea levels and increasing temperatures. By the beginning of the Neolithic the environment was relatively stable with the climate remaining warm and constant. Sea levels throughout much of the Irish Sea were more or less at the levels they are today. At the most southern extreme of our study area, the sea levels in south-west Wales may have been slightly lower than today, perhaps as much as 10m lower than present (Heyworth and Kidson 1982): this would also have been the case with the southern coast of Ireland. At the opposite end of the study area, sea levels may actually have been slightly higher than today, as northern Scotland was still undergoing isostatic lift at the beginning of the Neolithic (Jardine 1964, 6). Sea levels for most of south-west Scotland, north-west England and north-east Ireland (Jardine 1975) would have been much as they are today, with slight regional variations.

By the beginning of the Neolithic much of the study area would have been forested, comprising oak, hazel and elm throughout, with birch, sloe, ash, poplar and yew also found in the southern part of the Irish Sea zone (Caseldine 1990; Edwards and Whittington 1997; Linnard 2000). There is evidence of woodland clearance throughout the Irish Sea zone in the Neolithic, but it is mostly suggestive of small-scale clearances, which also occurred in the late Mesolithic (see previous chapter). However, the pattern is not identical throughout the area: some places saw more sustained clearance, while others remained wooded (Cooney 2000, 36; Cummings and Whittle 2003; Tilley 2006). Some areas that were initially cleared later returned to woodland. Like most of Britain and north-west Europe, the study area has evidence for the elm decline around 3850 BC (M. Robinson 2000; Sutherland 1997). Cefn Gwernffrwd, in Carmarthenshire, for example, has evidence of several episodes of vegetation clearance (Chambers 1983) and has also produced dates for the elm decline (Burrow 2003). At Langdale Coombe in Cumbria the elm decline is clearly documented in the pollen record followed by a series of woodland clearances (Bradley and Edmonds 1993, 139). In the past the elm decline has been interpreted as evidence for the beginnings of agriculture, but the decline in elm may be a more complex process, perhaps involving tree management strategies or disease (Edwards and Whittington 1997, 73; M. Robinson 2000; Williams 1989). The same range of wild plants and animals that were present in the late Mesolithic would have been available to people in the Neolithic, the only exception being Ireland, where there were no deer or auroch, with red deer being introduced at some point during the Neolithic (Cooney 2000, 43; Woodman and McCarthy 2003, 37). I now want to explore the evidence for domesticated animals and plants in the Irish Sea area in more detail.

Domesticates

Domesticated plants

For many years, it was assumed that the beginning of the Neolithic was essentially an economic change from a hunter-gatherer lifestyle of the Mesolithic to full-scale farming (see papers in Whittle and Cummings 2007). It was naturally assumed that this shift to farming would involve the cultivation of domesticated plant species, imported into Britain from the Continent around 4000 BC. However, evidence for cereal cultivation proved harder to locate. Firstly, as we have already seen, there is only limited evidence for clearance, a pre-requisite for cereal agriculture in the otherwise forested environment. Secondly, not only did Britain and Ireland lack comprehensive evidence for widespread clearance, there were also very few cereal remains surviving in the archaeological record: in fact hazelnuts, supposedly indicative of a hunting and gathering lifestyle, were archaeologically more prominent in Neolithic contexts than cereals (G. Jones 2000; Milles *et al.* 1989). The post-processual backlash against the idea that the Neolithic was primarily an economic phenomenon suggested that the reason that there were few cereals in the archaeological record was because they were not used extensively in the Neolithic (e.g. Thomas 1999). It was suggested that cereals may instead have been grown in small garden plots (e.g. Whittle 2003), or even just grown for use in ceremonial contexts, as occurs in some ethnographic examples.

There is some evidence of cereal cultivation from our study area, and as with other aspects of the Neolithic it paints a picture of diversity across the region. For example, there is very limited evidence for cereal cultivation from much of western Britain: only small quantities of cereal grains and pollen survive in Wales and Cumbria for example (Bradley and Edmonds 1993, 140; Caseldine 1990, 43–7). Likewise, in western Scotland occasional finds of cereal, such as the charred grains of emmer and barley found in an early Neolithic pit at Carzield, Dumfries and Galloway (Maynard 1993), show that cereal was being cultivated, but probably not in massive quantities. However, there is more substantial evidence for cereal cultivation from eastern Ireland. For example, cereal pollen has been found at the site of Glencoy, Co Antrim, which shows that cereal was being grown over a sustained period (Cooney 2000, 36). Charred cereal remains also occur at a number of the settlement sites (see above) such as Ballygalley (Simpson 1996) and Ballyharry (Moore 2004, 144).

Therefore, cereals were clearly available and used by people throughout the Irish Sea zone from the early Neolithic onwards. However, it remains difficult to fully assess the scale of cereal cultivation throughout the area. It is only in recent years that a more thorough methodology has been employed at sites which enables the recovery of cereal remains (G. Jones 2000 and see Bogaard and Jones 2007). There remains the problem associated with context: the comparative lack of cereal remains from western Britain may relate more to the types of site being excavated, as opposed to a genuine difference of practice. At the same time, we must not rush to homogenise what may have been quite different practices either side of the Irish Sea zone, or even between different communities. Furthermore, it is perhaps not surprising that we do not find large quantities of cereal from chambered tombs or from the short-stay or ephemeral occupation sites which dominate the record in western Britain. The fact that cereal is much more common from the timber building sites (in Ireland and also at similar sites such as Balbridie and Claish Farm in eastern Scotland (Fairweather and Ralston 1993; Barclay *et al.* 2002) is also perhaps not surprising, if we consider the possible ways in which these buildings were used (see above). In summary then, cereals were used in the Irish Sea zone, but at present we are struggling to suggest the extent to which they contributed to people's everyday diet.

Domesticated animals
There is also fairly limited evidence for the use of domesticated animals in the Neolithic of the Irish Sea. Chambered tombs from across area have produced evidence for domesticates: pig, sheep/goat and cattle have all been found in court cairns in Ireland (Herity 1987, 121), sheep and cattle were found in Ballaharra on the Isle of Man (Burrow 1997, 13) and in Wales, domesticated animal bone has been found in some of the north Welsh sites (Cummings and Whittle 2004). However, the presence of domesticated animals in chambered tombs, as opposed to cereals, is almost certainly in part to do with the robust nature of animal remains and poor sampling strategies for cereals at early excavations. It is interesting, though, that animals were considered appropriate to be buried alongside human remains, perhaps showing the significance of these animals to a community.

Domesticated animal remains have also been found on other sites. Cattle teeth were found at Ballygalley in Co. Antrim (Simpson 1996, 129), cattle and sheep on Dalkey Island, Co. Dublin (Woodman and McCarthy 2003, 32) and cattle bones were found at Clegyr Boia (Williams 1953), for example. However, it is interesting how few domesticated animal bones have been found on Neolithic sites. This lack of domesticated animal bone must relate in part to the types of site excavated, as well as poor preservation in the soils of western Britain. Nevertheless, it must be significant that substantial assemblages of domesticated animals do begin to appear in the early Bronze Age (Woodman and McCarthy 2003, 33), suggesting that we might want to reconsider the assumed high contribution of domesticates. It would seem, therefore, that domesticated animals contributed to the economy of people along the shores of the Irish Sea, but again to what extent remains unclear (and also see various papers in Parker Pearson 2003).

Another strand of evidence which contributes to our understanding of diet in the Neolithic is stable isotope analysis. This assesses the impact of marine and terrestrial resources in an individual's diet (Richards 2003; Richards and Hedges 1999; Schulting 2004; Schulting and Richards 2002b and see Milner *et al.* 2004) and from all areas of the British Isles it seems that people switched from a marine-based diet in the late Mesolithic to a terrestrial diet in the Neolithic. This includes populations who lived extremely close to the sea (e.g. Schulting and Richards 2002b). The implication of this work is that people at the beginning of the Neolithic started relying heavily on domesticated animals, turning their back on the resources used by their ancestors (Schulting 2004). There have been suggestions that people may have started rely on terrestrial, but wild, resources at the beginning of the Neolithic, supported by the continued presence of wild foods at Neolithic sites (see below). While this may have been the case with some communities, we know for sure that this did not happen in Ireland, as there were no large wild animals to rely on at the beginning of the Neolithic (Woodman and McCarthy 2003). It seems more plausible that people throughout the Irish Sea zone were using the newly-introduced domesticates, if not purely for economic reasons, for reasons tied up with changing belief systems (Fowler and Cummings 2003; Thomas 2003; and see chapter 8).

The overall picture, therefore, is that people in the Neolithic of the Irish Sea had access to domesticated resources, and that they probably played a fairly significant part of people's diets. Keeping domesticates would have had a major impact on the way in which people lived their lives, not only in terms of diet but also in relation to lifestyle. People may now have had to move around the landscape with their herds, utilising particular parts of the landscape at different times of the year, and tied to specific routes and routines (cf. Edmonds 1999). Cattle in particular take a lot of looking after and the close relationship required to maintain a cattle herd would have entailed very different sets of relationships between humans and animals. The keeping of domesticates, therefore, would also have had an impact on peoples' mobility and settlement patterns (see above).

Wild resources
While it is clear that domesticated animals became available at the beginning of the Neolithic, if not before, there is continued evidence for hunting and gathering

throughout the Irish Sea zone. Settlement sites have produced evidence for wild resources: for example at Ballyharry, Co. Antrim for example produced large quantities of wild plant seeds (Moore 2004, 144). This site is not exceptional. Hazelnut shells have been found at many sites, including Billown on the Isle of Man (Darvill 2003) and Townhead, Isle of Bute (Ritchie 1997). Chambered tombs have also produced evidence for the utilisation of wild resources: bones from red deer, horse, birds and fish have all been found in Irish court tombs (Herity 1987, 121) and it is a similar pattern at sites in western Britain.

Furthermore, although the stable isotope analysis suggests that people did not eat marine foods in the Neolithic, there is some evidence for the continued importance of marine resources. For example, a number of monumental sites in western Scotland have produced remains of marine foods. At Crarae, 5000 marine shells were found in the chamber and forecourt (Scott 1960). A midden was also found across the river from Crarae. This site, Fairy Knowe, was investigated in the nineteenth century and it remains unclear as to its date (NMRS ref: NR99NE 1). However, a chamber not too dissimilar from a Clyde chamber was found in midden, containing 'bones and ashes' (Scott 1960, 22). Another Clyde monument, Glecknabae on Bute, was built over a shell midden, while Torlin on Arran also reportedly contained shells (Bryce 1902). Shells have been found in chambered tombs in Wales, including Bryn yr Hen Bobl and Pant y Saer (see Cummings and Whittle 2004). It would be possible to dismiss these finds as 'special' token deposits, associated with the burial of the dead (Fowler and Cummings 2003; Thomas 2003). However, shells have also been found on settlement sites, suggesting that marine resources were still utilised to a certain extent in the Neolithic. There are further hints at the potential significance of marine resources in the Neolithic. Evidence for the intensive utilisation of coastal zones has been found throughout the Irish Sea, for example masses of lithics have been recovered from the west coast of Cumbria (H. Evans 2004, 126) as well as Luce Sands in Dumfries and Galloway. While this does not represent direct evidence for the consumption of marine foods, it at least demonstrates the ongoing importance of the maritime environment and the sea (and see chapter eight). And finally, shell middens were also clearly being used in the Neolithic (see above), suggesting a continuity of practice in the utilisation of marine foods in this period.

With regards the economy we can therefore conclude that:

• Domesticated animals and crops were used throughout the Neolithic of the Irish Sea zone

- Their contribution of people's diets may have changed over time and differed from area to area
- Wild resources (or places associated with wild resources) continued to be used
- These different resources would have had a profound impact on people's attachments to different parts of the landscape, and their movements around that landscape
- These different resources would have played a crucial part of social relations, and were quite possibly connected with ritualised behaviour
- Domesticates may also have created further connections with origins in Europe. In Ireland, the introduction of large wild species such as red deer may also have created connections with communities elsewhere.

Conclusions

This chapter has summarised what we know about the Neolithic of the Irish Sea zone. We have a wealth of evidence for some aspects of the Neolithic, in particular stone axe factories, pottery, and increasingly, settlement evidence. However, much of our evidence still comes from the chambered tombs which are the subject of the next chapter, or from ephemeral traces of human occupation such as lithic scatters. It is clear that large field projects in some areas of the Irish Sea have greatly increased our knowledge about certain aspects of the Neolithic (see Cummings and Fowler 2004c). It is also clear that many areas still require further detailed investigation in order to gain more information on various aspects of Neolithic life. It is fair to say that at present, the Neolithic of the Irish Sea lacks the quantity and quality of data required for us to meaningfully compare this area to the more 'luminous' areas of Neolithic Britain such as Wessex and Orkney. Nevertheless, it is also clear that the Neolithic of the Irish Sea is not a 'poor cousin' to these more studied areas: this study area clearly had a different Neolithic sequence (or sets of sequences) to other areas of Britain, and to explore this difference, as well as diversity, is clearly one of the aims of further research.

4

The Neolithic chambered tombs
of the Irish Sea zone

Introduction

The aim of this chapter is to provide a comprehensive overview of Neolithic monumentality in the Irish Sea zone. The bulk of the chapter considers the early Neolithic megalithic monuments (chambered tombs), which are the focus of discussion in later chapters. The discussion is then broadened to include a brief summary of all chambered tombs in the Irish Sea area. Throughout this chapter I hope to emphasise some key themes. The first is that discussion of these monuments has focused very heavily on their form, over-complicating how we classify these sites. I will argue that while classification remains a useful and valid tool for getting to grips with these monuments, we should not place too much emphasis on precise architectural details. Instead, much more emphasis should be placed on other aspects of these monuments such as the materials from which they were built and their landscape setting, as we will see in later chapters. Thus, monuments that have been classified differently actually share many similarities. Secondly, this chapter will also emphasise that while these sites do share some similarities with their better-studied counterparts elsewhere in the British and Irish Isles, these sites should be understood very much within their own particular context: the Neolithic of the Irish Sea zone, as detailed in the previous chapter.

Early Neolithic chambered tombs

We begin by considering the early Neolithic chambered tombs of the Irish Sea region. These monuments are very distinctive: they consist of a stone-built chamber and are typically surrounded by either a round or long cairn. Although usually referred to as chambered tombs, they are also known as megaliths, long or round cairns and chamber cairns. Early Neolithic megalithic architecture is extremely well-represented in the Irish Sea zone (Fig. 4.1). There are distinctive clusters of chambered tombs in many of the areas bordering on the Irish Sea, in

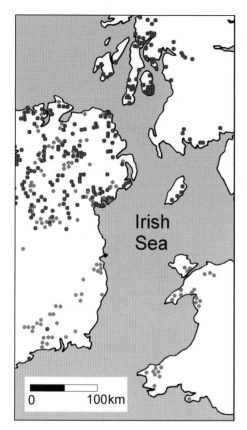

Figure 4.1. Early Neolithic chambered tombs in Irish Sea zone. Dark grey dots are court and Clyde cairns, light grey dots are dolmens

particular in west Wales, western Scotland, the Isle of Man and eastern Ireland. Chambered tombs are not found everywhere, however, and there are notable gaps in the distribution. Cumbria in particular is prominent for its lack of chambered tombs, and there are other blanks such as north-east Wales. While it seems likely that the absence of sites in these 'blank' areas may have been the result of more intense agricultural practices, this is not sufficient to explain the complete lack of monuments in some areas. Therefore this distribution should be regarded as a general reflection of the overall density of chambered tombs in the Neolithic.

The chambered tombs of the Irish Sea region have been written about in hundreds and books and papers since the Antiquarian age. This is almost certainly because these monuments are one of the most enduring visible remains of the Neolithic period in the region. Not only are they plentiful and well-preserved, they are also visually impressive and evocative sites which have captured the imagination of many generations of scholars and amateurs alike (Fig. 4.2). Because so much has been written about these monuments, there is now a rather confusing literature which can be off-putting when trying to

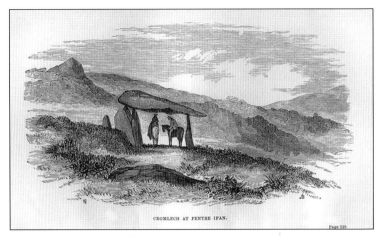

CROMLECH AT PENTRE IFAN.

Page 129.

Figure 4.2. Pentre Ifan chambered tomb in the nineteenth century

get a better understanding of these sites. The following sections are designed to look at the history of research into these monuments, followed by a simpler classification and description of these sites, which will be used throughout the rest of the book.

History of the Irish Sea megaliths

People have undoubtedly engaged with the chambered tombs of the Irish Sea zone for thousands of years. After they had been constructed their original purpose seems to have remained in the memories of people for a considerable amount of time, as Neolithic chambered tombs were frequently reused for burial in the Bronze Age (see below). However, at some point after this, these sites seem to have no longer been the focus for ritualised activities. They must have remained known points in the landscape though. Some were clearly reused: some chambered tombs in the Irish Sea zone were cleared out so people could use the chamber, and a number are simply incorporated into walls, their cairns a convenient source of walling stone. Others may have been ignored or avoided: certainly some seem to have become associated with a whole range of myths and legends, as were many other prehistoric remains (cf. Bahn 1996). The names of a number of sites in the Irish Sea zone give an indication of the histories surrounding them: the Devil's Quoit in Pembrokeshire, the Druid's Stone in county Antrim and the Giant's Graves on Arran all show the kinds of associations people have made with these sites in the past. By the time Antiquaries began recording these sites, many sites had obviously been investigated, probably by curious local people: it is frequently recorded by Antiquaries that bone and 'crude' pottery had been found in chambered tombs (for example see Inventory in Cummings and Whittle 2004). Antiquaries themselves undoubtedly did further damage, investigating the chambers but not recording their findings. This continued into the nineteenth century with sites being investigated using very poor excavation techniques and limited (or no) recording of the findings. Sites were also destroyed (Ffynnondruidion in Pembrokeshire, for example, is a good example of a known chambered tomb that was destroyed: Cummings and Whittle 2004, 154).

Chambered tombs were studied in depth for the first time as part of the growth of archaeology in the first half of the twentieth century. This was when archaeologists first started to recognise 'types' of monument, regionally distinctive styles that could be tied into the culture-historical approach to the archaeological record. The Clyde cairns of western Scotland seem to have been the first recognised group: this is down to the extraordinary work of Bryce in Arran in particular, but in western Scotland more generally (e.g. Bryce 1902). Court cairns were first recognised as a distinctive class of monument in 1932 (de Valera 1960, 10) and it is this year that also saw the first of a number of important excavations of Irish chambered tombs. The Welsh monuments proved harder to classify however (Grimes 1936) due to the diversity of types in this area, although a number of distinctive styles were identified, including outliers of the Cotswold-Severn group. In the 1930s and 1940s, excavations took place at a number of key sites, and there was discussion on their overall classification (e.g. Childe 1934; 1940; Davis 1945), however it wasn't really until the 1950s that a fuller classification of all of these sites was published. I want to here briefly highlight two key texts from the 1950s. The first is Daniel's 1950 *The prehistoric chamber tombs of England and Wales*. Daniel considered in detail the classification of sites in Wales, and came up with a rather bewildering set of classifications for the monuments in question. He described various west Welsh sites as passage graves, dolmens, gallery graves, and chambered long barrows (Daniel 1950). His work was important though for considering more than just the type sites, and for recognising that these were part of a broader 'Irish Sea group' (Daniel 1950, 86).

The second publication of particular note is Piggott's *The Neolithic cultures of the British Isles* (Piggott 1954). In this volume Piggott devotes a chapter to the Clyde-Carlingford culture, essentially those sites found in western Scotland and eastern Ireland (the northern part of the Irish Sea zone). He argues that while there is some variation amongst these sites, they share enough features to be indicative of an area of primary colonisation (Piggott 1954, 152). They are the result, therefore, of an incoming cultural group from the continent (Piggott 1954, 181). Critically, Piggott believed that primary colonisation took place in western Scotland, from where people spread over to Ireland. Piggott also considered some of the Welsh monuments to be derived from the western Scottish sequence (Piggott 1954, 179–181). Piggott's consideration of these sites was exceptional at the time: he drew on the excavation results from the 1930s and 1940s, including his own work at Cairnholy I and II (Piggott and Powell 1949), from which important information had been produced. He also fitted this into a coherent culture-historical narrative for the British and Irish Neolithic sequence: this was just before C-14 dating so we now know some of his ideas were incorrect, nevertheless it remains a fine piece of scholarly research. It also marks an important turning point in studies of these monuments.

From the 1960s onwards, studies of the chambered tombs of the Irish Sea zone became much more regionally focussed. While Piggott was able to use the plans from excavated sites, at the start of the 1960s a large number of sites were unplanned and little was published about the sites which had not been excavated. In 1960 de Valera published a seminal paper: The court cairns of Ireland. This detailed paper considered all the court cairns of Ireland complete with an extensive inventory of sites. The same year Corcoran published a review paper entitled 'The Carlingford culture' and these two papers mark a distinctive shift from Piggott's Clyde-Carlingford culture, *shared* across the Irish Sea, to separate cultures, based *either side* of the Irish Sea. 1963 saw the first of two volumes detailing the chambered tombs of Scotland (Henshall 1963; 1972), the second volume of which contained a full listing of all the Clyde cairns in western Scotland. Finally, the 1969 publication *Megalithic enquiries in the west of Britain* (Powell *et al.* 1969) summarised the chambered tomb sequences from Wales and western Scotland.

By the 1970s, then, we had a very good understanding of the structural remains of the chambered tombs throughout the Irish Sea zone, with different parts of the Irish Sea zone having different regional sequences. But the 1970s also marked the end of the 'golden age' as far as the excavation of chambered tombs in this area: a few were excavated in this decade, but the focus shifted, firstly geographically to more 'luminous' areas such as Orkney and Wessex, and secondly, towards different types of sites (later Neolithic monuments in particular as well as non-megalithic sites). Between the late 1970s and the present day, only a few chambered tomb sites have been excavated. While chambered tombs once filled the pages of Neolithic texts (e.g. Piggott 1954), the core Neolithic literature nowadays (e.g. Bradley 1998a; 2007b; Thomas 1999) has its focus elsewhere. There has been a revival in interest in these sites though as part of the broader post-processual approach: Tilley's 1994 *A phenomenology of landscape* makes a good starting point for the range of papers that followed considering a whole range of different approaches to these sites, focussing on landscape setting (Cummings and Whittle 2004; Tilley 1994), experience (Cummings 2002c; A.

Jones 1999) and construction processes (Richards 2004; Whittle 2004 and see other papers in Cummings and Fowler 2004c).

So what does this brief review of the history of studying these sites tell us? Firstly, that there has been considerable interest in them from the Antiquarian age onwards. This means that sites have frequently been robbed of their original deposits. This review also shows that a great deal of time has been spent recording and understanding the structural remains at these sites. On the one hand this is incredibly useful as we have really excellent inventories for these sites. It also means that there has been an over-emphasis on the architecture of these sites, in particular their classification, which post-processual archaeology has only just begun to address.

The classification of chambered tombs
The attention to the architectural details of chambered tombs over the past 50 years has left us with a confusing array of site names and types. A quick look at the literature will reveal almost as many names for these sites as there are monuments: Clyde-Carlingford long cairns, horned cairns, gallery graves, A and B type dolmens and so on. Instead of this, I want to suggest a much simpler approach. My classification of these monuments relies partly on their landscape setting (discussed in detail in chapter 6), but also considers their architectural design. While I do think that subtle architectural differences may be significant, particularly at a local level, I am more concerned with the overall impression that each monument creates. Having visited virtually every chambered tomb in the Irish Sea region, I would like to suggest that there are only two basic 'types' of early Neolithic megalithic monument in whole Irish Sea area. I will also argue that two of these types are so similar that they can be considered two parts of a broader whole.

The first type of chambered tomb in the Irish Sea zone are the 'Clyde' and court cairns of western Scotland and eastern Ireland (Fig. 4.3). These divide into two slightly different types. The first are the Clyde cairns which are found in western Scotland and as we have already seen, many authors have identified a number of similarities in form (Henshall 1972; Scott 1969; 1973). Essentially, these sites consist of a chamber area which is divided up into box-like compartments (Fig. 4.4). These box chambers lead directly to a forecourt area which is defined by a simple façade of stones (Fig. 4.5). The whole chamber is set within a long cairn. While no two sites are the same, these basic features are found repeatedly throughout western Scotland. Occasionally sites also have additional side (lateral) chambers, a feature of many chambered tombs throughout Britain (Fig. 4.6). Secondly, there are the court cairns of eastern Ireland (Fig. 4.7). These

*Figure 4.3. The court
cairns and Clyde cairns
of the Irish Sea zone*

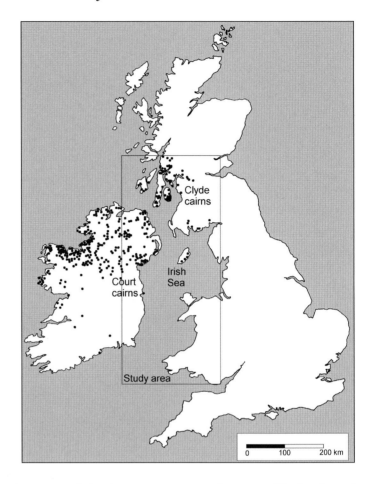

monuments share similarities with both court cairns in the west of Ireland, and
also Clyde cairns. This group includes all court cairns in eastern Ireland as well
as those on the Isle of Man. The court cairns of eastern Ireland and the Isle of
Man consist of a series of box-like chambers which lead directly into a forecourt
area (Fig. 4.8). The forecourt is more concave than those of Clyde cairns, as well
as frequently being overtly asymmetrical in form, but both create an enclosed
area. Court cairns are also set within a long cairns. A very small number of sites
are 'doubles': two court cairns set back to back (Fig. 4.9).

This group, the Clyde cairns of western Scotland and court cairns of
eastern Ireland, share so many similarities that the old classification of 'Clyde-
Carlingford' often seems relevant when discussing these monuments. This point
will be returned to in subsequent discussions.

The second group in the study area are what I have called 'dolmens' (Fig.
4.10): this includes all sites that have traditionally been described as portal

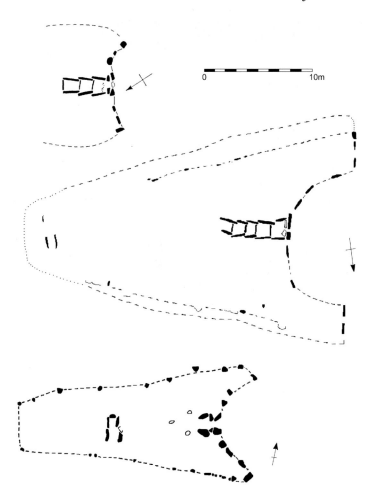

Figure 4.4. Clyde cairns of western Scotland. Top: Monamore, Arran, middle: East Bennan, Arran, bottom: Blasthill, Kintyre (after Henshall 1972)

dolmens and also those sites which are considered derivatives of the dolmen tradition. This group also includes small early Neolithic passage graves, found in scatters along the shores of the Irish Sea, especially in west Wales and north-east Ireland. These sites are virtually identical to the dolmens in the area, apart from the presence of a small passage tacked onto the entrance into the chamber. I argue that the presence of a passage at these monuments does not make a fundamental difference to these sites, and thus all sites should be considered under one heading. At a later date, however, the passage becomes of central significance (see below) and the passage grave tradition proper begins. Therefore, those monuments in the dolmen tradition consist of a simple open box chamber supporting a large and distinctive capstone (Fig. 4.11). This chamber is either a stand-alone box or entered along a short passage. The chamber is typically set within a round cairn, and there is no formal forecourt area (Fig. 4.12).

*Figure 4.5. The chamber
at Nether Largie, Argyll
(top) and the forecourt
at Cairnholy I, Dumfries
and Galloway (bottom)*

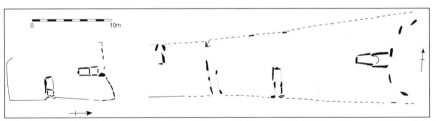

Figure 4.6. Lateral chambers at Glenvoidean, Bute and Gort na h'Ulaidhe, Kintyre (after Henshall 1972)

    Therefore I argue that there were essentially two different types of chambered tombs in the early Neolithic of the Irish Sea. The first group are Piggott's old Clyde-Carlingford group, which can be further subdivided into two: the Clyde cairns of western Scotland and the court cairns of eastern Ireland. The second main group are those monuments of the dolmen tradition, which can also be subdivided into simple box-like dolmens and those with small passages. My justification for this classification is based on a number of different strands of

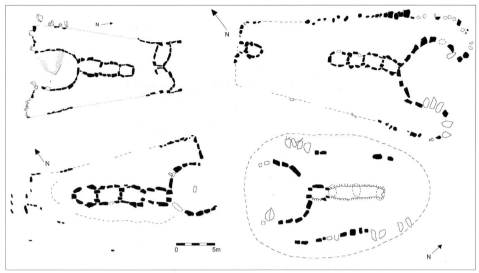

Figure 4.7. Court cairns of Ireland. Top left: Annaghmare, bottom left: Browndod, top right: Ballymarlagh, bottom right: Ballymacaldrack (after de Valera 1960)

Figure 4.8. The chamber at Annaghmare

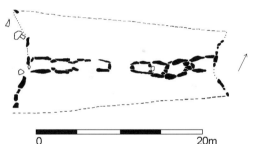

Figure 4.9. The double court cairn at Audleystown (after de Valera 1960)

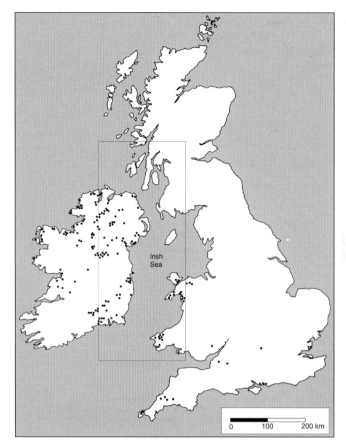

Figure 4.10. The dolmens of the Irish Sea zone

evidence. Firstly, while I think it is important that we recognise small architectural differences between sites (such as the presence of a small passage on some dolmens), I would argue that this should not affect the overall classification of sites. If we take all small differences into account we end up with, as with previous classification systems, a confusing array of sites. Furthermore, when you consider that Neolithic people were not working to precise architectural plans or blueprints, then small architectural differences between sites may well have been fairly insignificant. I think that we also tend to approach these sites from a modern perspective, and of course as archaeologists we are able to visit hundreds of these sites in a relatively short space of time. We are also equipped with plans and elevations of sites when we go. In the Neolithic, people may only have ever visited a few sites or were working to a very generalised plan of a site. They were also using unaltered stones to construct their sites (a deliberate choice here I would argue) so they were partly constrained by the stones available to them, although of course they could and did travel some distance to find

Figure 4.11. The dolmen at Proleek, Co. Louth

Figure 4.12. Dolmens in Wales (after Barker 1992 and Lynch 1969a)

stones to build the sites (see next chapter). Furthermore, at many sites, the actual chambers were encased in cairn material, meaning that people would not have been able to make out the precise architectural configuration of each site. Taking all this into account, would small architectural differences really have been that significant? Furthermore, as I will argue in subsequent chapters, when we look at the landscape setting of these sites, we will see that they are all set in very similar settings. In chapter 8 I will go on to argue that people were actually trying to create very similar places (in terms of both architecture and landscape) across the Irish Sea zone.

Before we move on to consider the early Neolithic chambered tombs in more detail, it should also be noted that there are several other types of chambered tomb in the Irish Sea zone, however, they are not included here as they are almost certainly not early Neolithic in date. This includes the large middle Neolithic passage graves of Ireland, the small group of 'Bargrennan' monuments in south-west Scotland and the small group of earth-fast megaliths in south-west Wales. These are discussed in more detail below.

The use of chambered tombs
One of the key elements of these monuments is that when we find monuments that have not been emptied in the past, they usually contain deposits in the chamber, with further deposits in the forecourt area. The next chapter considers the deposits at chambered tombs in detail, but here I just want to highlight the fact that these sites often, although not always, contain human remains: this is the reason these sites are known as chambered 'tombs'. It is a powerful idea, and of course assumes that the primary function of these sites were as houses for the dead. However, human remains at these sites may well have not been conceptualised as such (and see Whitley 2002), and these sites may well have been primarily designed as gathering places for the living. Nevertheless, I like the term chambered tomb, so here I will continue to use it, with this one noted caveat in its usage. Otherwise, typical deposits in the chambers of these sites include pottery, small quantities of lithics and animal bone, along with burnt material. The forecourt area also frequently contains material, again pottery, lithics and other burnt deposits.

Multi-phase monuments and pre-cairn activity

So far we have discussed the chambered tombs of the Irish Sea zone as complete monuments, considering the plans of these sites as they exist today. However, some sites in the Irish Sea zone have clear evidence of a number of different phases of construction, which means that, as archaeologists, we need to think about all of the different phases of the site and not just their final form. Multi-phase construction is not confined to a particular type of chambered tomb, but is documented at all different types. It is perhaps best known amongst the Clyde cairns, in particular those in south-west Scotland, due to discussion by Scott (1992) and Kinnes (1992). However, the whole debate surrounding the many phases of monument construction has had something of a renaissance in recent years as more detailed work has been conducted on the life histories of individual monuments (e.g. Benson and Whittle 2005; McFadyen 2006). The focus of this research though has been primarily on the Cotswold-Severn monuments and while we can draw some inspiration from the work on these sites, they are different in many key ways from the monuments of the Irish Sea zone (see below).

Amongst the Clyde cairns, a number of sites in south-west Scotland have evidence for multi-phase activity. At Mid Gleniron Farm, two early Neolithic Clyde cairns were excavated by Corcoran (1969). Mid Gleniron I was constructed in a number of phases. Firstly, a small and simple chamber was built, set within a small oval cairn. Next another chamber was added in front of the first chamber, and again set within its own round cairn. At a later date a third chamber was added between the earlier chambers, and the whole monument was incorporated into a long cairn with a façade set at one end (Fig. 4.13). A similar sequence of construction was also documented at Mid Gleniron II, just a short distance from the first site. Although the excavators (Piggott and Powell 1949) did not document any evidence of a multi-phase construction sequence at the two Cairnholy sites, also in south-west Scotland, there has since been considerable speculation that these two sites were also built in a number of phases just like at those at Mid Gleniron. At Cairnholy I in particular, it has been suggested that the primary phase was a small box-like chamber, which was elaborated at a later date with the addition of a 'porch', façade and long cairn (Scott 1969; Noble 2005). A little further afield, the site of Trefignath on Holyhead was also constructed in a number of discreet phases which draws comparison with the Clyde monuments.

The idea that the primary phase of some of these Clyde cairns consisted of only a simple box-like chamber set within a round cairn led Scott (1969, 212) to suggest that these early phases could be termed as 'proto-megaliths'. He suggested there may once have been a number of these simple proto-megaliths, which were later turned into much more elaborate megalithic structures. There are a number of candidates in western Scotland which may have proto-megalithic

*Figure 4.13.
The multi-phase
monument at Mid
Gleniron I, Dumfries
and Galloway*

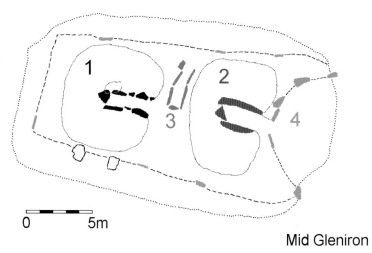

Mid Gleniron

*Figure 4.14. Multi-phase
construction at Slewcairn
and Lochhill, Dumfries and
Galloway (after Masters 1992)*

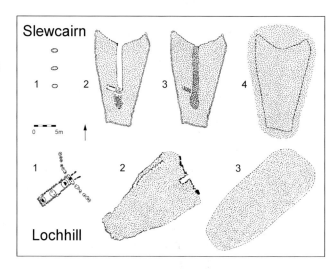

phases, but it is also clear that many sites were not built in such a way. Many of
the large and elaborate Clyde cairns of Arran, for example, could only have been
constructed if they were conceived and built in a single phase. So while some
Clyde cairns were altered over many years, most seem to have been built in one
go. A single construction event, however, may still have taken many years, if not
decades. For many of the builders of these sites they may have existed primarily
as 'construction sites' and not as finished monuments (McFadyen 2006).

In Ireland there is also some evidence for court cairns being built in a number
of phases. The primary phase at Dooey's Cairn in County Antrim consisted of
three large timber posts, over which a court cairn was later constructed (Cooney
2000, 101; E. E. Evans 1938). This example is particularly interesting as the site

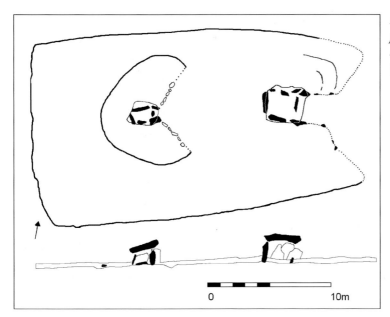

Figure 4.15. Multi-phase construction at Dyffryn Ardudwy (after Powell 1973)

has parallels with two sites in south-west Scotland. Lochhill and Slewcairn in Dumfriesshire both began life as timber monuments, consisting of three large timber posts, and in the case of Lochhill, with a wooden façade (Masters 1973; 1981). Both of these monuments were later converted into stone monuments, although neither became a classic Clyde monument (Fig. 4.14). At Annaghmare, Co. Armagh, two subsidiary chambers were added to the rear of the monument (Waterman 1965, 21), although the date of these is unclear and they may feasibly be early Bronze Age in date (see below). There is also the question of whether the double court cairns were built in a single phase or whether these may also represent multi-phase monuments. There is a sense, therefore, with the vast majority of court cairns that like most of their Clyde counterparts they were conceived and built in a single phase.

Amongst the dolmens, the site of Dyffryn Ardudwy in north-west Wales is the classic multi-phase monument. This site began its life as a small but 'classic' portal dolmen (Powell 1973) set within a small round cairn. At a later date another chamber was added and both chambers were incorporated into a long cairn (Fig. 4.15). A similar sequence can be seen at the site of Pentre Ifan in south-west Wales. Here the primary phase of the monument seems to have been the chamber set within a small cairn (Barker 1992, 23–6; Grimes 1948; Lynch 1972). At a later date the orthostatic façade and long cairn were added. There are other possible examples of multi-phase dolmens in Wales. The two sites at Carneddau Hengwm seem to have started life as dolmens, and again had additional chambers and long cairns added at a later date (Cummings and Whittle 2004, 131–2). The double chamber at Ballyvennaght in Co. Antrim may be an Irish example of a multi-phase dolmen. However, these examples seem to be more the exception than the rule for dolmens found in the Irish Sea area. For the most part, dolmens seem to be single-phase constructions, where the simple chamber and associated small cairn were conceived and built in one go. There is the possibility at those dolmens which have long cairns that the cairn was built at a later date than the construction of the chamber and primary core cairn. It seems likely that at many dolmens, however, particularly those in western Britain, that there was never a substantial cairn at most sites (Cummings and Whittle 2004).

It is significant to consider the different phases at these early Neolithic chambered tombs for a number of reasons. As already noted, we tend to study these sites in their final form, which although important, means we can over-emphasise similarities which were only present in the later stages of the monument's life. The earliest phases of many of these monuments were really rather different, and may well have held many different sets of associations for the people building and using them, particularly when we begin to consider the range of meanings assigned to different materials in the early Neolithic (see next chapter). A monument of stone may have been conceived completely differently from a monument of wood (e.g. Parker Pearson and Ramilisonina 1998). I shall discuss again in more detail the implications of monuments in the Irish Sea zone being remarkably similar, but it is key to stress that there was considerable diversity in the very earliest phases and development of some of these monuments. Secondly, there is the issue of why some monuments underwent changes in form while others seem to have been conceived and built in one go. There is clearly an issue of chronology here. It has been argued by Scott (1969) and others that the proto-megaliths were very early in the sequence, and it is only later that the larger and 'complete' monuments were built. This remains for the most part unproven in the Irish Sea zone sequence due to a lack of radiocarbon dates from the relevant monumental sequences, although an early date from Lochhill of 3950–3800 cal BC (I-6409) hints that this is a reasonable suggestion.

The fact that monuments were sometimes altered and reconstructed a number of times also indicates that people had a desire to return to a site many times and make substantial alterations. There is again a tendency to think of monuments as being built and finished rather quickly, then available for use by a community rather like a village hall or a church. It may well have been the construction process itself that was significant, the bringing together of people and materials at specific locations (Cummings 2007b; McFadyen 2006). It may be that these early sites were intended to be revisited and reworked at a later date. In fact, the decision to return to rework a monument may have occurred tens if not hundreds of years after the primary monument was built: indeed there is evidence for this at a number of sites where the material culture and/or radiocarbon dates show that sites were used for hundreds of years.

It is also worth mentioning that returning to a site already known about and used is not restricted to monumental phases. A number of sites also have evidence of pre-cairn activity which is distinct from the 'monumental' elements of the site. At Trefignath in north Wales, for example, a small lithic scatter was found underneath the cairn (Smith and Lynch 1987). In Scotland, a shell midden was found underneath the chambered tomb at Glecknabae (Henshall 1972). Considerable pre-cairn activity was found at Ballybriest in county Derry. At this site the remains of six hearths, pottery vessels, flint tools, charcoal and cremated human bone were found underneath the monument (Herity 1987, 126). Many authors have claimed that this pre-cairn activity is essentially domestic in nature, but as already outlined, this presupposes some dichotomy between ritual and domestic that was almost certainly not present in the Neolithic. It seems at a number of sites there was some form of occupation prior to the megalithic phase. Obviously we only have evidence of this at sites that have been fully excavated, so in the vast majority of cases we do not know whether pre-cairn activity occurred or not. It is also worth noting that pre-cairn activity has not been found at all sites which have been fully excavated, so it is not a pre-requisite or ubiquitous element of monumentality.

Monuments, therefore, may have already been locales for activity prior to construction. Pre-cairn finds such as lithics and pottery unequivocally demonstrate occupation, but there is also the possibility that clearings in woodland may have been chosen for monumental construction. These would not necessarily leave any archaeological trace in the record, but well may have been known locales in the landscape. Once people started to construct monuments there is also substantial evidence to show that not all sites were designed and executed in a single phase. Some sites seem to have been drawn out construction processes (cf. Richards 2004) with alterations and additions being made to some sites over hundreds of years. On the other hand, other sites *do* seem to have been conceived as a whole, and we must not lose sight of the fact that some sites may well have been planned, built, deposits made and the whole closed in a single persons lifetime (Bayliss and Whittle 2007). This brings us neatly to considering the dating of these sites.

Site name	Context summary	Uncal. date BP	Calibrated date
Western Scotland			**2 sigma**
Glenvoidean, Bute	Under main chamber	4860+115	3950–3350 BC
Monamore, Arran	Hearth in forecourt	5110+110	4250–3650 BC
Monamore, Arran	End of tomb use	4190+110	3100–2450 BC
Port Charlotte, Islay	Pre-cairn	5020+90	3980–3640 BC
Port Charlotte, Islay	Pre-cairn surface	4940+70	3950–3630 BC
Port Charlotte, Islay	Pre-cairn surface	4660+90	3650–3100 BC
Port Charlotte, Islay	Chamber 3 stone	4710+70	3640–3360 BC
Port Charlotte, Islay	Chamber 3 stone	4540+70	3510–3010 BC
West Wales			
Carreg Coetan	Beneath kerb	4830+80	3780–3370 BC
Carreg Coetan	Socket of chamber stone	4700+80	3700–3300 BC
Carreg Coetan	Old ground surface	4560+80	3550–3000 BC
Carreg Coetan	Within mound	4470+80	3360–2920 BC
Trefignath	Old ground surface	5050+70	3980–3690 BC
East Ireland			
Ballymacaldrack	Wooden structure	5150+90	4250–3700 BC
Ballymacaldrack	Wooden structure	4940+50	3920–3630 BC
Ballymacaldrack	Pottery	4630+130	3700–2900 BC
Ballymacdermot	Chamber 3	4830+95	3800–3350 BC
Ballymacdermot	Chamber 1	4715+190	4000–2900 BC
Ballybriest	Pre-cairn activity	5045+95	4040–3640 BC
Ballybriest	Pre-cairn activity	4930+80	3950–3530 BC
Dunloy	Façade	4980+40	3940–3650 BC

Table 4.1. A selection of the C-14 dates from the chambered tombs of the Irish Sea zone

Dating the monuments of the Irish Sea zone

The recent dating programme on a number of Cotswold-Severn chambered tombs has radically altered our understanding of these monuments (Bayliss and Whittle 2007). It would be desirable to undergo a similar dating programme on the monuments of the Irish Sea zone, but this may be a trickier exercise: quite simply, we do not, for the most part, get the bone preservation in chambered tombs in this area. This limits the material we can date, and more critically, the ability to model those dates.

Table 4.1 gives some indication of the dating of these chambered tombs. You will see that many of the dates, however, are fairly useless as they cover such broad time frames. At present all the dates are able to do is to confirm that these sites were probably built sometime in the early Neolithic, but we cannot pin down precise dates beyond that very general statement. What is clearly needed is a series of excavations of sites with good stratified material which can be subjected to both a suite of radiocarbon dates which can be modelled using

Bayesian statistics. This must be one of the highest research priorities for this group of monuments.

Monumental reuse

Although we struggle to date precisely the construction and primary use of these chambered tombs, we know that at some point people stopped using the chambers. At a number of Clyde and court cairns people seem to have had access to the monuments deliberately halted by blocking the entranceway into the chamber and infilling the forecourt area. At Cairnholy I in Dumfries and Galloway, a slab was placed between the portal stones to prevent access into the chamber, and the forecourt was blocked with stones (Piggott and Powell 1949). Many of the court cairns in Ireland have a similar blocking episode, for example at Ballyalton, Co. Down (Evans and Davies 1934, 83) and Ballymacdermot, Co. Armagh (Collins and Wilson 1964). There is less evidence for blocking episodes at the dolmen sites. The nature of these sites mean that many of them are already essentially closed boxes (see above). Access may have been restricted to these chambers simply by virtue of a cairn which could conceal the chamber. However, dolmens never seem to have received the quantity of material culture found more typically in courts and Clydes, which may indicate that the primary use for these sites was not for the deposition of material culture (see chapter 8).

An interesting facet of these chambered cairns is that they were frequently reused in the Bronze Age. This is particularly apparent in the western Scottish sequence, where people seem to have regularly reused Clyde tombs (and other tombs for that matter: Cummings and Fowler 2007) for Bronze Age mortuary practices. A number of sites have Bronze Age deposits, for example at Cairnholy I (Piggott and Powell 1949) and Brackley (Scott 1955). In both these examples, people seem to have cleared out any Neolithic material still present in the chambers and added their own deposits which included human bone and artefacts. For example, at Brackley, Argyll, a cremation deposit was found with 44 jet beads, a food vessel, a plano-convex knife, flints and pitchstone (Scott 1955, 34–5). These deposits are intriguing for a number of reasons. It hints at the possibility that these early Neolithic sites were still important places in the landscape well into the Bronze Age. By the end of the early Bronze Age when these deposits were being made (c1500 BC), these sites would have been close to 2500 years old. Did people remember what these sites had originally been used for or were they appropriated for the same use? What did people think of the older deposits that they came across? For that matter, what did they do with the remains that they found when reusing these sites? Did they become artefacts or heirlooms or were they redeposited? Although it may be difficult to answer these questions, the reuse of these sites does demonstrate the potency of these places to endure in the memories of people over long periods of time.

A note on similarity and difference

For those perhaps more familiar with the Cotswold-Severn monuments of southern Britain, many of the aspects of the monuments of the Irish Sea area will seem very familiar. The monuments included in this study, just like those of the Cotswold-Severn region, are built of stone. In the case of the Clyde and court cairns, they also have a forecourt area and are set within a long cairn. They all have a chamber or chambers of some description. They usually contain the remains of the dead and were almost certainly used for the gathering of people for special events or ceremonies. Other objects were also deposited at these sites, in particular stone axes and pottery. Yet for all the similarities, there are also considerable differences. In the past some scholars tried to find connections, in particular in relation to morphology, between the sites of the Irish Sea and the Cotswold-Severn group. Aspects such as the façade were seen to have 'derived' from the Cotswold-Severn region. Such an approach is no longer in favour, with scholars emphasising the development of regional forms of monumentality from a shared suite of characteristics.

In more recent years, the ways in which sites were used, and what they might have meant to people has become the focus of attention, but this post-processual literature on Neolithic chambered tombs has been dominated by discussions of the Cotswold-Severn monuments, as well as later passage grave sites in Ireland and Orkney (e.g. from Shanks and Tilley 1982 to Thomas and Whittle 1986 to Benson and Whittle 2005). This is partly because a number of these sites have been excavated and have produced well-preserved remains. It is also partly because these monuments offer a wealth of evidence that invites constant reinvestigation and reinterpretation. It is not surprising, therefore, that new ideas have been explored by using the best material evidence. But while many of the ideas that have been suggested for the Cotswold-Severn monuments in particular, and also to a certain extent the later large passage graves, may be relevant to the sequence in western Britain, we are, at the end of the day, dealing with a unique set of monuments. The monuments found around the Irish Sea are not Cotswold-Severn monuments, and models or suggestions as to the use and meaning of the southern British sites should not be liberally applied to monuments elsewhere.

I think there are a number of reasons why this is the case. Firstly, the two different regions have very different histories. There seems to have been only limited Mesolithic occupation in some areas where Cotswold-Severn monuments were constructed (e.g. Whittle 1990), and those areas that did have Mesolithic populations would almost certainly have had quite different social structures and understandings of the world than our maritime fisher-hunter-gatherers of the Irish Sea zone (see chapter 2). The arrival of the Neolithic may well have also been rather different in these two broad areas: there is good evidence that the Irish Sea zone acquired the Neolithic (things, people or ideas) via the western seaways (e.g. Bowen 1970) while the Cotswold-Severn region was inspired from France or Belgium (see Cummings and Whittle 2004, 88–91). People in the Irish Sea zone seem to have retained a close connection with the sea into the Neolithic, while southern England clearly saw a shift to a terrestrial diet probably based on cattle (Schulting and Richards 2002b). Furthermore, the long-term trajectories of these different areas was quite different: one need only look at the late Neolithic sequences around Avebury and Stonehenge to realise how radically different this was from what was going on around the Irish Sea zone. I argue, then, that is it critical that we understand the monuments of the Irish Sea zone in their own individual context.

Middle and late Neolithic chambered tombs

The focus of this volume is the early Neolithic chambered tombs of the Irish Sea zone. However, the area also has a rich and varied set of middle and later Neolithic monuments. Unfortunately, the project could not incorporate all of these sites into the study, due to the sheer number of sites in the case study area. However, these monuments have been discussed in detail elsewhere (Cummings 2002b; Cummings and Fowler 2004c; Cummings and Whittle 2004; Eogan 1986; O'Kelly 1982; Murray 1992) and here I offer a brief summary of some key aspects of these sites.

Passage graves

There are two types of passage grave in the Irish Sea zone: the first are the small, early Neolithic sites which I have argued share so many characteristics with dolmens that we should consider them part of the same general group (discussed above). The second are the much larger, more visually impressive passage graves which are frequently, although not exclusively, found in 'cemeteries': the most famous collections of passage graves are the Brú na Bóinne monuments,

Figure 4.16. Passage graves at Knowth, Co. Meath

Figure 4.17. Passage graves at Loughcrew, Co. Meath

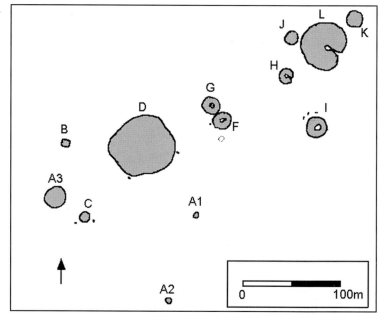

Loughcrew and Carrowmore (Fig. 4.16). Passage graves come in a variety of sizes from the small 'satellite' tombs found in clusters around the much larger and visually very impressive central passage graves (Fig. 4.17). The large passage graves seem to date to the middle Neolithic (Cooney and Grogan 1991), however some of the smaller satellite tombs may be earlier. This is primarily an Irish phenomenon, with all the major passage grave cemeteries being there, although there are two large 'Irish-looking' passage graves on Anglesey in north Wales (Barclodiad y Gawres and Bryn Celli Ddu).

   These passage graves as a whole are a complex group of monuments, the study of which could fill several large volumes (indeed, there is a considerable literature on these sites: e.g. Bergh 1995; Burenhult 1984; Cochrane 2006; Fraser 1998; Herity 1974; Shee Twohig 1981). Here I want to just briefly highlight some of their key features, primarily to illustrate how different these sites are from the early Neolithic chambered tombs in this study.

- The passage is an important component of these sites, a space designed for people to move between the inside of the monument (the chamber) and the outside. The passages at these sites are quite sizeable in length and narrow, so that only one or two people could enter the chamber at any one time.
- A key characteristic of many of these sites is that they are grouped together so that entire landscapes became filled with monumental spaces. These are not single isolated sites, and this contrasts dramatically with early Neolithic sites which do not create entire landscapes of monuments.
- The largest of the passage graves within any one group is usually set on top of a hill or mountain, meaning that from these sites there are wide-ranging views of the surrounding landscape. Furthermore, the passage graves themselves can be seen from a large area. These were sites that were meant to be seen: highly visible nodes in the landscape. As we shall see in the next chapter, this contrasts with the early Neolithic chambered tombs in the area.
- Most sites are associated with rock art. At a site like Newgrange, part of the Brú na Bóinne complex, many of the stones have rock art on them, both within the monument and around its periphery. None of the early Neolithic chambered tombs in this study have rock art, and again, it seems to have been something that was particularly appropriate at these sites.
- The large passage graves in particular would have taken a massive amount of time and effort to construct. These were either long, drawn-out projects, or a significant number of people were involved in their construction.
- Human remains have been found within these passage graves, so clearly these sites were partly about creating a space for the storage of the dead. However, this was clearly not their only function. Furthermore, excavated sites such as Knowth and Newgrange reveal that these sites were also used (before and after) for settlement (Cooney 2000, 30), meaning these chambered tombs may actually share more in common with British henge monuments than their chambered tomb predecessors.

Bargrennan monuments

The Bargrennan monuments are found exclusively in south-west Scotland in western Galloway (Fig. 4.18; Cummings 2002b; Cummings and Fowler 2007; Murray 1992). This small group of chambered tombs is completely different

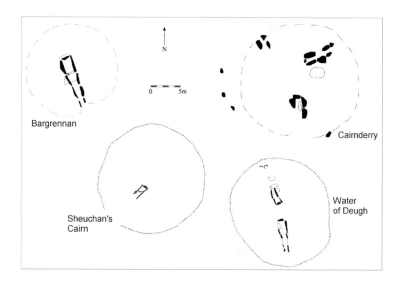

*Figure 4.18.
Bargrennan
monuments (after
Murray 1992)*

from the Clyde monuments found along the coasts of western Britain. Firstly, Bargrennan monuments are passage graves: sites consist of a small chamber or chambers with a passage set within a round cairn. This is in complete contrast to the nearby Clyde cairns which do not have passages and are set in long cairns with impressive façades. Secondly, the Bargrennan sites also have a very different distribution to the Clyde monuments: the Bargrennan sites are all found in upland and inland Galloway, on what is now marginal land (Cummings 2002b). Again, the setting of these sites is radically different from Clyde monuments in the area (Cummings 2002b and see chapter 6). Older (Piggott and Powell 1949) and more recent excavations (Cummings and Fowler 2007) have found little evidence for a construction date for these sites. At the type site Bargrennan White Cairn, and at Cairnderry, pre-cairn activity has been found, dating to the later Mesolithic at the former and the early Neolithic at the latter. However, the chambers at both sites had been robbed out giving no indication of when the sites may have been constructed. At both sites, however, there was substantial evidence for early Bronze Age reuse, including the digging of pits with cremated bone and grave goods at both sites as well as the insertion of a cist at Bargrennan White Cairn. Links with Irish passage graves have led to suggestions of a middle Neolithic date (Murray 1992), but the sheer quantity of early Bronze Age material, and parallels with the Clava cairns (Bradley 2000b), must also point to a possible early Bronze Age date. The excavation report of Bargrennan and Cairnderry (Cummings and Fowler 2007) includes a full review of these sites including their possible date, but it is sufficient here to say that these are not early Neolithic chambered tombs, so will not be considered any further in this study.

Figure 4.19. The earth-fast monument of Carn Wnda, Pembrokeshire

Earth-fast chambers of south-west Wales

Another small group of chambered tombs are found in south-west Wales: these are the earth-fast monuments (Cummings and Whittle 2004), so named as one end of the capstone rests on the earth (Fig. 4.19; Daniel 1950). Even less is known about these sites that the Bargrennan monuments, and none have been subject to recent excavation. These sites are fairly insubstantial, and many could easily have been destroyed, thus it is difficult to say whether this monumental tradition was small-scale and restricted or much more widespread. So far, they have only been found in south-west Wales. Elsewhere, I suggested that these monuments may be later Neolithic in date (Cummings and Whittle 2004), however similarities with caves utilised in the late Mesolithic may indicate an early date (Tilley 1994, 96–9). The Antiquarian investigation of Carn Wnda (Fenton 1848) did uncover a small urn and cremated bone, which may equally suggest an early Bronze Age date for either construction or reuse. It is likely we may never resolve the dating of these sites: all seem to have been robbed out. However, due to their uncertain date and unique landscape setting in contrast with known early Neolithic sites (see Cummings and Whittle 2004), they were not included in this study.

A brief note on other Neolithic monuments

Chambered tombs are not the only type of monument found in the Irish Sea zone. Cursus monuments (Thomas 2006a), enclosures (Darvill 2003; Thomas forthcoming), stone and wooden circles and henges (Bradley 1998a; Burl 1995; Cooney 2000; Gibson 2005; Hartwell 1998) are all found within the study area. These monuments are very different from chambered tombs and the vast majority of these sites are later than the chambered tombs, although people may well have still been using or visiting the chambered tombs when the later sites were being built and used. These sites differ from the chambered tombs as they are all much more substantial structures, with more permeable boundaries. The Irish Sea zone has some spectacular examples of these other monumental forms, a set of sites which would also benefit from further investigation into their landscape settings.

Conclusions

In this chapter we have considered the chambered tomb tradition of the Irish Sea zone, focussing primarily on the early Neolithic sequence. I have argued that there were essentially only two different types of monument in the early Neolithic of the Irish Sea zone, the Clyde and courts found in west Scotland and east Ireland, and the dolmen tradition found in south-east Ireland and west Wales. Other monuments are found in the study area, but do not date to the early Neolithic. We have also seen how these sites have been the focus of attention for hundreds of years, yet in the last few decades, interest has turned away from these sites to other types of evidence. I would argue that if we move beyond considerations of the architectural form of these sites, which has dominated the literature in the past, there is still much to be gained from studying these monuments. In the next chapter I move to a more detailed consideration of these sites, in terms of the materials used to construct them as well as the materials deposited in them. In the following chapters I will then consider their landscape setting, drawing all of these strands of evidence together in the final chapter.

5

The materiality of monuments

Introduction

This chapter will consider the issue of the materials used in the construction, use and experience of megaliths. I will emphasise how specific substances with distinctive properties were repeatedly used to construct monuments, as well as being deposited in the chambers and forecourts. There will be a consideration of the origin of the materials used to construct megaliths. I will also consider the textures, colours and shape of the stones, and how megaliths essentially bring together different pieces of the landscape. I will then go on to consider how sites were used once they had been constructed. We will look in detail at the deposits found in these megaliths (burnt soil, charcoal, human bone, lithics and pottery) and what we can begin to understand about the material substances being evoked and performed at these megaliths.

A brief introduction to materiality

Before we look at in detail at the megaliths of the Irish Sea zone, I want to consider the term materiality very briefly. The word materiality has been used a great deal over the last few years, and it is a concept of increasing importance when it comes to theoretical considerations of the material world. I understand materiality to refer to the material from which a thing is made (for example wood, stone or bone), so 'the state or quality of being material': critically, though, materiality is *contextual*. Therefore, this definition also relates to what a thing actually *is* (e.g. a bow, axe or pendant) and all the social sets of meanings attached to that thing. The fact that something is made of stone is not enough to ascribe it meaning, although the fact something is made of stone can help define its character and therefore its meaning. The quality of things are inherently socialised and as such, part of existing ideologies and understandings of the world. However, this is not a one-way process: people ascribe meaning to things, but those things have an effect on people, thus making materiality a key part of the dialectical engagement of people and things (Demarris *et al.* 2004, 2; Meskell 2005b, 4).

The very fact that something is made from a particular substance can imbue it with a whole range of significances. In the Neolithic world, for example, exotic stones such as that from Tievebulliagh mountain in Co. Antrim were made into axes that were then distributed or exchanged over a wide area. It has been argued that the source of stone axes was one of the most significant parts of the object (e.g. Bradley and Edmonds 1993). Here, then, part of the meaning and significance and value of the object relates to the material from which it was made. Yet this is not the whole story. It would seem that Tievebulliagh stone was not inherently valuable, or, for that matter, particularly rare: large quantities of flakes can still be found at the site. The material substance was not enough – what it was made into or how it was used was also significant. Perhaps who made the object or its life history also added to the meaning of the object. Robb summarises this rather neatly: 'an artefact, thus, cannot be considered as a single physical thing, but rather possesses a culturally-attributed extension of beliefs, practices, contexts and extensions in time; and it is this extension of the artefact that gives it the power to structure human lives' (Robb 2004, 135). A study of materiality, therefore, is bound up with many other key conceptions such as the biography of an object, its aesthetics as well as its functionality within society.

Discussions of materiality have, for the most part, focussed on objects (e.g. papers in Demarris *et al.* 2004; Meskell 2005a). However, materiality also relates to materials which are not 'material culture' in the formal sense (and also see Scarre 2004). The focus in this chapter is not only on those objects found in megaliths, such as axes, pots and arrowheads; I am interested in the materiality of the stones which make up the megaliths as well as the substances deposited such as charcoal, quartz and bone. I make no distinction between objects made by people and natural objects when considering possible meanings. I also consider human and animal bodies (bones) to simply be part of the suite of things considered appropriate to be deposited in monuments: material substances imbued with their own sets of cultural meanings. However, it is important to stress again that materiality is contextual: here I only consider the meanings of substances found in chambered tombs, while drawing on the network of connections of these substances in other contexts in the Neolithic world.

Construction of megaliths

I want to begin by considering the construction of the chambered tombs. This issue has been discussed recently by a number of scholars. Colin Richards (2004), for example, has examined the different aspects involved in the construction of a monument. He suggests that in order to construct a chambered tomb people needed to do a number of things before they were actually ready to build the monument. Firstly, they needed to find an appropriate source of stone, which for many chambered tombs of the Irish Sea region was probably local, although some distant sources were also used (see below). Secondly, people would need to make ropes in order to move the stones around, as well as prepare timbers for rollers and props. Thirdly, people would need to store up enough food to feed people while they were building the monument. And finally, a work force would need to be gathered at an appropriate time in order to actually build the megalith. All of this required a considerable investment of time and labour even before the construction of the megalith had begun. Richards (2004) also suggests that building a monument therefore involved a considerable amount of risk. This was risk not only in terms of the possible dangers surrounding the construction of megalithic architecture, but also in terms of social investment and risk. He suggests that there might have been quite serious social consequences for failed attempts at megalithic construction. For example, if a stone that was being dragged across the landscape broke *en route*, that might mean more than simply the loss of time and energy.

Interesting work has also been done on the construction process itself, particularly in relation to long barrows and cairns. McFadyen (2006) has studied the composition of Cotswold-Severn chambered tombs and discovered that many seem to have been built from a series of very carefully selected materials. She has argued that monuments were 'construction sites' where people came together at different times to add to the monument, weaving in different materials and substances. Long cairns were often constructed in small sections or bays where particular sets of materials were brought together to make up one particular part of the monument. All the materials selected and used in each monument were significant to the people building the site, perhaps coming from a significant place or incorporating material that belonged to particular people. In this way, chambered tombs were carefully composed, constructed and reworked, with materials and biographies of people and places interwoven into the fabric of the monument (McFadyen 2006).

Following on from McFadyen and Richards' work on the construction process, I want to consider the megaliths of the Irish Sea zone. Sadly, for the most part, there are not the detailed excavations of the cairns of the megaliths of the Irish Sea zone which has enabled McFadyen to discuss the precise composition of her sites. However, there are still some interesting observations to be made with the Irish Sea megaliths which suggest that the composition of these sites was very carefully orchestrated.

Pre-cairn and prepared surfaces
A number of megaliths seem to have been built onto carefully prepared surfaces. While some preparation of the ground was obviously required, such as the clearance of vegetation, some sites had surfaces of specific materials laid down prior to megalithic construction. At Ballyedmond, Co. Down (E. E. Evans 1938a), for example, the cairn seems to have been built on a prepared surface of gravel. At other sites, brightly coloured materials seem to have been used. At Browndod, Co Antrim, the monument was built over a layer of red soil, which the excavators claimed had been brought to the site and laid out prior to megalithic construction (Evans and Davies 1935). A yellow clay layer was found under the cairn and in the forecourt at Clontygora Large, Co. Armagh (Davies and Paterson 1937). In these examples, the ground surface prior to construction seems to have been marked out in a visually distinctive way. It is also worth noting that specially imported materials were used to floor the chamber at some sites. At Kilchoan, Argyll, for example, imported yellow sand was used to line the base of the chamber (Henshall 1972, 340–2). At Barmore Wood, Argyll, a yellow clay layer had been added to the base of the chamber (Henshall 1972, 322).

At other sites, megaliths seem to have been constructed over earlier activity. For example, at Trefignath in North Wales, small hearths and a scatter of finds were found underneath the primary monument (Smith and Lynch 1987). Further north on Islay, the chambered tomb at Port Charlotte was preceded by a deposit of hazelnut shells, sheep bone and flints (Harrington and Pierpoint 1980). And the chambered tomb of Glecknabae, Bute, was built over an earlier shell midden (Henshall 1972, 411–14). This pre-cairn activity is often considered to be the remains of occupation but at some sites it seems that funerary or more ritualised activity was taking place on site prior to the construction of a megalith. For example at Ballybriest, Co. Derry, a quantity of cremated bone, pot sherds and a hearth were found underneath the court cairn (Herity 1987, 126). Both the primary and secondary phases at Bryn yr Hen Bobl on Anglesey covered quantities of pottery and flint tools as well as scraps of human and animal bone (Hemp 1935). At these sites, then, the presence of cremated human bone suggests that more ritualised activities were already occurring at these sites prior to megalithic construction. Once again, the usefulness of the domestic-ritual dichotomy can be questioned.

It seems that in many cases it was appropriate to build megaliths over earlier material which had been produced through ritualised activity. This suggests that some of these locations were already associated with the remains of the dead prior to megalithic construction and offers hints that these locales were already important places in the landscape (cf. Tilley 1994). At other sites, it seems to have been appropriate to import material, often brightly coloured, prior to the main construction phase: this imported material may well have had a whole series of links with other places, people or events. So far there is no evidence from the study area for monuments being built over preceding 'settlement' structures, as has been found at megaliths elsewhere (e.g. at Ballyglass one in Co. Mayo: Ó Nualláin 1972) but this may well have also occurred at some of the Irish Sea sites. However, it is also relevant to note that pre-cairn activity or deposition is not present at every site, showing diversity across and within this area.

Construction methods
As we have seen in chapter 4, megaliths throughout the Irish Sea zone share a number of characteristics such as the presence of a chamber or chambers and forecourts. However, the same construction methods were not employed by all builders of these megaliths. For example, in some areas, the stones which make up the chamber area were simply bedded on the ground surface (for example at Annaghmare, Co. Armagh, Din Dryfol on Anglesey and Clontygora, Co. Armagh). At other sites, holes were cut into the ground in order to take the orthostats (for example Carreg Samson, Pembrokeshire and Ballyalton, Co. Down). At some sites, a combination of these methods was used. Furthermore, the type of site (court cairn, dolmen etc) does not dictate which construction method was employed, with considerable variety evident in all forms of megalith. These different construction methods shows a level of improvisation and it is therefore clear that the builders were not simply following a set 'pattern' but willing and able to adjust the construction methods in order to create a monument using specific stones in specific locations.

Many of the monuments in the Irish Sea zone utilise really massive stones in their construction. The largest capstones in this area are well over 50 tonnes: the capstone at Goward dolmen, Co. Down is one of the largest, but other large examples include Proleek, Co. Louth, Garn Turne, Pembrokeshire and Arthur's Stone on the Gower (Fig. 5.1). Elsewhere, it has been suggested that one of the essential qualities of these monuments was the lifting up and displaying of large and impressive capstones (Cummings and Whittle 2004; Whittle 2004). It is not just the capstones at megaliths which are large stones: there are also examples of massive stones used as uprights in either the chamber or façade of sites. Brackley in Kintyre, Boreland in Dumfries and Galloway and King Orry's

Figure 5.1. The massive capstones at Goward (top) and Brennanstown (bottom)

Grave SW, Isle of Man all use very big stones in their façades, for example (Fig. 5.2). The level of engineering demonstrated at all the megalithic sites, therefore, is very impressive, but particularly extraordinary at sites where really massive stones are used. It would be possible to suggest that the builders of these sites were not experimenting with a new technique, but were already competent at the methods required for moving massive pieces of stone around the landscape. This has implications for the origins of the Neolithic and will be discussed in more detail in chapter 8.

It is interesting that while people were obviously extremely skilled at moving large stones, they do not, for the most part, seem to have shaped the stones used in megaliths. At a few sites there is some evidence of stones being worked.

Figure 5.2. King Orry's Graves SW, Isle of Man

At Carreg Coetan in south-west Wales it seems that at least one stone in the chamber had been deliberately shaped, although the possibility exists that some apparently worked stones may actually have been 'accidentally' altered, simply by virtue of moving them around. However, even if this is not the case, we are clearly not seeing the level of stone-working that is found at later Neolithic sites such as Stonehenge (for example see figures in Whittle 1997). Most stones used in the monuments of the Irish Sea zone seem to be unworked, so stones were being used more or less as they were found. Therefore, one of the key characteristics of these megaliths is that they incorporate unworked stones into the fabric of the monument. This contrasts dramatically with other stones in the Neolithic world, such as stone axes and flint tools, which were carefully shaped into distinctive artefacts (see chapter 3).

Although the vast majority of stones were unworked, it seems some may have been very subtly altered through the addition of rock art. None of the megaliths of the Irish Sea zone being considered here have the type of art found on the later passage graves of the region. However, a few sites do have some evidence for what has more recently been termed as scratch art (Bradley 1998a and see Shepherd 2000). The sites of Ballymarlagh, Co. Antrim and Goward court cairn, Co. Down, have evidence of shallow lines carved onto the chamber stones. There is no evidence to show whether these are primary features or added at a subsequent date. Furthermore, this subtle alteration of stones may not have survived at many sites, which have been exposed to the elements for hundreds if not thousands of years. However, it does suggest that the very elaborate rock art of passage graves may have a precursor in early Neolithic chambered tombs, and that some very subtle alteration of these stones was appropriate. We must also consider the possibility that some stones may have been painted with pigments, as has been suggested for Neolithic sites on Orkney (e.g. Isbister 2000).

A variety of construction methods were therefore employed in order to make megalithic architecture out of unworked stones. Some of these stones may have been very subtly altered through incised lines or pigments. In some cases it seems that it was desirable to utilise really massive pieces of stone, stones that may already have been significant (see below). I now want to move on and consider the individual properties of the stones that make up the megaliths of the Irish Sea zone, beginning with quartz.

The stones of chambered tombs

One of the most distinctive types of stone used in the chambered tombs of the Irish Sea zone is quartz. It is perhaps not surprising that quartz is found at a number of sites, as it is the most common mineral in the world and is ubiquitously found on the shores of the Irish Sea. However, chambered tombs are never built solely of quartz stones, perhaps because the shape of quartz boulders were not suitable for chambered tomb construction, but also because it seems not to have been appropriate to solely use this substance to make a monument. Only a couple of sites employ extensive amounts of quartz in their construction: the chamber at Cragabus on Islay is built from a quartzite, as is Loch Nell in Argyll. Both of these sites would have been visually quite distinctive.

At the vast majority of sites utilising this substance, quartz seems to be positioned quite subtly and carefully, seeming to mark out important parts of the monument. For example, at Brackley, Kintyre, the large surviving portal stone has many quartz lumps in it. This marks out the entranceway into the monument in a distinctive way. Similarly, a number of stones in the chamber at Carreg Samson in west Wales have quartz inclusions, including the capstone. At this site, the largest piece of quartz is found at the point in which a participant would enter the chamber. King Orry's Grave NE on the Isle of Man has quartz in the portal stones only (Cummings and Fowler 2004a, 117), as does Cashtal yn Ard, also on the Isle of Man (Fig 5.3.). At other sites, quartz seems to have been used to make the backstone visually distinct. At Glecknahavill, Kintyre, Greenamore, Co. Antrim and Sannox on Arran, for example, quartz is found in the backslab of each chamber. Some sites seem to have the most quartz as part of the capstone, particularly dolmen sites which will be discussed again in chapter 7. For example, the impressive dolmen at Ballyvennaght in Co. Antrim, is made from a stone containing many lumps of quartz, however, this is the most distinctive in the capstone which has massive quartz chunks in it. At Tamlaght, Co. Derry, quartz is

Figure 5.3. Cashtel yn Ard, Isle of Man

Figure 5.4. Quartz in one of the chamber stones

only found in the capstone and this emphasis of quartz in the capstone is mirrored at other dolmen sites such as White House, Pembrokeshire. Some megaliths utilise quartz in other ways, emphasising a particular side of the monument (Fig. 5.4). At Ossian's Grave, Co. Antrim, for example, the stones on the right side of the chamber (looking in from the façade) have chunks of quartz, which is also the side of the monument with a sea view. Single quartzite stones are also employed at a number of the north Welsh sites, which again makes one side of the chamber particularly visually distinctive. At other sites, quartz is not employed in the chamber, but is found in the cairn itself. At Carnbaan, Glenvoidean and Michael's Grave, all on Bute, quartz is clearly visible as part of the cairn.

Figure 5.5. Carreg Samson, Pembrokeshire

It is clear, then, that quartz is not used consistently in chambered tombs in order to repeatedly emphasise one part of the monument only. Instead, quartz is employed differently at different sites, sometimes seemingly to emphasise the entrance into chambers, or the back of chambers, but in other cases sides of monuments or the large capstones on the tops of monuments. We will see below that quartz is also deposited at chambered tombs in a variety of ways which further emphasises its unique properties.

It is clear how carefully quartz is located when you visit these sites, marking out transitional areas such as the entrance into, or the end of, the chamber. However, it could be argued that the use of quartz is simply fortuitous. The stones chosen for the backslab or entrance portal may possess other qualities which make them appropriate for use in these places, such as size and shape. However, there is other evidence which supports the idea that the stones used to build chambered tombs *were* very carefully and deliberately chosen by the builders of each site. At Glenvoidean on Bute for example, people primarily used schistose grit to construct the monument, even though quartzite was plentiful in the area, a deliberate avoidance, apart from at very specific and presumably appropriate points, of this stone (Marshall and Taylor 1976, 5). At other sites, people used non-local stones in a megalith, even though there was suitable quartzite building stone in the immediate vicinity. This is particularly distinctive at one site in west Wales, Carreg Samson, where three of the six uprights were built from stone that does not outcrop in the immediate vicinity (Fig 5.5. and see Cummings 2002c). The three stones which make up the front of the chamber and the capstone are all made from a conglomerate containing lumps of quartz which outcrops in the immediate vicinity, however, the remainder are not and must have been imported from another location. Other sites in west Wales have stones which are not from the local area: Parc y Cromlech, Pembrokeshire and Ty Newydd in north Wales. In Ireland, Mourne Park, Co. Down (Davies 1938) was mostly constructed out of granite boulders, but one upright was of quarried shale. At these sites, other stones have been brought in from other parts of the landscape. All of this suggests that the builders of these sites did not simply use the most convenient source of stone in order to construct each site. Instead, stones were carefully chosen for their properties, which in some cases involved moving stones across the landscape. This should perhaps come as no surprise, since there is substantial evidence for the movement of stones in later Neolithic contexts (e.g. Avebury and Stonehenge), yet arguments persist that people in the early Neolithic built their monuments at the most convenient place for acquiring stone (e.g. Fleming 1999). Instead, it is possible to argue that people were carefully and deliberately composing their monuments using appropriate stones, and in some cases they had to travel a good distance in order to acquire specific stones, which may relate in part to the presence (or absence) of quartz.

The stones that were brought together to make the chamber and cairn at sites around the Irish Sea may have had other properties which made them significant. For examples, stones may already have had a history before they were even incorporated into the monument. The idea that each stone had its own biography prior to monumental inclusion has been discussed in a neat paper by Pollard and Gillings (1998) in relation to the Avebury stones and similar ideas could be employed here (and see Cummings and Whittle 2004, chapter 7). Alternatively, stones may have related to different family groups or communities, and the bringing together of these stones representative of the bringing together of different social groups. Ethnography also provides us with some ideas worth considering. Some non-western peoples see stones as active entities in their own right. For example, to the Wamira of Papua New Guinea, each stone in their landscape has a history, name and life of its own (Kahn 1990). Some stones represent where elders sat in the past while others are considered to be the ancestors themselves. The Wamira believe that stones and rocks actually move around by themselves. Stones representing named ancestors walk about, particularly at night, sometimes even disappearing for years at a time (Kahn 1990). While it would be inappropriate to suggest that an identical situation occurred in the Neolithic of the Irish Sea, we could suggest that the stones used to make megaliths were imbued with significances or identities of their own. While quartz might be the physical manifestation of essences or other beings (see below) there may also have been properties of rocks that made these stones significant.

Figure 5.6. Pentre Ifan, Pembrokeshire

Figure 5.7. Kilfeaghan, Co. Down

Significant stones

There is evidence which suggests that, particularly at dolmens, stones were simply dug from the earth and lifted up (and see Cummings and Whittle 2004, chapter 7). At Carreg Samson in south-west Wales a large pit was found underneath the chamber which was the right size and shape to have once held the capstone. The excavator suggested the stone had been dug up from that spot and lifted up to create the chamber (Lynch 1975). A similar situation seems to have occurred at Pentre Ifan in south-west Wales (Fig. 5.6) where a large pit was also found underneath the chamber (Grimes 1948) and we could also envisage a similar situation in the construction of the monument of Arthur's Stone on the Gower

Figure 5.8.
Trefignath, Anglesey

(see Cummings and Whittle 2004) as well as possibly at Kilfeaghan (Fig. 5.7) and Proleek in Co. Down. At other sites pits have not been found underneath the chamber and at these monuments stones lying on the ground surface may have been used for the capstone. It could be suggested that the capstones at Garn Turne, south-west Wales and Goward, Co. Down may have been literally lifted up and supported from where they lay. In these cases it could be argued that these stones may have already have been significant prior to being turned into megaliths (see Cummings and Whittle 2004, chapter 7). They may well have been associated with a whole series of myths and stories, were known locales in the landscape and perhaps were even the focus of acts of deposition.

At some sites then, significant stones were excavated from the earth and turned into a megalith. Other sites seem to be positioned in relation to stones or outcrops that may also have been known locales in the landscape. A number of sites seem to have been built directly on top of visible and distinctive outcrops. For example, the court cairn of Ballymacdermot, Co. Armagh, was built directly on top of a solid granite outcrop (Collins and Wilson 1964, 6). This meant that a large boss of granite protruded into the third chamber as well in the forecourt, which was framed on one side by the outcrop. A similar situation is found at Annaghmare, Co. Armagh, where the forecourt contained outcropping rock as well as a large natural hollow (Waterman 1965). Due to the presence of outcropping rock, the builders at this site chose to use a whole variety of different construction methods in order to create the forecourt and chambers. In Wales, Din Dryfol on Anglesey was constructed on a distinctive elongated rock outcrop and Trefignath on Holyhead Island (Fig. 5.8) was also constructed

Figure 5.9.
Cairnholy II,
Dumfries and
Galloway

directly on top of an outcrop. And in western Scotland Cairnholy II (Fig. 5.9) was built on top of a domed rock outcrop. At all of these sites, it would seem that the builders of each monument could have made the construction process considerably easier by avoiding outcrops and natural features. Instead they seem to have deliberately chosen distinctive outcrops on which to construct sites which adds weight to the suggestion that the precise location of each site was much more important than mere 'convenience' or practicality. This was confirmed by the excavation at Beacharra, Kintyre, where the excavator found that it would have been much easier to built the site in a slightly different location (Scott 1954, 148).

Use of colour
Another component in the experience of sites is colour. The use of colour at megalithic architecture has been discussed more generally by a number of authors (Bradley 2000b; Lynch 1998) and the colours of the chambered tombs of Arran has been considered in detail by Andy Jones (1999). Jones notes how different colours are employed in the construction and use of each megalith. Sites seem to have been made using a combination of red and white stones, and each colour seems to have been carefully positioned in relation to its original source, so red stones are on the side closest to the source of these stones. Jones also argues that artefacts of different colours were deposited in different ways in each monument. Dark Arran pitchstone was mostly deposited in the rear chambers, while bright quartz was deposited in the forecourt. This mirrors the 'natural' colours of monument in relation to areas which received light and those which were dark. Jones (1999)

goes on to suggest that red, black and white formed a symbolic code on Arran. He suggests that white was connected with the north of the island, quartz, and the outside of each monument. Black, however, was associated with darkness, the interior of monument, and the dead. Red, found in monuments in the form of sandstone from the coasts and also red knives represented flesh, blood and fertility (A. Jones 1999, 348). This careful use of colour created connections between different parts of the landscape as well as being part of a broader symbolic code concerning life, death and the body (A. Jones 1999).

While it would be insightful to conduct a similar analysis on all the megaliths of the Irish Sea zone, unfortunately we are restricted by the quantity and quality of excavations. Sadly, no other area has seen the levels of investigation achieved by Bryce in his prolific excavations of the chambered tombs of Arran (Bryce 1902). This means it is not possible to meaningfully tie the deposition of coloured substances in relation to the chambers. There are hints that colour was carefully employed at other sites however. At Browndod, Co. Antrim, for example, there is the varied use of colour in the deposits. We have already noted how there was red soil underneath the cairn, including in the forecourt. There was also the usual black earth deposits in the chambers (see below). Furthermore, the pot sherds found in the forecourt were also mostly red, and three rounded yellow pebbles were also deposited there (Evans and Davies 1935, 87). At the site of Pant y Saer on Anglesey, there is also clear evidence for the use of a number of coloured substances. At this site the chamber was cut into the limestone which was then covered with a red layer of clay. On top of this was a layer of charcoal and sea shells, and on top of this, the main deposit of bone and pottery. The excavator also noted that all the arrowheads found on the site were different colours (W. Scott 1933, 215–6).

We can also comment on some other interesting uses of colour at some monuments. Firstly, we have already considered the incorporation of stones containing quartz in the fabric of the monument, as well as quartz deposits in the chambers and forecourts. White was therefore repeatedly present at chambered tombs in the Irish Sea area. Elsewhere it has been suggested that white may be representative of bone, the moon, semen, ice, snow and water (Bradley 2004; Fowler and Cummings 2003; A. Jones 1999). I would be wary of suggesting that the presence of quartz was ubiquitously representative of these substances at chambered tombs throughout the area, but these may have been associations which were drawn upon at specific times and in specific contexts. Secondly, I have also noted that virtually all megaliths have a black or charcoal layer deposited in the chambers, as well as frequent burnings in the forecourt. Again, we could envisage connections here with burning (cremations), the hearth, darkness and the night. There are other, very distinctive uses of colour in the megaliths of the Irish Sea. Some sites employ brightly coloured stones in their architecture: for example some of the stones in Mourne Park, Co. Down are a pink quartzite. Creag Mhor and Crarae in western Scotland both use a shiny blue stone, which would have been very conspicuous and intense when freshly quarried/exposed. Granite is also occasionally used to make megaliths: for example Kilfeaghan, Co. Down is constructed from a dark mica-rich granite.

The vast majority of chambered tombs in the Irish Sea region, however, do not incorporate brightly coloured stones in their fabric, apart from quartz. So while it is interesting to note the presence of coloured stones at some sites, it was not 'mandatory' to use distinctive colours in construction. This does not mean that colour was not significant, or that megaliths did not incorporate colours in other ways: the presence of dyes, paints and pigments may well have been employed at these sites. Other organics may well have played an important role at these sites such as plants and coloured fabrics.

Texture
Elsewhere I have discussed in detail the use of texture in monuments (Cummings 2002c). Carreg Samson, Pembrokeshire, for example, is constructed from two different rock types which have distinctively different textures. The stones are arranged so that all three smooth stones are positioned to one side of the chamber, while the other side of the chamber is constructed from rough stones. Other megaliths in the study area have stones with distinctive textures which could be understood in a similar way. For example, at Nether Largie, Argyll, the three stones at the rear of the chamber are all rough, while the backslab itself is smooth. I have suggested that these different textures may have imparted meanings to people encountering these monuments, either through visual engagement, or through touch if light levels were low or people were actually entering the monument (Cummings 2002c). These contrasting textures may have helped to designate different areas of each monument, themselves associated with different substances or uses.

Shape
The shape of the stones used in megaliths is also worth commenting on. I have already noted the use of large chunky capstones at a number of dolmens in the Irish Sea zone (see above and also Cummings and Whittle 2004, chapter 7). At a number of sites there is also the use of water-worn stones, especially in the supports for the capstone (sidestones). It is interesting in itself that some sites incorporated stones from watery places into the fabric of the monument (see discussion on

Figure 5.10.
Wateresk, Co. Down

connections between stone and water in Fowler and Cummings 2003), but it also gives these stones a very distinctive shape, especially in comparison to angular stones from terrestrial sources. Examples of sites which incorporate water-worn stones are Carreg Coetan in Pembrokeshire and Moinechoill, Arran.

Individual sites often seem to have distinctively shaped stones included in the chamber. An excellent example of this is the dolmen of Wateresk in Co. Down where one of the uprights which supports the capstone has a triangular top which tessellates with the capstone (Fig. 5.10). At Ballynichol in Co. Down the entrance into the now-destroyed chamber is through two thin and narrow stones, one of which is shaped so that it touches the other stone at the top. This also happens at King Orry's Grave north-east on the Isle of Man. Another interesting arrangement of portal stones is also found on the Isle of Man at the site of Cloven Stones, where one stone is literally 'cloven' into two. Thus, stones which were distinctively shaped were often chosen for inclusion in megalithic architecture. It is also worth noting that the shape and form of many stones means that chambers in particular are not symmetrical. This point will be developed further in chapter 7 with a discussion of sidedness.

Some megaliths also incorporate distinctive natural features into their fabric. Most commonly in the Irish Sea zone are sites with 'natural cupmarks' – these are small hollows created through natural processes. In some cases they are difficult to tell apart from cupmarks made by people, and this ambiguity may have been as relevant in the Neolithic as it is today. The most extreme example of this is the site of Trefael in Pembrokeshire, which is a single stone, possibly once part of a burial chamber. The slab is covered with both natural and humanly constructed cupmarks (see Barker 1992, 52). Cairnholy I in south-west Scotland has a number of stones with natural hollows and these are most obvious at the portal stones, one of the key transition points at the site (Cummings 2003).

Composition of the cairn

So far we have only considered the composition of each monument in terms of the stones which make up the chambers and façades. However, a significant part of many chambered tombs were the cairns which surrounded the chambers. There is some debate with regards the phasing of cairns at chambered tombs and it seems likely that in some cases the main bulk of the cairn was added on a later date (for example at Pentre Ifan, Pembrokeshire and Cairnholy I in Dumfries and Galloway). In other cases, particularly the dolmens, it is debatable whether there ever was a substantial cairn (see Cummings and Whittle 2004). However, other sites such as the Clyde and court cairns of western Scotland and eastern Ireland clearly had large cairns as an integral and primary part of the megalith. The logistics of cairn construction are radically different from the chamber construction: the stones used to make up a cairn are much smaller and could easily be lifted by one or two people. For the most part, people seem to have used local stones to make the cairn and therefore cairn construction would not have required the level of planning needed to build a chamber. Although a considerable number of stones are required in order to make a cairn, even a few people can amass a large number of stones over quite a short period of time (approximately 15 people rebuilt a third of a round cairn in less than a day after excavations at Bargrennan in south-west Scotland, although the cairn stones were next to the monument in this example: Cummings and Fowler 2007).

The overall visual appearance of the cairn also seems to have been carefully orchestrated at these megaliths. It is frequently difficult to get a good sense of what these cairns would originally have looked like as almost all have been robbed to a greater or lesser extent. However, it is clear that many cairns incorporate visually distinctive stones such as quartz or granite boulders. It would appear that these are carefully distributed amongst the cairn, not clustered together around the edges or at particular points. This makes an interesting contrast with later sites such as Newgrange in Ireland which had a concentration of quartz stones around the perimeter of the cairn.

Multi-phase constructions

As we saw in the last chapter, a number of sites in the Irish Sea zone were not constructed in a single phase. Instead, many sites show evidence of reworking at a later stage in their history. At some sites this involves the addition of chambers (e.g. Trefignath, North Wales and Mid Gleniron I in Dumfries and

Galloway) and at others it may have involved the extension of the cairn (e.g. at Pentre Ifan, Pembrokeshire and Bryn yr Hen Bobl: Barker 1992; Leivers *et al.* 2001). It is difficult to know when these additions were made: in some cases it seems that there was a fairly quick succession of chamber additions (like at Trefignath and Mid Gleniron) whereas other chambers or smaller cists may well have been added in the early Bronze Age (for example at Gartnagreanoch and Nether Largie, Argyll). With the lack of decent dates from sites, we struggle to date precisely when these different events occurred.

Another later addition at megaliths is the infilling of the forecourts. Again, this does not happen ubiquitously at all sites, although there are problems in telling the difference between a deliberately filled forecourt, and cairn collapse. Some sites have also seen much cairn material robbed from the forecourt area that potential evidence has been destroyed. Nevertheless, it is clear that at some sites, people returned to the site and sealed up the forecourt. In Ireland, the forecourt at Dooey's Cairn, Co. Antrim was blocked, which included pottery fragments, flint flakes, cores and chips and quartz flakes (Collins 1976, 5). The blocking of the forecourt dated to several centuries after the main construction of the chamber and cairn. The court cairn of Ballymacdermot, Co. Armagh, also had its forecourt blocked, and at this site, the chambers were also filled with granite boulders (Collins and Wilson 1964, 14). At Cairnholy I, Dumfries and Galloway, a slab was inserted into the gap between the two portal stones and the forecourt carefully sealed with stones (Piggott and Powell 1949). Other sites in western Scotland also show evidence for the blocking of the forecourt such as Glenvoidean on Bute and Monamore, Arran (Henshall 1972). At a number of sites, then, people came back to a site and made the forecourt inaccessible and sealed up the chambers. It may appear that people were therefore making sure that no further deposits could be made in the chambers. However, in many instances chambers were re-accessed, particularly in the early Bronze Age, and additional deposits were made, which may suggest that the primary aim of forecourt blocking was not to make the chambers inaccessible but to stop people being able to congregate in the forecourt.

All of this suggests that the reworking of these places at some point after their initial construction was a highly significant act. The careful reworking of elements of these monuments, the addition of chambers or the lengthening of the cairn, for example, suggests the long-term significance of these locales: these were still important places in the landscape. The addition of chambers suggests that people simply needed more space for deposition, but we should be wary of such a simplistic interpretation. It may equally have been the case that they no longer wished to disturb earlier deposits, while still depositing material at the site. Another chamber, then, may represent the desire of communities to continue to use a site while respecting earlier deposits. The blocking of the forecourt suggests a similar situation: the restriction of access to places which had been used for a considerable period of time. At these sites, then, there is the sense of sealing off the past and restricting access for living communities. But the reworking of sites may also relate to a desire to impart new senses of identity and community onto these places. The addition of a chamber may represent a social alliance, or the addition of new members into the community. As communities grew, so, perhaps, was it appropriate for monuments to grow along with them.

Constructing places
We have seen how the megaliths of the Irish Sea zone were carefully constructed. I have argued that the materiality of stone imbued megaliths with a whole range of meanings and significances even before they had been used for deposition activities. I have also emphasised the diversity of these structures not only in terms of the stones used to build them, but the techniques in which chambers were built.

There would have been another side to the construction of megaliths in the Neolithic and this relates to the human experiences generated by the construction process. Just as with an excavation, the construction of a megalith would have been a messy experience. Moving around big stones would have required rope, rollers, grease and many people trampling over a site repeatedly. It may well have been very muddy and chaotic, quite possibly with children and animals running around the site. Moving heavy stones around may also have injured people, from a twisted ankle to something more serious. These 'construction sites' (McFadyen 2003) would have become part of peoples' biographies, places not only in the landscape but also in peoples' life histories. These were places where relationships were formed, social relations negotiated and altered. These were places about which stories would be told, perhaps for generations to come.

Using megaliths

I now want to move on and consider the deposits made in chambered tombs. For the most part, these deposits were almost certainly made once the monument had been built, particularly those in the chambers, although some sites do have evidence of deposits being made while the site was 'under construction'. We should also be wary of suggesting that there was a point when the monument was considered 'finished' and ready for use: it may have been the case that these sites were considered as always being built and never finished (cf. Barrett 1994). Indeed, as we have seen, many sites were remodelled at some point,

Figure 5.11.
Bicker's Houses,
Bute

and sites seem to have received deposits right from the early Neolithic into the late Neolithic, and often into the early Bronze Age. Equally, others were sealed and inaccessible prior to this (see above) so we are clearly looking at different practices of deposition over time. Since the focus on the volume is the early Neolithic, I will focus here on the deposits made at this time.

One of the most intriguing aspects of the megaliths of the Irish Sea zone is the fact that the deposits in these monuments are remarkably similar throughout this area. Of course there are limitations to this discussion, as we can only consider those sites that have been excavated. As mentioned in the previous chapter, only a small number of sites have been excavated in our study area, and a fair proportion of these revealed that many sites had been robbed prior to excavation, but there remains a remarkable degree of similarity with regards the deposits made at these sites. I want to consider this evidence in more detail and then think about what it might have meant. Let us begin by considering the deposition of burnt material.

Burnt deposits
Firstly, almost without exception, megaliths contain burnt material. This includes charcoal or burnt wood, dark or black earth (which is dark from burning or has a high charcoal content), burnt stones, and also burnt bone, although the latter will be considered separately below. Burnt objects are also considered below (and see Herity 1987). These burnt remains occur in a number of contexts. At many sites the primary deposit made in the chambers consisted of dark or black earth with charcoal fragments. For example, Michael's Grave, Glecknabae and Bicker's Houses (Fig. 5.11), all on Bute, contained dark earth, charcoal

Figure 5.12.
Audleystown,
Co. Down

and burnt bones in the chambers. Similarly, Ballyalton and Ballynichol in Co. Down both contained dark earth and charcoal (Collins 1956; Evans and Davies 1934). And in Wales, Bachwen and Dyffryn Ardudwy both contained dark earth in the chamber areas (Hemp 1926; Powell 1973). The presence of dark earth and charcoal in the chambers is repeatedly found at almost all excavated sites where the primary deposit has remained intact. Burnt material does not just occur in the chamber areas, it is also repeatedly found in the forecourt area as well. Spreads of charcoal have been found at a number of sites, especially those where the forecourt was blocked or sealed at a later date. For example, at Cairnholy I in south-west Scotland a whole series of charcoal spreads were uncovered in the forecourt area, probably indicative of small fires (Piggott and Powell 1949). At Ballymarlagh, Co. Antrim, burnt deposits were uncovered in the forecourt, the possible remains of a pyre (Davies 1949). And at Pentre Ifan, Pembrokeshire, the remains of fires as well as charcoal were found in the forecourt (Grimes 1948).

Burnt material and burning also occur in other contexts at megaliths. For example, at Audleystown, Co. Down, burnt chips of shale were found in one of the chambers (Collins 1954, 17). At Ballymacaldrack, Co. Antrim, two pots deposited at the site contained charcoal (Collins 1976). There is also evidence for burning happening *in situ* at a number of sites. At Barmore Wood, western Scotland, the floor of the chamber was burnt in patches (Henshall 1972, 322). At Audleystown, Co. Down (Fig. 5.12), chamber three seems to have seen a large fire *in situ*. The pre-cairn timber structure at Ballymacaldrack, Co. Antrim was also burnt down prior to the construction of the megalithic monument (Collins 1976). Other sites have evidence of substantial burning events prior to the construction of the monument: at Ballybriest, Co. Derry, six depressions interpreted as hearths were found along with charcoal, carbonised hazelnuts, lumps of clay and cremated bone (Herity 1987, 126). This has led to suggestions that this site may have been used for funeral activities prior to the monumental phase (Shee Twohig 1990, 24).

Therefore, there is a remarkable amount of evidence for burning and the deposition of burnt material at megaliths. It seems that in some instances burning actually went on within the megalith itself, although this clearly did not happen at all sites. At other sites, burning seems to have occurred in the forecourt, with evidence for small localised fires or hearths. At the vast majority of sites, however, it seems that burnt material was brought in from elsewhere to the megalith (as no burning has been found in or around the monument itself) and deposited in both the chambers and forecourt area. It would be tempting to see the addition of this burnt material into the chambers of megaliths as simply the remains of a funeral pyre. In Ireland in particular many of the human remains seem to have been cremated before being interred in a megalith (see below), and cremation was also clearly present in other areas along the Irish Sea zone. However, this interpretation would be too simplistic. The dark/black soil as well as the charcoal added into chambers frequently does not contain cremated bone, although it does in some cases. While it would be possible to remove cremated bone from the remains of the funeral pyre, it would be an assumption that all burnt material came from cremation pyres. There are many other contexts from which material could have derived, including the deliberate burning of other timber structures. We know, for example, that the vast majority of timber structures (both 'wooden mortuary structures' as well as 'houses') built in the early Neolithic were fired at the end of their lives. It is not inconceivable that the remains of these structures were incorporated in the chambers of megalithic monuments (and see Bradley 2007a). It is also equally worth considering that the burnt material in monuments was a token deposit of other events such as feasts, pottery firings or the results of slash and burn tree clearance. All of these events may have been key to the life history of each megalith and broader notions of 'being Neolithic'. It is worth considering, therefore, that the burnt deposits in chambered tombs may in actual fact relate to other forms of material culture from the Neolithic, and other events in the Neolithic world. In this sense, people were adding fragments of other places, other events, other people, into each monument.

One of the key elements of events that involve fire or the burning of material is that they are visually very spectacular. The firing of a house structure or a wooden monument, for example, would have been a visual spectacle (e.g.

Figure 5.13.
Walton Farm,
western Scotland

Tringham 2005), something not quickly forgotten. The creation of memories at these events may have meant that they endured in the minds of Neolithic people (cf. Barrett 1994; A. Jones 2003). In most discussions, the burial of the remains of the deceased are always given prominence over other forms of material culture, so that pots and flint tools in megaliths are simply considered as grave goods, accompaniments to the main human burials. However, if we consider the possibility that the deposition of pots and flint tools were just as significant, then burnt remains may just as likely refer to key events associated with their creation or transformation, as with the transformation of the human body to cremated remains. We return to the issue of whether these monuments were 'burial places' in more detail below.

Quartz
Another remarkably ubiquitous substance found deposited in chambered tombs is quartz. We have already seen how quartz stones are frequently incorporated into the fabric of the monument. Smaller quantities of quartz are also deposited in the monument itself. Many sites have the deposition of quartz pebbles. For example, 50 quartz pebbles were found at Walton Farm in western Scotland (Fig. 5.13; J. Scott 1969, 206). Split quartz pebbles were also found at Glecknabae, Kilchoan and Nether Largie, all in western Scotland (Henshall 1972). Ty Newydd and Pant y Saer, both on Anglesey had quartz pebbles deposited in the chamber (Phillips 1936; W. Scott 1933), and at Cashtel yn Ard quartz pebbles were scattered at the rear of the chamber (Cummings and Fowler 2004a, 125). And at Goward, Clontygora and Ballintoy in Ireland (Davies and Evans 1933; Mogey 1941), quartz pebbles were also deposited. It is interesting that quartz pebbles have been noted in other

Figure 5.14.
Clontygora Large,
Co. Armagh

contexts in the early Neolithic of the Irish Sea: they were found in quantities at Billown enclosure on the Isle of Man for example (Darvill 1996; 2002).

Quartz is also found in other forms in chambered tombs. Occasionally, worked quartz pieces are found alongside worked flint. At Audleystown, Co. Down, for example, 2 flakes of quartz were found, along with a bigger assemblage of flint (Collins 1954). At Cairnholy I in south-west Scotland, quartz chunks were scattered in front of the revetment (Piggott and Powell 1949). Another intriguing quartz deposit was made at Glenvoidean on Bute: here a triangular lump of quartz was placed in a pot and deposited in the chamber. The excavators suggested that the lump of quartz had been shaped in order to fit into the pot (Marshall and Taylor 1976, 9). In Ireland, quartz crystals were also deposited in at sites. At Clontygora Large, Co. Armagh (Davies and Paterson 1937, 41) a broken crystal of translucent quartz was found in the disturbed contents removed from either the second or third chamber (Fig. 5.14). At Ballyalton, Co. Down, a crystal of smoky quartz, which originated in the Mournes, was found as well as several pieces of vein quartz deposited in little pockets (Evans and Davies 1934, 98). The most interesting example is that from Annaghmare, Co. Armagh. Here a prism of smoky quartz was found in the chamber. This piece of quartz is very distinctive and thought to be too large to have come from the quartz source in the Mournes (Waterman 1965, 35). It is suggested that this piece of quartz may come from outside Ireland.

We have seen then that quartz was deposited in a variety of ways at chambered tombs as well as being incorporated into the fabric of the monuments. It has been suggested elsewhere that quartz may have been a highly potent substance in the Neolithic (Darvill 2002; Fowler and Cummings 2003), which I want to briefly explore in more detail here. Firstly, there seems to be strong connections between quartz and water. Quartz pebbles in particular would have come from the beach or rivers and as we have seen these are frequently deposited at chambered tombs. Elsewhere it has been argued that the builders of the chambered tombs of western Britain were concerned to create places which connected the land and the sea, stones and water, at particular liminal places in the landscape (Fowler and Cummings 2003). Quartz shares a number of properties with water such as its translucence, reflectability and colour. We will see below that other substances from the sea were deposited at some chambered tombs. Another possible connection is between quartz and the human body. Darvill (2002) notes that quartz pebbles resemble skulls when being excavated and the white of quartz could also be analogous to other parts of the body such as bone, fat or even the eyes.

Another suggested significance of quartz is its connection with the moon. Quartz has been found in quantities at later recumbent stone circles, and there seems to be a strong correlation between the location of the recumbent, quartz and the rising of the moon (e.g. Bradley 2004). There is less evidence for alignments on the moon at early Neolithic chambered tombs, however, this does not negate a possible connection between the moon and quartz. The two share many properties, including colour, translucence and in the case of quartz pebbles, shape. The use of quartz takes on an interesting role if we also envisage chambered tombs being used at night. Quartz would reflect and sparkle in moonlight or firelight. As we have seen, there is also substantial evidence for the use of fire at these sites, with many good examples of fires being lit in both the forecourt and chamber areas which also saw the deposition of quartz. It is an easy assumption that these sites were only used in the daytime, but the connections between fire, quartz, death, the moon and the night may be an interesting way of thinking about these sites.

It could also be suggested that quartz may have been considered the physical manifestation of essences or other beings. In a paper about the use of particular stone sources in Australia, Taçon (1991) notes how Aborigines understand the landscape to be the remains of ancestral beings. To make a tool from what is essentially the petrified remains of the ancestors imbues enormous significance to that tool. It is possible that quartz was understood in this way in the Neolithic, with the use of pieces or boulders of quartz at sites analogous to the deposition of ancestral beings at the site. The example from Glenvoidean, Bute, is particularly interesting here. The triangular piece of quartz contained within a pot, deposited in the chamber, could possibly represent the containment or burial of particular spirit or being. We could also consider the quartz crystals found in some of the Irish monuments in a similar way.

Figure 5.15.
Brackley, Kintyre

Exotics

Another intriguing deposit made at the chambered tombs of the Irish Sea region is that of exotic material. We have already seen quartz crystals from the Mournes and further afield deposited in Irish megaliths. Another lithic that moves considerable distances in the Neolithic is Arran pitchstone and it is frequently found in chambered tomb contexts. Perhaps not surprisingly, pitchstone is found in a number of the Arran sites. The chambers at Tormore, Carn Ban and East Bennan all contained pitchstone (Williams Thorpe and Thorpe 1984, 7) and pitchstone was also found outside chambers at Monamore (MacKie 1963), Tormore Farm, Giant's Graves, Dunan Beag and Dunan Mor (Williams Thorpe and Thorpe 1984, 7). Pitchstone is found further afield, at Brackley (Fig. 5.15) and Beacharra, in Kintyre (J. Scott 1954; 1955), Michael's Grave and Glecknabae on Bute and Barmore Wood, Argyll (J. Scott 1973). There is only ever a very small quantity of pitchstone deposited at these sites, apparently a token deposit (and see Wickham-Jones 1986).

Other exotics are recorded at chambered tombs. For example, a fragment of a jadeite axe was found at Cairnholy I (Piggott and Powell 1949) which would have originated in the Alps. Giant's Graves on Arran contained six axes, four from Cumbria and one from northern Ireland (Group IX: J. Scott 1969, 218). A number of large flint tools have been found in the chambered tombs on Arran, and many of these are made from Antrim flint: plano-convex knives have been found at Sliddery Water, Torlin, Tormore and Giant's Graves (Saville 1999). One deposit found at many of the court cairns throughout north-east Ireland is flint from Antrim. This may not seem remarkable, since the main outcropping source of flint in northern Ireland was in Antrim (see chapter 3).

However, virtually all sites also contain flint tools made from beach pebbles, showing that a local source of flint was available. It would seem, then, that imported flint was deliberately deposited.

There is also much discussion in the older literature that pottery may well have moved around the Irish Sea. For example, the pottery from Cairnholy I, Dumfries and Galloway and Monamore, Arran were compared to Irish Lyles Hill ware (J. Scott 1969, 220). Similarly, a number of assemblages from Irish court cairns have been compared to Beacharra ware. It is now difficult to assess these claims: we have already noted in chapter 3 that a number of pottery styles, especially the early Neolithic pottery styles found either side of the Irish Sea share a number of similarities. What is clearly needed is a full assessment of the origins of the clay used to make pottery either side of the Irish Sea, a project sadly beyond the scope of this study. A reassessment of lithics may also illuminate further examples of material moving across the Irish Sea (a project in Kintyre has been initiated with this research question in mind: see, for example, Cummings and Robinson 2006).

We have some examples, therefore, and hints of further cases, of exotic material being deposited at chambered tombs. It seems to have been appropriate to deposit non-local material, but only ever in small token quantities. Some of this material seems to have come from the across the waterways of the Irish Sea (in the case of Antrim flint and Arran pitchstone) while other examples come from further away still. This material may have been highly desirable as exotic substances connected with distance places and people, however, it would be too simplistic to see this material purely as grave goods for the deceased. I will argue in chapter 8 that this material was intrinsically linked to broader connections and notions of identity across the Irish Sea.

Marine deposits

A few sites have famously produced the remains of marine resources, especially shells. The deposition of marine shells was not considered remarkable prior to the advent of stable isotope evidence, but we now know that people do not seem to have been eating marine resources in the Neolithic, with some of these results coming from human bone from the Irish Sea chambered tombs (e.g. Schulting and Richards 2002b). There are actually only a few examples of marine resources from chambered tombs: 5000 shells were found at Crarae (J. Scott 1960, 7). Here, a pit at the southern end of the forecourt contained 2500 marine shells, mostly of pullet carpet. In the second chamber compartment a few shells were found along with the main deposit of charcoal, pottery, flint and bone. In the third compartment, more shells were found with the main deposit, and underneath the floor level was a further deposit of 2500 shells, mainly of periwinkle (J. Scott 1960, 25). Another possible Clyde cairn was located close to Crarae at Fairy Knowe, built into a shell midden (J. Scott 1960). At Torlin on Arran, marine shells were reportedly found in the chamber, and at both Lligwy and Pant y Saer on Anglesey, shells were recovered from the chambers (Baynes 1909; W. Scott 1933). There are also some examples from Ireland: at Clontygora Large, Co Armagh, (Davies and Paterson 1937) a few fragments of marine shells were found, and at Ballinran, Co. Down, a nest of winkleshells were found in a stone socket, although there is the possibility that these are post-Neolithic. The strongest connection between marine resources and chambered tombs, however, comes from the site of Glecknabae on Bute. Here the chambered tomb was actually built over an earlier shell midden (Henshall 1972, 412).

These deposits could be interpreted as a continuity of hunting and gathering practices in the Neolithic, as well as a continuity of place in the case of Glecknabae and possibly Crarae. Furthermore, these deposits could strengthen connections between monuments and the sea, already suggested for the deposition of quartz at these sites. The next chapter also outlines how these monuments are positioned in relation to water. However, these deposits could also be considered as tokens of the sea, something that was clearly important to people in the Neolithic. This reference to the sea may relate to origins of the Neolithic (see Cummings and Whittle 2004, chapter 7), to connections across the Irish Sea (see later chapters this volume) or even the rejection of the sea as a resource. It has been suggested that the sea might increasingly be connected with the dead in the Neolithic (Fowler and Cummings 2003; Thomas 2003), one of the reasons people no longer relied heavily on marine resources and relevant for our discussion here, why bits of the sea might end up in a megalithic context.

The deposition of human remains

Human remains are one of the commonest finds at chambered tombs in the Irish Sea zone. In fact it is considered unusual if no human bone is recovered during an excavation and when this occurs acidic soils are often blamed for the absence. Both cremations and inhumations are found in the chambered tombs of the Irish Sea zone. In Ireland, cremated human bone is more common than inhumations, although both do occur at some sites (Herity 1987, 111). In the rest of the Irish Sea zone inhumations seem to be deposited more frequently than cremations, although both are present. Because of the problems of estimating the number of individuals represented by cremation deposits (e.g. Mays 1998, chapter 11) it is difficult to estimate the minimum number of individuals deposited. Only a few scraps of bone could actually be the remains of several individuals: this draws on the idea that only 'tokens' of other events/objects were deposited at these sites which we have seen again and again in relation to other forms of material culture.

The number of individuals deposited at chambered tombs varies enormously. In some cases large numbers of individuals have been found. At Pant y Saer on Anglesey a total of 54 people were found (W. Scott 1933). In Ireland, at Audleystown, Co. Down, the excavator claimed there were the remains of at least 34 people (Collins 1954). And on the Isle of Arran, Clachaig produced the remains of 14 individuals (Henshall 1972, 392). At the other end of the scale, sites have frequently been excavated and produced only small scraps of human bone, probably representing only one or two people (see Cummings and Whittle 2004; Herity 1987; Henshall 1972). Although acidic soils or later disturbance are cited as reasons why some sites have produced no human bone, we must also consider the possibility that some sites were not built to be used in this way (Leivers 1999). It is entirely possible that human remains were considered objects, sometimes appropriate to be deposited at these sites as was flint, pot and other objects. It may be the case that people in the Neolithic had a very different idea of how to treat and dispose of the dead than we do. Firstly, there is plenty of evidence from Neolithic Europe that parts of bodies, particularly bits of bones, were artefacts in their own right (see Fowler 2004, chapter 5). Although found less frequently in British contexts, human bone seems to have been curated and carried about by the living (Bradley 1998a). This suggests that parts of people may have become artefacts in their own right, with bone being another material through which meaning could be assigned. It is interesting that at some sites there is evidence for the careful ordering and placing of human bone. At Audleystown, Co. Down, for example, ten small long bones and ribs were laid out in parallel rows on a flat stone slab in chamber one (Collins 1954, 17).

Secondly, there is an overall absence of burials throughout the Neolithic period. Although some people clearly do end up being interred in chambered tombs, the small quantities of bone do not represent the entire population. We must therefore imagine that people disposed of the dead in other ways than 'formal' burial in a monument. There are hints that excarnation was an important rite in the Neolithic, with bits of bodies frequently turning up at sites such as causewayed enclosures (Oswald *et al.* 2001, 126–7). There are suggestions that human remains were also deposited in rivers, with a number of examples particularly of skulls from the Thames and Trent perhaps indicative a broader tradition (Pearce *et al.* 1997). There is a strong possibility that bodies were deposited on beaches or in the sea, perhaps indicating why people were increasingly reluctant to eat marine resources in the Neolithic (Fowler and Cummings 2003). It may not, therefore, have always been considered appropriate to bury people in a monumental setting, with the vast majority of people deposited in 'natural' locations. And as already mentioned, even when the remains of the dead were deposited in monumental places such as chambered tombs, it was not necessarily the case that people in the Neolithic understood these remains as either named or unnamed 'ancestors' (cf. Whitley 2002). Therefore, the presence of human remains in chambered tombs does not mean that these places should simply be understood as burial monuments.

Deposition of material culture

Pottery

Another common find in the megaliths of the Irish Sea is pottery. Pottery has not been found at all sites that have been excavated, but is present at a large number of sites, in the chambers, in the forecourts and also associated with pre-cairn activity. It is also worth noting that considerable quantities of later Neolithic and Bronze Age pottery have been found at sites, evidence for the later re-use of these sites (see below). A number of sites have produced early Neolithic bowl pottery, in particular developed bowls (see chapter 3). These occur both whole (for example in Beacharra in Kintyre and Carreg Samson in Pembrokeshire) and in fragments. The issue of fragmentation is interesting at chambered tombs, as it seems to have been appropriate to deposit both whole and fragmentary (token) deposits at sites, and some sites contain both. For example, at Glenvoidean, Bute, both whole and partial pots were uncovered, and some of the whole pots seem to have been smashed before deposition (Henshall 1972, 408). At other sites, only fragmentary pottery was deposited, for example at Audleystown, Co. Down, the remains of at least 16 pots were deposited in the chambers. Here some fragments were substantial while others were much smaller and more fragmentary (Collins 1954). This has interesting parallels with fragmentation of material and deposition in the late Mesolithic (see chapter 2).

The presence of pottery at chambered tombs has been interpreted in a number of ways. In the earlier literature pottery was thought to be indicative of the presence of different cultures of people, who were responsible for the spread of the Neolithic way of life throughout Britain. Pottery at chambered tombs then, was understood very much in this light and was seen to demonstrate broader cultural affinities and groupings in Britain. In a culture-historical paradigm pots were primarily grave goods, placed at sites to accompany the deceased (e.g.

Powell *et al.* 1969). More recently, pottery has been interpreted much more in terms of understandings of sociality and materiality. In early post-processual literature, with the emphasis on megaliths as places for the living to negotiate their place in the world (e.g. Shanks and Tilley 1982) pots were interpreted as the remains of feasting or other social events. Pottery, then, became increasingly associated with the living and not the dead.

More recently still, pottery at megaliths has been considered in a number of ways. Firstly, while whole pots do occur at these sites, it is much more common for pieces of pot to be found. These may well be token deposits from other events, possibly from other places, such as middens (J. G. Evans *et al.* 1999) or signifying other rituals. This could tie into ideas of material composition and the bringing together of different components of the material world at one specific locale. Pots may well have represented other places, as much as they represented other events or other people (cf. Fowler 2004), and the interweaving of pottery, with its own specific biography, and place, associations may have been part of the process of bringing things together at these site. An attempt to manipulate the material world was clearly deemed either necessary or desirable by the people involved. Pottery, like other substances deposited at these megaliths, was also transformative, potentially one of the key metaphors being drawn on at these sites.

Pottery continued to be an appropriate substance to deposit at chambered tombs in the late Neolithic and early Bronze Age. There is considerable evidence for the reuse of these, and other, chambered tombs in these periods (see Cummings and Fowler 2007). A number of sites have produced evidence for both Grooved Ware and Beaker, suggesting late Neolithic/early Bronze Age depositional activity. Food vessels and collared urns have also been found illustrating that deposition continued well into the early Bronze Age. Frustratingly from our point of view, people often cleared out earlier deposits in order to make way for these later ones.

Axes
Although a common find from the Neolithic period as a whole (see chapter 3), axes are only occasionally found in megaliths. This may be in part because axe production intensified after the main phase of deposition at these sites (after about 3600 BC). It may equally be the case that they were not considered appropriate deposits at many sites. Some axes have been recovered, however, for example from Giant's Graves, Arran, Bryn yr Hen Bobl, Anglesey and Ballymacaldrack, Co. Antrim. In Ireland, it has been noted that axes are primarily found in relation to entrances and chamber-sealing events (Sheridan *et al.* 1992, 394) and this seems to be consistent at other sites in the Irish Sea area. This may mean that axes were deposited later on in the early Neolithic. However, at

Ballyalton, Co. Down, two axes along with other flints were found at the base of a socket for a forecourt orthostat (Sheridan 1992, 394), suggesting in some instances axes were part of primary depositional activity. There is also variation in the types of axes deposited: at some sites, whole axes have been found, which often do not seem to have been used. However, a number of sites have produced fragments of axes, including Pant y Saer, Anglesey (W. Scott 1933), Cairnholy I (Piggott and Powell 1949) and Ballymacaldrack, Co. Antrim (Collins 1976, 5). Again, the idea of token deposits could be suggested, with it being appropriate to leave just a fragment of the object at the site. This is particularly resonant if we consider the idea that axes had their own biographies (see chapter 3) and that the sealing of the monument was analogous to the end of its life.

Stone tools
Stone objects are found fairly ubiquitously at the chambered tombs of the Irish Sea zone. For the most part, these consist of the occasional flint flake or chip, although flakes of quartz, pitchstone and other stones are also sometimes found (see above). Occasionally, larger assemblages of debitage have been found, such as the 90 flint flakes from Ballymarlagh, Co. Antrim, which were found in a depression in the court (Herity 1987, 129). Similarly, the large number of flints found at Ballintoy, Co. Antrim, were either from a pre-cairn phase or were associated with later blocking of the chamber (Mogey 1941, 53). However, for the most part, these larger assemblages tend not to associated with the primary use of the chambers.

These flakes and chips have not warranted the detailed discussion that other objects receive (see, for example, Herity 1987). However, it is interesting that flakes are found so frequently at chambered tombs as it seems unlikely that these were simply casual 'waste', inadvertently deposited at sites by a careless flint knapper. Instead it seems that waste material was deliberately being deposited. Perhaps these were tokens or fragments again, this time of knapping events, or events associated with the production of stone tools.

Another possibility is that these stone fragments are representative of other places. At Ballymacdermot, Co. Armagh, the 21 flints recovered from the site were identified as having a variety of origins (Collins and Wilson 1964, 17). Some flint was from Antrim, the largest source of flint in northern Ireland (see chapter 3), however, some was derived from beach sources. This is repeated at other Irish sites: at Audleystown, Co. Down, most of the flint originated from the Antrim sources, but again one piece was beach flint (Collins 1954, 28). Unfortunately we have a poor understanding of the sources of the flints found in the western Scottish and Welsh megaliths, but the presence of pitchstone and other exotics at these sites suggests that we are seeing a similar pattern there too. These flints from different places, then, may be representative of those locales, symbols or 'bits' of other places. Equally, they may refer to other people or other events. It is also interesting that at the Irish examples above people seem to have deliberately incorporated worked beach flint into megalithic architecture. There was no shortage of high quality Antrim flint in Ireland, suggesting the possibility that the source was either controlled or that beach flint was still considered a valuable resource despite its poorer quality.

A quantity of arrowheads have also been found in some of the megaliths of the Irish Sea zone. These are more common than axes but still a fairly rare find overall. The largest number of arrowheads comes from the court cairns of north-east Ireland, where a number of sites have produced arrowheads, in particular lozenge-shaped arrowheads (see Herity 1987): the double chambered site of Audleystown, Co. Down producing a total of 12. On the other side of the Irish Sea, arrowheads are rarer finds: only a few are known from the Welsh sites, and some of these (for example those at Ty Newydd and Bryn yr Hen Bobl on Anglesey) are almost certainly later additions. Arrowheads have been found in some of the western Scottish sites, including lozenge-shaped forms, with the most coming from sites on Arran.

While arrowheads are commonly considered a typical part of a Neolithic flint assemblage, they do not always turn up in large numbers on occupation sites, found instead as isolated finds, presumed to be lost on hunting trips. However, the role of hunting is still contested in relation to the Neolithic. How should we then understand their occasional deposition in the Irish Sea megaliths? While they may have belonged to individuals interred in the monuments, or representative of hunting events or the killing of domesticates for a feast, we must also consider possibility that they were embedded in people deposited, or at least representative of violent events. Recent work on human remains from other chambered tombs in Britain has illustrated the high incidence of interpersonal violence in Neolithic society (Schulting and Wysocki 2005). I have repeatedly drawn on the idea of megaliths as places where other events were cited and recomposed: it seems plausible that these places, then, may have been about coming to terms with violence within society, surely one of the most powerful and transformative mechanisms of social change.

Later deposits
A few sites have also produced some rather spectacular finds which are later Neolithic or early Bronze Age in date. For example, Tormore I on Arran produced

a gabbroic macehead, and this was almost certainly deposited at the same time as the Grooved Ware or Cinerary Urn found at the site (Henshall 1972, 372). Jet has also been found on some sites: at Beacharra, Kintyre, a jet slider was found (J. Scott 1954) and at Brackley, also in Kintyre, 39 jet beads, an end plate and four spacer plates were found (J. Scott 1955, 28). Secondary deposits of flint knives have been found at a number of sites, including Ballymarlagh, Co. Antrim (Herity 1987, 125), Sliddery Water, Arran, (Henshall 1972, 393) and Port Charlotte, Islay, (Harrington and Pierpoint 1980). These are the most spectacular finds from what was a quite widespread practice throughout the Irish Sea zone: the reuse of chambered tombs in later periods (see chapter 4). It demonstrates their ongoing significance into later periods (and see Cummings and Fowler 2007).

Conclusion

In this chapter we have considered the substances used by people to build the megaliths of the Irish Sea zone. I have argued that the construction process drew upon a whole series of meaningful materials, people, communities, places and events, and that each megalith was carefully composed from different essences of these things. The construction of a monument was an inherently material exercise: it involved ordering and composing substances. I have argued here that the substances chosen to be transformed into a megalithic structure were those already significant to people: outcrops already named and visited places, stones already redolent with meaning, locales already associated with activity and occupation. Materials were carefully chosen to be incorporated into a megalith: particular textures, colours, shapes and sizes of stone were picked. Working or shaping a stone was not an option: unworked stones only seem to have been acceptable. In a similar way, subsequent depositions were also fragments of other events, people and places, as well as being symbolic substances in their own right. It seems to have been key to emphasise transformation, not just of bodies but of other substances too, and experience, making the construction and use of these places highly emotive and memorable for people. Although many substances were drawn upon again and again at megaliths throughout the Irish Sea, people were not following a set pattern of composition and deposition at all sites. Although there were common themes, people were almost certainly drawing on local meanings and symbolism in the construction and use of sites. These issues will be further explored in the final chapter where I will consider the Irish Sea zone as a whole, and within a broader British and European context.

6

Megaliths and landscape: the setting of the chambered tombs of the Irish Sea zone

Introduction

In this chapter, our attention turns to the landscape. Chapters two, three and four painted a general picture of life in the Irish Sea zone, and set the scene for a more detailed discussion of the early Neolithic chambered tombs. In chapter five, we considered the materials used to construct these sites, as well as the depositions made at the monuments. This chapter focuses on a different aspect of the chambered tombs: their landscape setting. In a way, this draws on earlier work: Cummings and Whittle (2004) considered the landscape settings of all of the chambered tombs in Wales. This chapter is a consideration of the landscape settings of all of the chambered tombs in the whole of the Irish Sea zone, including west Wales, discussed in that earlier volume (Cummings and Whittle 2004) but also referred to again here. This chapter then is a broad overview of the landscape settings of the chambered tombs of the Irish Sea zone, discussing similarities and themes amongst this group. The next chapter will go on to discuss the details, with a series of regional case studies.

The significance of landscape

I think it is fair to say that landscape archaeology really began life in the 1990s. This is not to say that authors had not considered the landscape prior to this, but the focus of interest had been rather different. Scholars had been interested in the landscape as environment in particular (e.g. Clarke 1952; J. G. Evans *et al.* 1975; Hawkes 1946) and there was also an interest in landscape distributions of sites since the turn of the century (see, for example, Crawford and Keiller 1928; Fox 1932). A few groundbreaking studies came before their time, of particular note here is Frances Lynch's paper 'The impact of the landscape on prehistoric man' (Lynch 1975), but otherwise it is the publication of two key texts, *Landscape: politics and perspectives* (Bender 1993) and *A phenomenology of landscape* (Tilley 1994), which really mark the birth of landscape archaeology as we know it today.

In these two texts, and in many others since, the concept of landscape has been thoroughly discussed and debated. I myself published a summary of the discussions on landscape in 2004 (see Cummings and Whittle 2004, chapter two) and I have no wish here to reiterate these theoretical arguments. I do want to make one point however: there is a unanimous agreement that landscape is significant to modern populations and it would also have been significant to people in the past.

The sheer quantity of literature written about the significance of landscape has not stopped criticisms of a landscape approach. Jo Brück (1998) wrote an important critique of some of the theoretical points in Tilley's *A phenomenology of landscape* and Tilley's original case studies in were also questioned in a paper by Fleming ((1999), and see a subsequent critique by Fleming in 2005). Putting aside the debate on phenomenology (see below), one of the key problems of a landscape approach seems to be how you can *prove* the significance of setting. The argument seems to revolve around the idea that just because a landscape feature is visible from a particular site does not mean that that landscape feature was important or meaningful to people in the past (see Fleming 2005 in particular on this). In the same way that we cannot 'prove' many things when discussing the past, nevertheless the evidence for landscape features being meaningful and significant is overwhelming. Time and again, ethnographies reveal that landscape features (mountains, rivers, trees, outcrops and so on) are imbued with significance, tied to myths, legends, personal and group identity and worldviews (e.g. Ashmore and Knapp 1999, 14–16; Basso 1984; papers in Bender and Winer 2001; Ingold 1996; 2000; Morphy 1995; Tilley 1994, chapter two). I take this as my starting point: the landscape meant something to people in the past. I have argued elsewhere (e.g. Cummings and Whittle 2004, 15), that at monuments (places with a particular emphasis on ritualised behaviour and tied to dominant ideologies and worldviews), the surrounding landscape was of particular significance. It was at these places that the significances tied to particular features such as mountains was brought into sharp contrast. Fleming (2005) in particular seems unable to grasp this particular idea, even when the evidence for this kind of relationship with the landscape in ethnographic examples is overwhelming, and when scholars have consistently and repeatedly demonstrated a relationship between the location of sites and the visibility of features in the surrounding landscape. Fleming's (2005) arguments against landscape features being significant are, at best, based on his functional interpretations of the past (people built chambered tombs where the raw materials were), and at worst, based on incorrect field observations or a plain unwillingness to see relationships when they are crystal clear. I do not wish to go over the evidence that landscape features were demonstrably visible in the landscape *again*, since it is well-rehearsed and Fleming's (2005) paper does nothing to undermine it. I will say that, theoretically, there is unequivocal ethnographic support for the idea of landscape as meaningful and that as you will see below, this is further supported by the archaeological evidence. As far as I am concerned, there is no further debate to be had here.

A second critique of a landscape approach concerns the presence of vegetation surrounding a site, and how this may affect visibility. Seen as particularly relevant to the Neolithic, where much of the landscape would have been forested (Pollard 2000b; Tilley 2007), the actual visibility of the landscape has been questioned. This has come to be known as the 'tree problem'. Myself and Alasdair Whittle (2004, 69–72) have considered this issue elsewhere, and argue that in many cases (using the environmental evidence from Wales as a case study), vegetation and trees would have been cleared around a monument meaning the landscape *was* visible. In cases where monuments would have been in forested environments, we also demonstrated that the presence of woodland did not restrict visibility in winter, when the landscape is clearly visible even through woodland. Of course, people also had the option of clearing woodland to create visual corridors through the trees, something we have argued elsewhere may in fact have been precursors to avenues on later Neolithic sites (Cummings and Whittle 2004, chapter 7). Thus, I do not consider the 'tree problem' to be an issue when considering landscape setting.

A note on phenomenology

One of the original and most influential studies of landscape was *A phenomenology of landscape* (Tilley 1994) and this book has received an enormous amount of criticism over the years, quite clearly reflecting its importance within archaeological discourse (see above). Regardless of these criticisms, studies of landscape have become virtually synonymous with the word phenomenology. For those of you who have (either miraculously or deliberately) managed to miss the entire phenomenology debate, as a philosophy it has quite clearly inspired Tilley and others in their considerations of landscape. Phenomenology, quite simply, is the study of phenomena (Karlsson 1997; Thomas 1996). Phenomenology does not care whether things are real or not, only how people *experience* things. So we might see things that do not exist, such as hallucinations, but we still experience them. Phenomenology, then, involves describing things rather than explaining them. It gets beyond the problem of realism (whether or not there is an external reality, a world that exists out there, whether or not we can see it or not) as phenomenologists argue that the world is not objective, but subjective. That all sounds rather handy for archaeologists, in particular post-processual archaeologists, who are obviously interested in how people experienced the world in the past. It also embraces one of the key tenants of a post-processual approach: that the archaeologies we write are subjective (see, for example, Hodder 1986, chapter 7).

One of key proponents of phenomenology was Merleau-Ponty, and he has inspired modern archaeologists, in particular his interest in phenomenology and perception. Merleau-Ponty (1962) describes perception as being the faculty of perceiving; the faculty, or peculiar part, of mankind's constitution by which he or she has knowledge through the medium or instrumentality of the bodily organs; the act of apprehending material objects or qualities through the senses. Critically then, phenomenology enables you to take into account subjective and non-measurable entities such as colour, taste and smell, all extremely important elements of how we encounter the world. So Merleau-Ponty argues that it is through the *perception of the body* that we engage with the world. In relation to objects he claims an object has no real shape or size, it is all down to how we perceive it. This has been illustrated in recent years by some excellent ethnographic examples. The Umeda of Papua New Guinea are a good example of how things are perceived subjectively (Gell 1995). The Umeda live in a forested environment and as such, struggle to perceive long distance views. Their eyes are, of course, identical to ours, but they struggle to perceive depth of field. Another good example regarding perception involves how we perceive colour, gloss, brightness and size. These are critical when we engage with them but cannot be described scientifically. So *perception* is entirely *subjective*. This is a key component of phenomenology: how people perceive phenomena, and it relates not just to objects, but also to the landscape.

And this is where the problem with phenomenology lies. How can we know how people in the past perceived things? We may have some idea what they were looking at, but how they perceived those things is clearly a much more difficult task. We may be able to come up with some good ideas however. Recent work on personhood, inspired by anthropological studies, has suggested that people in the past may not have conceived of themselves as individual beings (Brück 2004; Fowler 2004). Instead, they may have understood themselves as being more integrated with the material world. One suggestion has been that people may have thought of themselves as 'dividual' and that their belongings were as much a part of themselves as their body. These are exciting and interesting propositions which may make us think differently about the archaeological record. We can also make strong claims for what particular landscape features might have meant to people in the past (i.e. that they were connected to belief systems). However, what people *perceived* when they looked at the landscape is clearly a complex and culturally specific issue. Whether or not Tilley achieved a phenomenological approach has been much debated. He does not really talk about perception in his case studies (Tilley 1994, chapters 3–5), only what *he* can see from various monuments. It is interesting to try and consider how people may have understood the landscape forms visible from the chambered tombs of the Irish Sea zone, and I shall try and do this in the final chapter. I am constrained by the same limitations as Tilley in his original case studies though. All I can relate is what I myself have seen from the various chambered tombs of the Irish Sea zone. I have no way of knowing how people in the Neolithic may have perceived these landscape features, although I will make some suggestions of what they might have meant to people. I am assuming that people in the Neolithic had a grasp of depth of field, and that they were able to therefore perceive distant mountains and watercourses. However, unlike Tilley I shy away from using the phrase phenomenology, and prefer to use the term 'landscape archaeology'. This is simply a preference. In both cases, the interest lies in what particular landscapes may have meant to people in prehistory.

Methodology

There has been surprisingly little discussion about the methodologies employed by landscape archaeologists, apart from within GIS studies (e.g. Wheatley and Gillings 2002). I developed and discussed in a previous work a landscape methodology for visiting chambered tombs and assessing and recording their landscape setting (see Cummings and Whittle 2004, chapter 3). I do not, therefore, wish to go into as much detail again here, suffice to say that the basic methodology outlined there was employed at all of the chambered tombs in the Irish Sea zone. On visiting a chambered tomb, I recorded the view from each site in a number of ways:

- A 360° photographic panorama, which could later be stitched together to form a continuous landscape image.
- A 360° representational sketch of the landscape setting (Fig. 6.1).
- A written description highlighting any seemingly important relationships.

Obviously, OS maps are also extremely important in this process, and I used 1:25,000, 1:50,000 and sometimes 1: 250,000 to locate sites and work out their broader setting.

Figure 6.1. Representation of the landscape
from Dyffryn Ardudwy

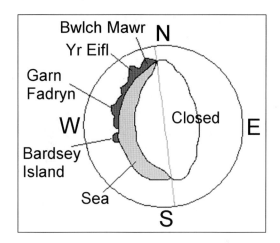

The key exception between the methodology employed here and the one from the previous 2004 study was that I did not create a GIS viewshed for each site. This was deliberate: I felt that the GIS viewshed did not demonstrate anything that could not be observed at ground level (except in the cases where sites were surrounded by dense modern forestry, or were inaccessible). Moreover, while GIS viewshed analysis is useful at one level for demonstrating which landscape features are visible or not, they do not give any sense of what those landscape features may have looked like from each site: a landscape feature may technically be visible, but if it is virtually indistinguishable on the ground, it begs the question of whether people would have assigned significance to it. Furthermore, many potentially significant landscape features (especially rocky outcrops) do not show up on GIS viewshed analysis using 1:50,000 maps. To calculate the viewshed from every chambered tomb in the study on 1:25,000 or 1:10,000 maps would be a massive and time-consuming undertaking, one that I felt would not enhance the study significantly for the amount of time it would take. Quite simply, GIS cannot replicate the experience of being in the landscape, so was not used here (see Cummings and Whittle 2004, 21–22 for a fuller discussion on GIS).

Similarly, I did not use control points to demonstrate how carefully sites had been positioned in the landscape. Again, this method was employed with some of the Welsh examples (Cummings and Whittle 2004, chapter 3), and I felt that those case studies were sufficient to prove the point: monuments were carefully positioned so that specific landscape features were visible. As I have said above, I take it as given at this stage that monuments were meaningfully located in the landscape, and it was not part of this study to reiterate this point again.

The focus within this study, then, is where sites are positioned in the landscape and what is visible from each chambered tomb (i.e. what parts of the surrounding landscape are visible from each chambered tomb). In an ideal world, it would have been fruitful to consider a whole of range of different landscape views: what was visible on the approach to the site (see Cummings 2007b on journeying to chambered tombs), and how each monument looked from the surrounding landscape. In particular it would be interesting to see what each chambered tomb looked like in the landscape from the areas used for settlement. However, this was not possible for several reasons. Firstly, we simply do not have this level of information for most parts of the Irish Sea zone, and secondly, where there are known lithic scatters which are potentially contemporary with the monuments or rarer still, known houses in the vicinity, this approach would have been massively time-consuming. This is clearly something to aim for in the longer term, but was beyond the scope of this particular study.

Introducing the landscapes of the Irish Sea zone

Before we move on to consider the setting of the chambered tombs, I want to very briefly introduce the study area in sections: west Wales, north-west England, western Scotland, north-east Ireland and south-east Ireland. I wish to discuss each of these areas in turn, to give a sense of the landscape overall as well as the landscapes in which the chambered tombs are located. This is quite difficult in this format, as here we are obviously restricted to the printed page: visiting these areas gives the best sense of what they are like. In an ideal world, this account would be accompanied by video footage, to show the different areas, and perhaps this is an area landscape research can develop and incorporate in future years as the technology becomes easier to acquire and quicker to download on the internet (and see Cummings 2008).

West Wales incorporates a considerable amount of the Welsh coastal zone, with the wide stretch of Cardigan Bay of particular note (Figs 6.2 and 6.3). West Wales is hilly and for the most part, not densely populated. A few sizeable towns (e.g. Aberystwyth, Pembroke Dock, Haverfordwest and Milford Haven) are found in this area, but no large towns are found in the areas with chambered tomb distributions. There is a general distinction between the north and south: the north is mountainous, while the south-west is more gently hilly. The exception to this is Anglesey: this island is low-lying and for the most part flat, a rich agricultural area in the otherwise mountainous north-west. The chambered tomb distribution focuses on two key areas: in the north, on Anglesey, the Lleyn peninsula and between Porthmadog and Barmouth, with a few outliers

Figure 6.2. South-west Wales

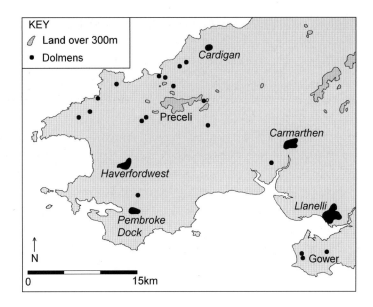

Figure 6.3. North-west Wales

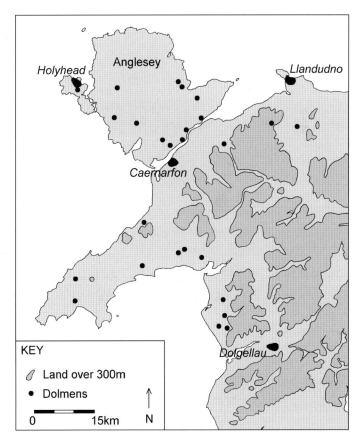

Figure 6.4. The landscapes of north-west Wales

Figure 6.5. The landscapes of south-west Wales

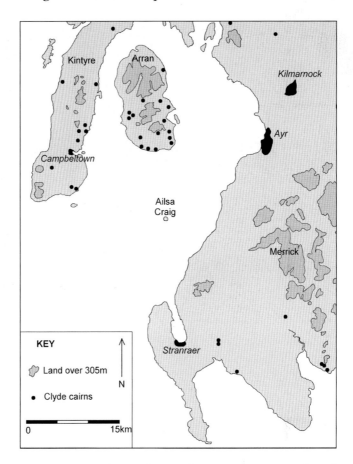

Figure 6.6. South-west Scotland

along the rivers Conwy and Dee (Fig. 6.4). In the south, monuments are found around the Preseli mountains and out towards Strumble and St David's Head (Fig. 6.5). This leaves considerable 'blank' areas in terms of the distribution of chambered tombs: none are found between Cardigan to the south and Barmouth to the north, a considerable swathe of this area. Much of this landscape would have been rich for fishing, hunting and keeping/growing domesticates in the Neolithic, so the lack of monumental architecture seems to be a deliberate one (see below for reasons why this and other blank areas did not see monument construction).

Next we move to north-west England, incorporating the western parts of Merseyside, Lancashire and Cumbria. This area contrasts with the rest of the study area in many ways. Firstly, there are no definite chambered tombs in this area (one, the Calderstones, is probably the remains of a later passage grave, another at Great Urswick in Cumbria is only a possible). One could argue that the mass of modern settlement in the southern area here (from Liverpool up to Preston)

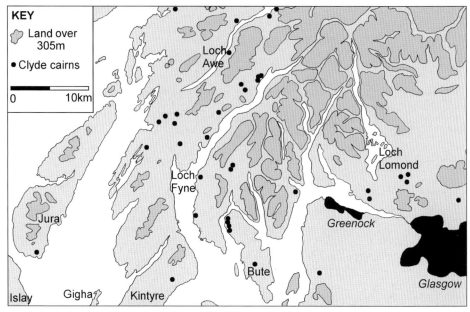

Figure 6.7. Western Scotland

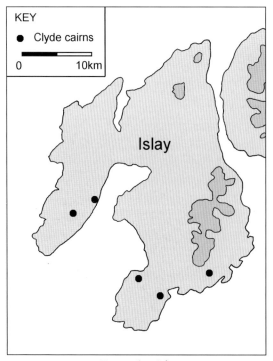

Figure 6.8. Islay

has obliterated any remains, but much of Lancashire and Cumbria is rural, and one would expect the survival of a few sites had they ever existed. Indeed, later Neolithic sites are found in both these areas. We seem, therefore, to be looking at a genuine gap in the distribution. Much of this area is low-lying and pretty flat, although Cumbria of course has central mountains with flatter areas on the coasts. Again, below I discuss why this area did not see chambered tomb construction in the Neolithic.

We move further north again into south-west Scotland,

Figure 6.9. The landscapes of western Scotland

which did see chambered tomb construction in the early Neolithic. While this part of the Irish Sea zone incorporates a considerable landmass, there is a great deal of similarity here. The chambered tombs have a notable coastal distribution in this area (Fig. 6.6), with a cluster in south-west Dumfries and Galloway, a blank area from Stranraer to Ardrossan, then a scatter of sites along the Clyde estuaries and lochs (Fig. 6.7), on Bute, Arran, Kintyre, Islay (Fig. 6.8) and Jura. This part of the Irish Sea has a real maritime focus, with waterways, islands and mountains being the key features (Fig. 6.9). Apart from Glasgow

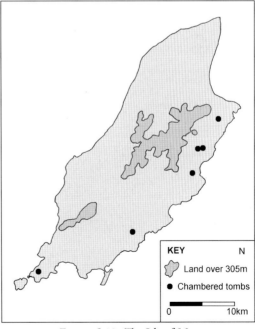

KEY   N

Land over 305m

● Chambered tombs

0   10km

Figure 6.10. The Isle of Man

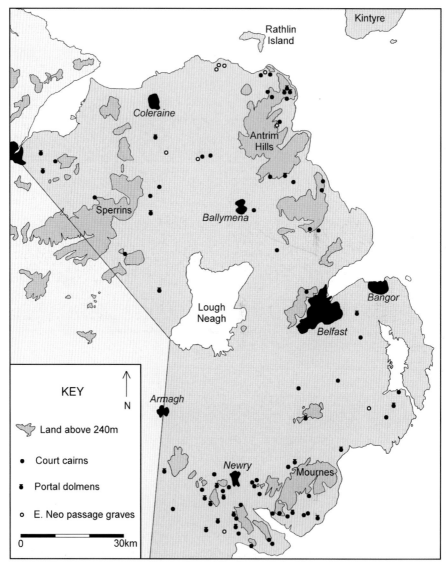

Figure 6.11. North-east Ireland

itself, it is sparsely populated in modern times and many of these areas are fairly inaccessible by car.

The Isle of Man sits at the very heart of the Irish Sea zone. Roughly 65km long and 15km wide, it comprises high mountains, the tallest of which is Snaefell (621m). There are also lower-lying areas, particularly to the north of the island. Modern populations are concentrated along the eastern shores, as are the chambered tombs (Fig. 6.10).

Figure 6.12. The landscapes of north-east Ireland

Moving over now to the western part of the Irish Sea zone, the Irish part of the Irish Sea zone divides neatly into north-eastern Ireland and south-eastern Ireland. In this study, the north-east section incorporates County Derry (from Londonderry to Lough Neagh), Counties Antrim, Down and most of Armagh, and all of county Louth (Fig. 6.11). There are plenty of low-lying agricultural zones in north-eastern Ireland, particularly around Lough Neagh and either side of the River Bann. There are also plenty of hilly and mountainous zones, of particular note the Antrim hills, the Mourne Mountains and the Sperrins (Fig. 6.12). These are also the areas with the concentrations of chambered tombs. Apart from Belfast itself, north-east Ireland has a fairly low density of population, and much of the area is agricultural land, suggesting the distribution of monuments is representative of the original quantity and location of sites.

Finally, south-eastern Ireland is the final portion of the Irish Sea zone. There is a notable blank in the distribution of chambered tombs between Dundalk in county Louth and Dublin: the southern part of county Louth, county Meath and most of county Dublin do not have early Neolithic chambered tombs. This is particularly interesting given that in the middle Neolithic there was an explosion of monumental construction in county Meath at the Bru na Boinne complex (and discussed below in more detail). Instead, there is a spread of chambered

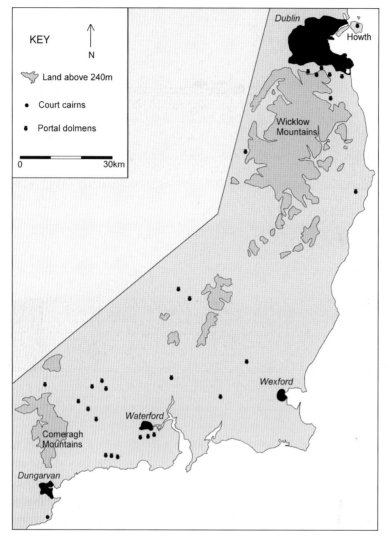

Figure 6.13. South-east Ireland

KEY

Land above 240m

• Court cairns

▪ Portal dolmens

0   30km

Dublin

Howth

Wicklow
Mountains

Wexford

Waterford

Comeragh
Mountains

Dungarvan

tombs starting south of Dublin itself, down into counties Carlow, Wexford, Waterford and Kilkenny (Fig. 6.13). Much of this landscape is low-lying rich agricultural land, again with a limited and dispersed population. Two mountain ranges are notable in this area: the Comeragh mountains in county Waterford and the Wicklow Mountains south of Dublin (Fig. 6.14).

General setting of the Irish Sea megaliths

There is surprising uniformity in the location of the chambered tombs of the Irish Sea zone. As I was visiting all of the sites in the study area, I was quite

Figure 6.14. The landscapes of south-east Ireland

surprised by this, as I assumed there would be some sort of regional variation in setting, as there is in monument form (see chapter 4). However, this is not the case and sites throughout the Irish Sea zone are located in remarkably similar settings. Below I will detail the precise location of the early Neolithic chambered tombs in terms of what is visible from each site. Briefly here I want to give some sense of where sites are positioned in the landscape.

Some parts of the landscape were completely avoided for monument construction. Chambered tombs were not located in the mountains, although they do cluster around mountainous regions (see below). Likewise, monuments were never constructed on the beaches or the intertidal zones of the Irish Sea. This means that considerable swathes of the Irish Sea zone did not see monument construction. Instead, the vast majority of sites are fairly low-lying, although some sites are found a few hundred metres above sea level. The vast majority of these early Neolithic chambered tombs are located on what is now agricultural land. This statement does not imply that these landscapes were utilised in a similar way in the Neolithic. Nevertheless, the landscapes where chambered tombs are

*Figure 6.15.
Ballybrack in
Dublin*

*Figure 6.16.
Auchachenna,
western Scotland,
visible on the
skyline on approach*

located are almost always suitable for agricultural use. This is in direct contrast to some parts of the Irish Sea zone which would have been, and still are, marginal areas. Because many of the chambered tombs are in agricultural land, they have frequently been used as a source of raw material (cairn stones primarily, taken away to construct walls or incorporated into walls). While the vast majority of sites are rural, which probably goes some way to explain why they have been preserved, a few sites are also located in more urban areas, found amongst houses (Fig. 6.15). Early Neolithic chambered tombs are frequently found on the side of hills: never on steeply-sloping ground but usually on a gentle slope. This creates a restricted view in one direction (i.e. a person standing at the site is unable to see very far on the horizon in that direction). In many instances, chambered tombs are located close to water: rivers, streams, lochs and the sea (see below for details).

When mid-twentieth century writers discussed the location of these sites (for example, Piggott 1954), they frequently commented on the fact that these sites were located on prime agricultural land. They were of course assuming that the Neolithic in Britain and Ireland was the result of colonisation from Europe, and that agriculturalists were arriving by boat and building monuments to their dead close to these virgin agricultural communities. We now know that the Neolithic package arrived on these shores around about 200 years *before* communities starting building monuments (see Bayliss and Whittle 2007), and that many communities

Figure 6.17.
Ardnadam, Argyll

probably integrated the keeping of domestic livestock with a hunting and gathering lifestyle (see papers in Whittle and Cummings 2007). Nevertheless, it is striking that earlier writers noticed a consistency in the location of sites, and that related to the agricultural potential for these landscapes.

As already noted, monuments are typically located on the side of hills or slopes and this means that when one approaches a site from the lower-lying coastal zone (where many of the lithic scatters have been found, probably representing occupation sites), a chambered tomb is then visible on the skyline on approach (Fig. 6.16). Of course, we cannot be sure from which direction people approached a site, although in the next chapter I argue that at many sites, people may have arrived at sites by boat and then walked uphill towards each monument. If one walks towards a monument from the opposite direction (essentially inland) as modern accessibility sometimes dictates, it can be very tricky to actually locate a site, and the monument of course also does not appear skylined on approach.

Thinking about moving around landscapes and visiting chambered tombs is a frustrating process. Many later Neolithic sites were embellished with avenues, formalised approaches which enable us to describe precisely what people saw and encountered on a specific approach to a site. Not so at chambered tombs. However, Tilley (1994) has an interesting idea here. The subtitle of his original *Phenomenology of Landscape* was *Places, Paths and Monuments*. Perhaps approaches to monuments were marked out by pathways through the landscape, sadly nothing we can identify in the archaeological record, but a prescribed route nevertheless. I have suggested elsewhere and above that the felling of trees in linear swathes may have acted in a similar way to an avenue, creating a formalised approach of sorts to a monument.

Mountains

One of the most striking aspects of the chambered tombs of the Irish Sea zone is their location in relation to mountains (Fig. 6.17). I have commented on this

Area	Total of sites (classification)	Number	Percentage
West Wales	45 (dolmens)	35/45	78%
W. Scotland and IoM	81 (Clyde cairns)	57/69	83%
NE Ireland	83 (53 court cairns, 22 dolmens, 8 passage graves)	74/78	95%
SW Ireland	27 (26 dolmens, 1 court cairn)	16/22	73%
Total	**236 sites in study**	**182/214**	**85%**

Table 6.1. Summary of visibility of mountains from chambered tombs by region. Column three (number) relates to how many sites had views of mountains out of a total number of sites where this could be ascertained. At some sites (for example those in dense modern forestry) this could not be ascertained, hence the total may be less than the number of sites in the study area.

before in relation to Wales (Cummings and Whittle 2004), but it is a consistent theme throughout the Irish Sea zone. It is true that there are considerable mountainous areas around the Irish Sea zone, but as already described above, there are also considerable swathes of the landscape which are not mountainous, so the location near to mountains seems to have been a deliberate choice. Indeed, monuments are not positioned in the flatter expanses of the Irish Sea zone – in north-west England, for example Lancashire and Merseyside, nor from Louth down to south of Dublin in Ireland. As I will detail below, people seem to have deliberately located their chambered tombs so that there were views of mountains on the horizon.

This is not to say that every single last chambered tomb in the Irish Sea zone has a view of a mountain. At some sites other concerns seem to have been paramount: for example the coastal location amongst many of the western Scottish sites seems to have been of more significance than a view of a mountain. Nevertheless, I argue that there is a genuine relationship between chambered tombs and mountains. There is also the problem, of course, of how one actually defines a mountain or mountains. For the sake of ease here I have followed the original methodology laid out in 2004 (Cummings and Whittle 2004, 30), of describing a mountain as a landmass over 1000ft (304m). This means that the Preseli Mountains, the smallest of the mountains in the Irish Sea zone, are classed as mountains here. Of course, people in the Neolithic had no knowledge of the relative heights of different peaks, and as such really the definition of a mountain is arbitrary. Nevertheless, there are peaks which are visually distinctive in the landscape both now and in the Neolithic, and it is these (called mountains here) that sites seem to have been built around.

The relationship between monuments and mountains is a fairly simple one: people did not build early Neolithic chambered tombs in the mountains themselves. Those critical of a landscape approach may argue that locating

Figure 6.18.
Goward court
cairn, Co. Down

Figure 6.19. Creag
Mhor, Argyll

sites in the mountains is not practical (in terms of access to raw materials and the day-to-day practicalities), however, there is plenty of evidence from the middle Neolithic for people doing just that: middle Neolithic passage graves are frequently located on the tops of hills, and in our terminology here, mountains. This occurs primarily in Ireland, where the passage grave tradition flourished in the middle Neolithic. But it serves to illustrate a point: people could choose where to build monuments wherever they wanted in the landscape and they were not constrained by the topography or by availability of raw materials (contra Fleming's (2005) functional arguments). In the early Neolithic people simply did not choose to build chambered tombs on top of peaks or mountains. What people in the early Neolithic seem to have been concerned about was positioning their monuments with *views of* mountains. Again and again, sites are located so that mountains (and prominent hills in some cases) were visible on the horizon. Usually, monuments were located so that there were views of mountains in one direction only: people did not want to surround monuments with mountains, but instead to have a view of mountains on one part of the horizon only. Again, Fleming (2005) would argue that surrounding a site with mountains is very hard to achieve, yet again, in the later Neolithic people managed to do just that.

*Figure 6.20.
Bachwen,
Caernarvonshire*

*Figure 6.21.
Llech y Dribedd,
Pembrokeshire*

Take, for example, the setting of stone circles such as Swinside and Castlerigg, where these monuments were set so that mountains were visible on the horizon in all directions (and see Bradley 1998a, chapter 8).

There are a number of major mountain ranges in the Irish Sea zone: in Ireland the Wicklow Mountains in the south-east and the Mournes in the north-east are prominent and both have concentrations of monuments around them (Fig. 6.18). In western Scotland it is the mountains of Arran which seem to have been a particular focus of monumentality, but the mountains of Jura, Ben Lomond and Ben Cruachan are also visible from sites (Fig. 6.19). In Wales, it the Snowdon range and the Lleyn mountains in particular in north-west Wales (Fig. 6.20), and the Preselis in south-west Wales that were visible from many chambered tombs (Fig. 6.21). In each of these cases it is not always the highest mountain that is visible from chambered tombs. Instead, people seem to have built chambered tombs so that it is the most visually distinctive profiles that were visible from each site.

Mountains seem to have had a particularly important place in Neolithic cosmology. From the early Neolithic onwards people were going up mountains to get materials for making polished stone axes. A quick look at the distribution map of stone axes sources reveals a large number in the Irish Sea zone (and see chapter 3). Indeed, there are major axe factories in the Precelis in south-west Wales (Group VIII), in Snowdonia (Group VII) and at Tievebulliagh (Group IX) in north-east Ireland. Later in the Neolithic, stones were actually removed from the Precelis and moved to Stonehenge in Wiltshire, and it has been suggested it was the source of these stones that made them so significant (Bradley 2000a, 95). Mountains were also clearly significant in the location of other Neolithic monuments, including passage graves and stone circles (see above). There is a wealth of ethnographic material which shows that mountains have a central place in mythology and cosmology which I do not wish to rehearse again here. Elsewhere, I have also described how the properties of mountains as places where the earth meets the sky, where you experience extremes of weather and wide vistas of the surrounding landscape (Cummings and Whittle 2004, 85–6) also makes them very special in the Neolithic. The mountains of the Irish Sea zone are also intervisible: standing on top of one of the peaks in the mountains means you can see out over other mountains in the Irish Sea zone. The mountains connect you to other parts of the Irish Sea zone (see Cummings 2004). Quite simply, mountains seem to have been highly significant places in the Neolithic hence the positioning of chambered tombs in relation to them.

As well as being places that were highly significant in the Neolithic in terms of cosmology and mythology, mountains may well have played other roles in the Neolithic. Since mountains are highly visible locations, they may well have been used for navigation, particularly when crossing the Irish Sea itself. We really do not have any real idea of how often people navigated this waterway: we know that they did from evidence like Arran pitchstone in Ireland and Antrim flint in Scotland, as well as the movement of polished stone axes (see chapter 3). But were people regularly crossing the Irish Sea, or were these periodic or sporadic visits? It is this particular topic which needs clarification, and a fieldwork project is underway to address this issue (Cummings and Robinson 2006). I think many archaeologists have perhaps thought that contact was sporadic (e.g. Burrow 1997; Sheridan 2004), and certainly the first scholars who considered this area in detail thought there was initial movements of people (the primary Neolithic), followed by a period of stability and presumably sedentism, with a second wave of population movements later in the Neolithic (the secondary Neolithic: e.g. Piggott 1954).

Area	Total of sites	Number	Percentage
West Wales	45 (dolmens)	37/45	82%
W. Scotland and IoM	81 (Clyde)	61/77	79%
NE Ireland	83 (53 court cairns, 22 dolmens, 8 passage graves)	32/74	43%
SW Ireland	27 (26 dolmens, 1 court cairn)	2/24	8%
Total	**236 sites in study**	**132/220**	**60%**

Table 6.2. Summary of visibility of the sea from chambered tombs by region. Column three (number) relates to how many sites had views of the sea out of a total number of sites where this could be ascertained. At some sites (for example those in dense modern forestry) this could not be ascertained, hence the total may be less than the number of sites in the study area. You can clearly see large differences here between western Britain and eastern Ireland.

Figure 6.22. Achnagoul, Argyll

Figure 6.23. Ballyvoy, Co. Antrim

This scenario was based on a much shorter chronology, and since the collapse of the old chronology with the radiocarbon revolution, our attentions have been focussed elsewhere.

There is no doubt, however, that people in the Neolithic were more than capable of crossing the Irish Sea on a regular basis. They certainly had the appropriate technology (cattle, sheep, pigs, cereals and people made it from the Continent to Britain by boat). A seaworthy boat, knowledge of tides and the right weather, therefore, is all that is needed to cross the sea. Mountains would have acted as key reference points, being the most visible landmasses across the sea. In the next chapter I argue that the western Scottish sites in particular seem to suggest a maritime community, and these may well have been people who utilised boats a great deal. It may be no surprise to hear that in recent times, people in Kintyre went for their Sunday lunch in county Antrim (Angus Martin *pers. comm.*), and it is not beyond the realms of possibility that in the Neolithic people had very close personal or community ties across the Irish Sea. Mountains may well have played a practical, as well as symbolic, role in the lives of seafaring communities.

Water: sea, lochs and rivers

This brings us neatly onto a consideration of the positioning of early Neolithic chambered tombs and water. One of the other key features of the early Neolithic chambered tombs seems to be their position in relation to water, in particular the sea. In particular, many sites (60% in total) have views out over the sea or sea lochs (see Table 6.2.). Many sites have been very carefully positioned in the landscape so that a sea view is present: at a number of sites had the chambered tomb been positioned a few metres from its present locale, then the view of the sea would be lost Figs 6.22–6.24).

It is obvious looking at the table above that there are considerable differences between areas around the Irish Sea. High percentages of the west Welsh and western Scottish sites are positioned in relation to the sea (82% and 79% respectively). However, in eastern Ireland, the number of sites drops dramatically: in the north-east, only 43% of sites have a sea view, even though these chambered tombs have a general coastal location. In the next chapter I argue that it was a mountain view that was of the greatest significance in this area. Even more striking is that only two sites in south-east Ireland have a view of the sea. Here, the opposite seems to be the case: people were deliberately *avoiding* a sea view. Mountains are ubiquitously visible from early Neolithic chambered tombs, yet

*Figure 6.24.
Carreg Samson,
Pembrokeshire*

*Figure 6.25. Loch
Nell, Argyll*

*Figure 6.26.
Druid's Stone,
Co. Antrim*

the sea is not, and this is the best evidence that we have for some smaller-scale regional differences, especially in the case of south-east Ireland (see below and chapter 7). Nevertheless, even with these regional variations, nearly two-thirds of sites have a view of the sea or a sea loch.

I have already discussed above the idea that people were moving across the sea frequently, and that there may well have been strong connections between communities either side of the Irish Sea. The sea may well have been a conduit for movement, not a barrier. The sea may well have also been an important symbolic feature, just like mountains, tied to mythologies and cosmologies. Other authors have detailed the significance of water at other Neolithic monuments (e.g. Bradley 1998a; Richards 1996; Tilley 2004), and all of those arguments may well be relevant here too.

We know that people in the Neolithic sailed across the sea, and we know that considerable parts of the population probably avoided eating foods from the sea (Schulting and Richards 2002b; 2006 and subsequent debates by Milner *et al.* 2004 and Thomas 2003). While many communities were quite clearly not eating fish in the Neolithic, others were (see, for example, Sturt 2004 on the Orcadian evidence), and to assume that stable isotopes from chambered tombs (and causewayed enclosures outside the study area here) are representative of the whole of the early Neolithic is perhaps not wise. People were clearly fishing in some areas, so many people's lives would be very strongly focussed on the sea. Talking to people in fishing communities, it is clear what an overarching theme it is in their lives (also see G. Robinson 2007). There are many rich ethnographies as well as personal stories about living life on the sea and the shore. For some, the sea and tides would have structured their lives (G. Robinson 2007).

I have previously suggested that perhaps people were buried at sea in the Neolithic, stemming back to a Mesolithic tradition (see Cummings 2003; Fowler and Cummings 2003). This idea has been used to suggest why people in the Neolithic avoided eating foods from the sea (Fowler and Cummings 2003; Thomas 2003) and also why monuments used for the burial of the dead were located with views of the sea. It is an appealing idea, but one which we shall struggle ever to prove. I wonder also whether there were tales or folklore which spoke of times when the sea removed land: even though the rising sea levels took place over a long period, it is likely that large chunks of land disappeared in one go, instead of there being a slow and steady rise in sea levels (and see Warren 2005). Some of these inundations may have happened within folk memory, and the sea could well have been revered for its tremendous and destructive properties. We often wonder why people changed from a hunting and gathering lifestyle to one focussed more on farming (and less on fishing).

Figure 6.27.
Hendre Waelod,
Denbighshire

Hunter-gatherers typically have a sharing relationship with the natural world, a 'cosmic economy of sharing' as it has been called (cf. Bird-David 1992). Could it be that amongst communities who relied on the bounty of the sea, yet had growing trepidation about the power of the sea as a destructive force, did the prospect of utilising domestic animals offer a 'way out' of a 'sharing' relationship with the sea? The apparently 'fast-change' from a hunter-gatherer lifestyle to one reliant on domesticated animals may have had less to do with what was on offer (the Neolithic package) and more to do with what people could now actively avoid? If this was the case, the sea may well have been a highly potent substance indeed.

This is only one idea. The sea probably meant many different things to different communities on its shores. What is clear is that early Neolithic chambered tombs in western Britain were deliberately and carefully located in relation to the sea. This was less relevant to communities in eastern Ireland, who may well have had a rather different relationship with the sea in any case (see, for example, discussion on the different resource base of late Mesolithic communities in Ireland as compared to Britain: Cooney 2000; Woodman 2004). In north-east Ireland, where the sea was visible from 43% of sites, the sea still clearly had an important role in symbolic and historic terms. In the south-east, people seem to have been deliberately avoiding a view of it from their monuments (see next chapter).

A few sites in the Irish Sea zone are also carefully positioned so that there are views of rivers (Fig. 6.27). Rivers may well have acted in similar ways to sea lochs and the sea: as conduits for movement through an otherwise predominately forested environment. Not only do rivers act as quick and easy ways of moving

Outcrop

*Figure 6.28.
White House,
Pembrokeshire*

around the landscape, but there are further hints of their potentially ritual significance. Large quantities of axes have been found in rivers, most notably in Ireland (Cooney and Mandel 1998) but also in Britain, as well as human bone (Bradley 2000a). It seems rivers received deposits, including human bodies, which could link them further to the depositional acts taking place at chambered tombs.

Other landscape features

A few sites in the Irish Sea zone are positioned in relation to a very striking landscape feature: rocky outcrops (Fig. 6.28). I noted this in relation to the sites in south-west Wales (Cummings and Whittle 2004, 29–30), and some of the sites in south-east Ireland also seem to be positioned close to outcrops (see next chapter). Clearly, then, this is not a feature of all early Neolithic chambered tombs. Certainly, not all of the landscapes in the Irish Sea zone have outcrops for a start, and in other areas land improvements may well have removed others. But where there are prominent outcrops, some chambered tombs at least seem to have been positioned in relation to these features as well. In all cases, the chambered tombs are located so that the outcrops are visible on the horizon. This makes their profile stand out on the horizon when one is standing at the monument.

Rocky outcrops are interesting features, and I have written elsewhere about them being ambiguous places, looking like built architecture but being what we would describe as 'natural' (Cummings 2002a). This ambiguity may have been less clear in the Neolithic and I am intrigued as to what Neolithic populations thought about outcrops, and the stories and myths surrounding them. Certainly in the case of some of the dolmens, people seem to have turned outcrops of rock into monuments, lifting up and displaying outcrops as the capstone (see Whittle 2004). At some sites, people raised massive chunky stones into the air, extremely impressive feats of engineering. Some of the largest capstones in the study area are on the dolmens of Goward (county Down), Brenanstown (county Dublin) and Garn Turne (Pembrokeshire). It is very tempting to suggest that these outcrops were already significant places in the landscape prior to be turned into monuments. Sadly, the nature of the archaeology means we know frustratingly little about these sites, and of course just because a site was significant, it did not mean that people left material culture there (parallels with Native American sites can be made here, where it is not considered appropriate to leave offerings at special sites: Carmichael *et al.* 1994)).

Orientations and symmetries

For many years, there has been interest in the orientation of chambered tombs. In particular this related to the direction of the entrance (the portal or façade or forecourt, dependent on the type of monument involved). Henshall (1963; 1972), for example, considered the orientation of all of the chambered tombs in Scotland, and she noted a preponderance of orientation of the Clyde cairns towards the north-east (Henshall 1972, 99). But unlike later Neolithic monuments such as Stonehenge and Avebury, and indeed later Neolithic chambered tombs such as Newgrange, Maes Howe and the Clava cairns (e.g. Bradley 2000b), scholars have struggled to find definite correlations between the orientation of early Neolithic chambered tombs and celestial events such as midsummer sunrise and midwinter sunset (e.g. Ruggles 1999). This does not mean that these chambered tombs were not orientated deliberately in the landscape, but just that their orientation does not seem to relate to celestial events.

Indeed, in Tilley's original case study of the Black Mountains group (Tilley 1994, chapter 4), he suggested a general orientation of sites towards escarpments. He suggested that the long cairns of the Black Mountains monuments were positioned in relation to those mountains. On visiting these sites, this relationship did not seem as clear cut to me as Tilley had suggested and a paper followed which suggested that the monument builders were not orientating their sites on landforms, but were more interested in creating opposing 'sides' to each monument, so that views to one side or the other of a monument were different (see Cummings, Jones and Watson 2002). In particular, we felt that monuments were not 'pointing' towards landscape forms at all: instead we argued that the builders of each site were positioning sites so that, for example, there were wide views out to one side of a long cairn, and closed and restricted views to the other, what we called 'axial asymmetry'. This worked particularly well with the Black Mountains group of long cairns, but was harder to work out at many of the west Welsh sites where the orientation of many of the sites was hard to ascertain due to the lack of a surviving cairn (see Cummings and Whittle 2004).

A number of sites in the Irish Sea zone do exhibit 'sidedness', so that there are direct contrasts between the landscape views along one side of the cairn as opposed to the other. This relationship is particularly noticeable amongst the court cairns of north-east Ireland. For example, at the site of Grange Irish in County Louth, the court cairn is orientated roughly north-south. Standing on the axis of the cairn, to the western side the view is restricted, looking inland at the immediate landscape. To the east, however, distant landscapes are visible, of mountains (the Mournes), Carlingford Lough and the sea. Many sites, but not all, exhibit similar views of the landscape in relation to how the long cairn is orientated in the landscape. In contrast, very few sites directly 'point' at specific landscape features. This may suggest that our way of pointing things out was simply not how things were done in the Neolithic, or that certainly this way of doing things was not appropriate at chambered tombs. My feeling is that in the Neolithic, people were more concerned with positioning sites within the landscape as a whole, than 'pointing out' specific features. I would suggest that once a specific location had been chosen for monument construction (and there may have been many reasons for choosing a specific site, including which landscapes were visible from the site, but also relating to settlement (new and old), mythologies, histories and pathways), people fitted monuments into that space as best they could. Not every site could have views of a mountain or mountains, a view of water, be positioned with a restricted view and have sided views either side of the long cairn.

Regional differences

In the next chapter I discuss the details of individual regional sequences, in terms of what is visible from specific sets of sites. Here I want to comment more generally on the overall setting of sites in the Irish Sea zone, and note any broad-scale regional differences. As I mentioned at the start, there is a remarkable consistency in the setting of early Neolithic chambered tombs throughout the Irish Sea zone. They are not in mountains, not on the shore, but set in the space between. Mountains are visible at most sites in Irish Sea zone, and the sea is visible at most sites in western Britain, but much less so in eastern Ireland. Sites that do not have views of the sea or sea lochs are often located close to rivers, and most sites are located on the side of gentle hills so that a view in one direction is restricted. I would argue, therefore, that there is remarkable similarity in the setting of chambered tombs throughout the Irish Sea area. I discuss what this may have meant in the final chapter.

While there are broad similarities between all sites in the Irish Sea zone, there are also some clear-cut differences. The group that stand out the most are the dolmens of south-east Ireland. These sites seem to deliberately avoid a view of the sea. They are considered in more depth in the next chapter but seem to be indicative of people doing things slightly differently there. The north-east Irish sites are also frequently placed so that a view of the sea is not present, and this contrasts neatly with the Clyde monuments of western Scotland where a view of the sea was paramount, whereas mountains were not always visible. It seems, then, that there were slight regional differences which should be noted. Again, what this might have meant is raised in the next chapter.

One might argue that it is the local topography which essentially creates these regional differences I have noted, and that simply by virtue of being in different parts of the Irish Sea zone, different landscape features are visible. Even the briefest look at other types of Neolithic monument (for example, middle and late Neolithic passage graves or stone circles) will demonstrate that where these sites have an overlapping distribution with early Neolithic chambered tombs, they are located in very different parts of the landscape. I did this with the original Welsh case study (Cummings and Whittle 2004) and clearly demonstrated how other types of monument have their own place in the landscape (and read Bradley 1998b; Richard 1996). People had a choice as to where they built their sites, and they seem to have very carefully located sites in very specific parts of the landscape. I have argued here that the settings are broadly the same throughout the Irish Sea zone, but with a few regional variations on those broader themes.

Blanks in the distribution

There are three key areas in the Irish Sea zone which have no known chambered tombs. I have argued above that these two blanks are genuine and not the result of modern destruction. The first area with a notable lack of early Neolithic monuments is between Dundalk in county Louth in north-east Ireland, to county Dublin. Here there is a stretch of nearly 70km which saw no known megalithic construction in the early Neolithic. Interestingly, this area does see middle Neolithic chambered tomb construction, with a large number of passage graves being constructed here (the Bru na Boinne complex being of particular note: Cooney 2000, 153–8). I would argue that this particular landscape was not suitable for the construction of early Neolithic chambered tombs as there were no views of significant mountains. The landscape between Dundalk and Dublin is of gently rolling hills but lacks the visually striking mountains which seem to have attracted the builders of the early sites. Middle and late Neolithic passage graves, however, are set in different landscape settings to early Neolithic chambered tombs, so this area saw considerable activity at a later date. So for this area I am arguing that the landscape dictated what could and could not be built there. This was, if you like, the active and potent agency of landscape, which prescribed how it could be used. We could use a similar argument to explain why there are no chambered tombs in mid-west Wales, where again there is a blank area between the north and south distributions.

The third blank area is north-west England (western Merseyside, Lancashire and Cumbria). It is perhaps not surprising that much of this area did not have chambered tomb architecture if we again consider the importance of the landscape setting. Quite simply, most of this area does not have the combination of mountains and sea that define the setting of other chambered tombs in western Britain. Cumbria here though, remains the one area where one might expect to find a considerable number of chambered tombs. We know that people utilised the Cumbrian shores in the late Mesolithic (e.g. Bonsall *et al.* 1990), and that there is a strong Neolithic presence in the form of a major axe factory (Langdale: Bradley and Edmonds 1993), a number of late Neolithic stone circles (Burl 1995), as well as assorted other forms of evidence (see H. Evans 2004). Furthermore, Cumbria is not intensively occupied so the modern destruction of chambered tombs can probably be ruled out. Quite simply, this area has the right sort of landscape for chambered tomb construction but no chambered tombs (although there are some long cairns) I am not sure why people did not build chambered tombs here in the early Neolithic. Perhaps the population was slower than others to change from a hunting and gathering lifestyle to one that included domesticates and monument construction. Or perhaps people here did things differently to other communities around the Irish Sea. Perhaps they did not wish to ally themselves with the Irish Sea traditions, seeking links and connections with the east of England, which did not see chambered tomb construction in the early Neolithic. Perhaps the absence of chambered tomb architecture is a reflection that not everyone in Britain and Ireland did things the same way. Whatever the case, Cumbria remains the one area which does not seem to fit the pattern.

Conclusions

In this chapter I have considered the location of the early Neolithic chambered tombs of the Irish Sea zone, highlighting the similarities in their setting within the landscape. In particular, I have emphasised the landscape features which were visible for people building, visiting and using these places. It seems to have been mountains which were of particular significance to the builders and users of these sites, although the sea, sea lochs and rivers were also important in particular areas. These may well have had a multitude of meanings and significances in a Neolithic worldview, relating not only to navigating and movement around the landscape and seascape but also in terms of symbolism and mythology. I have argued that people had a choice as to where they built their monuments. Critically, the location of sites in relation to the landscape seems to have been shared across a broad area, certainly within the study area of the Irish Sea zone here and also possibly beyond. While there were elements of commonality in the setting of sites throughout the entire Irish Sea zone, there are also hints of regional variations, where people were following, very broadly, some general structuring principles, but they were being manifest in slightly different ways in certain parts of the area. In the next chapter I go on to consider some of these regional areas in more detail, teasing of the specifics in setting out groupings of sites in the Irish Sea zone.

7

Attention to detail: regional landscape case studies

Introduction

In the previous chapter I concentrated on the settings of all of the chambered tombs of the Irish Sea zone, focussing on what was visible from the sites in general. I noted a series of regularities in the setting of the chambered tombs throughout the Irish Sea zone, particularly the tendency for the builders to locate their sites so that there were mountains and water visible. In this chapter I want to go into more detail, focussing on particular sets of monuments within the Irish Sea zone. First of all I will discuss the settings of sites in western Scotland, firstly those in Arran, Kintyre, Islay and Jura, then those chambered tombs found around the Firth of Clyde and the western lochs. I will then turn my attention to eastern Ireland with detailed case studies of monuments in the Mournes, the Glens of Antrim and the dolmens of south-east Ireland. I have already discussed in detail the settings of the Welsh sites and those on the Isle of Man (see Cummings and Whittle 2004 on the former and Cummings and Fowler 2004a on the latter), and I so I will not repeat those discussions here.

Western Scotland

There are a number of concentrations of early Neolithic monuments in western Scotland which were discussed more generally in the previous chapter. They stretch from the 'outliers' in Dumfries and Galloway (see Cummings 2002b), to a few around Glasgow, all the way up to Oban. Beyond Oban, another early Neolithic megalithic tradition is found, that of the Hebridean chambered tomb, a different style completely from the Clyde tombs being discussed here (see Henshall 1972). In the following two sections I will discuss two particular concentrations in more detail. I am not suggesting here that these two groupings form distinctive regions in the Neolithic, although there are some striking similarities in the precise settings of sites. Instead, I will suggest that there are some interesting themes that these sites have in common which may have been an expression of identity or indications of areas of close contact.

Arran, Kintyre, Islay and Jura

A total of 32 definite early Neolithic chambered tombs are found on the islands of Arran, Islay, Jura and the Kintyre peninsula (Fig. 7.1). Within this distribution, Arran has the densest concentration with a total of 16 definite sites as well as additional possible sites (these are not included in this study, but see Henshall 1972). At those sites where it was possible to see the landscape, 87% of the chambered tombs in this area have views of mountains and 86% have views of the sea, meaning they are typical setting-wise within their broader Irish Sea zone context.

The set of chambered tombs in Kintyre are interesting in comparison to those elsewhere in the Irish Sea zone. Kintyre is a long thin finger of land set between Arran to the east, Islay and Jura to the west and Ireland to the south-west: even though it is attached to mainland Scotland, it has very much a feeling of being an island (it's motto: Scotland's only mainland island, and see Scott 1955). Kintyre is primarily hilly although some of its peaks are mountains by the definition employed here, including the Mull of Kintyre which has a highest

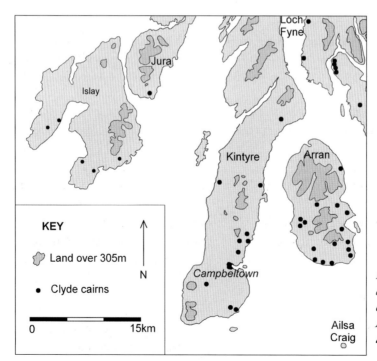

Figure 7.1. The distribution of chambered tombs in Arran, Kintyre, Islay and Jura

point of 428m OD. The west coast is fairly exposed while the east coast is more sheltered: the biggest town, Campbeltown is on the east coast in a sheltered harbour (Campbeltown Loch). Nine out of ten of the chambered tombs are found on the east coast or inland, with only one site, Beacharra on the west coast. Jack Scott used to holiday in Kintyre (Frances Hood *pers. comm.*) and excavated a number of chambered tombs while there, including Beacharra (Scott 1954), Brackley (Scott 1955) and Ardnacross II (Scott 1973). Beacharra was originally investigated in the late nineteenth century and again by Scott in 1954. Of particular note are the group of round-bottomed pottery vessels found in the original excavations, all early Neolithic Carinated Bowls and now named after the site: Beacharra Ware (Scott 1997, 76). Likewise at Brackley, Beacharra Ware was found (Scott 1955, 27). There is also evidence that these sites were reused (or continued to be used) in the Bronze Age. At Brackley, the chamber seems to have been emptied out and subsequently paved in the Bronze Age and pottery, jet beads, flint and cremations added.

The majority of sites in Kintyre are in 'typical' locations for early Neolithic chambered tombs, as outlined in the previous chapter. A number of sites seem to have been carefully positioned so that the spectacular profile of the Arran mountains is visible on the horizon, and sites in southern Kintyre also frequently have views of Ailsa Craig, the distinctive domed island off mainland Scotland at Girvan. All but one of the sites are positioned so that the sea is visible. Other, more distant landmasses are also visible. At Blasthill in southern Kintyre, the chambered tomb is located close to, but not on top of, a hill. The chambered tomb has been positioned as such that there are views towards Arran in one direction and Ireland in the other (Fig. 7.2). Moving this monument slightly in any direction would result in one, or both, of these distant vistas being lost. This suggests that the builders of the site positioned their monument very carefully. The site of Beacharra is also carefully located in the landscape. It is the only chambered tomb on the west coast and is set up above the raised beach opposite the small island of Cara Island, and it commands spectacular views of Gigha and Jura (see Fig. 7.3). The west coast of Kintyre is quite exposed and also rises quite steeply here, not making it ideal either for travelling by boat or for settlement. However, Gigha would have provided shelter from westerly winds and an easier access point into West Loch Tarbert. Beacharra seems to mark the southerly entrance point into this calmer stretch of water, and interestingly, the location is also marked by a later standing stone. Throughout this region, standing stones seem to have been positioned to mark out key locales for navigation if one were moving around by boat (Gary Robinson *pers. comm.*), strengthening the argument that Beacharra also related to communities using boats.

Figure 7.2. Blasthill, with views out over Ireland

Ireland

Figure 7.3. The chambered tomb and standing stone at Beacharra, with Jura visible in the distance (photograph by Chris Jennings: www.pagetoscreen. net)

Figure 7.4. Brackley, Kintyre

Not all of the Kintyre monuments have views of both mountains and the sea though. The site of Brackley, one of those sites excavated by Scott, is a good case in point. This chambered tomb is less than 2km from the east coast, but is tucked away in a river valley (Fig. 7.4). From the site neither mountains nor sea are visible. Instead, the focus of this monument is Carradale Water, a river which runs close to the site and flows down to Carradale Bay a few kilometres to the south. Carradale Bay is another very sheltered harbour and would have made a safe landing place in the Neolithic. This chambered tomb, then, relates to sea travel, but this time via a river. The adjacent coastline to Brackley is very rocky and not the sort of location chosen for chambered tomb construction (see previous chapter), so the builders have chosen a riverine location instead.

Figure 7.5. Sannox, Arran

The chambered tombs of Arran have long been the focus of interest (for example see Bryce 1902; Henshall 1972; Renfrew 1973; A. Jones 1999). For this study I only included the definite Clyde tombs, a total of 16 sites. Henshall (1972) lists 21 sites in her inventory, but one is destroyed, another natural and three of these (Dunan Mor, Baile Meadhonach and Carmahome) are almost certainly later in date. The distribution map immediately reveals that all bar one of the sites are found in the southern part of the island which is less mountainous than the north. Virtually all the early Neolithic chambered tombs are found close to modern roads and settlements, the inland hilly and mountainous areas avoided. This coastal distribution means that from most sites it is possible to see the sea as well as mountains (Fig. 7.5). Other distant landmasses are also visible from sites, including Kintyre, Dumfries and Galloway/Ayrshire and Ailsa Craig. Some chambered tombs are located in rich modern agricultural land (particularly the southern monuments), others are positioned to overlook agricultural land (the eastern monuments). Monuments were also clearly built in relation to movements *around* the landscape. Three chambered tombs are located on Machrie Moor and following up Clauchan Water from Drumadoon Point you encounter each monument in turn, leading you to the heart of the moor. Machrie Moor is unique on Arran: it is the only large flat piece of land, connected to the sea yet with spectacular views of the mountains (Fig. 7.6). It later became the focus for even more monumental architecture (stone circles, cairns, burnt mounds and enclosures), clearly a highly significant locale on Arran. This point is further illustrated by the site of Moinechoill. This site

Figure 7.6. Tormore I on Machrie Moor, Arran

is located along 'The String', the road that runs through the centre of Arran connecting the east and west coasts. The String follows the course of Machrie Water and Moinechoill is located at the point that two streams meet to form the main watercourse. It is therefore effectively marking the routeway through the landscape, connecting east and west and the route from Brodick Bay to the east with Drumadoon Bay to the west. Again, like at Beacharra, this location was later marked by a standing stone.

In the past, Arran has been used as a case study because it is an island and therefore represents a bounded area for study. But is it clear that in the Neolithic Arran was connected to the landmasses around it by water, water that would have been easily navigable and calm: Kilbrannan Sound to the west, the Sound of Bute to the north and the Firth of Clyde to the east. Arran does have a genuine concentration of monuments on it, but so do the surrounding landmasses and it seems likely that these areas were of prime importance and significance to people in the Neolithic, not just in terms of subsistence (keeping animals, collecting plants and fishing), but also in terms of connection to place. These are visually distinctive landscapes, of mountains and sea yet with low-lying areas sheltered and ideal for settlement.

There are only five definite chambered tombs on Islay (Henshall 1972), and they are found only in very specific parts of the island. The early Neolithic chambered tombs are located only on the Rhinns and the Oa, essentially the two westerly headlands which protrude into the Irish Sea/Atlantic Ocean. At the top of each of these headlands, on the easterly side, are two modern ports: Port Charlotte at the head of the Rhinns, and Port Ellen at the head of the Oa.

Figure 7.7. Port Charlotte, Islay, with Jura in the background (photograph by Nicola Didsbury)

One might suggest that these would also have been suitable landing places in the Neolithic. The southern headlands of the Rhinns and the Oa would make tricky sailing, with numerous overfalls and riptides (see the Admiralty Chart), but they frame the protected waters of Laggan Bay and Loch Indaal. Two sites, Port Charlotte and Giant's Graves overlook Loch Indaal from the Rhinns, another site, Frachdale, is 1km inland from Laggan Bay on the Oa, and the final two sites, Cragabus and Ballynaughton, are either side of Port Ellen. While the positioning of these five sites seems to reference landing places, sites were also carefully positioned so that there were also views of distant places. Two sites have views over to the Kintyre peninsula, and at Port Charlotte there is a view out towards Ireland as well as Jura (Fig. 7.7). On Islay, then, the communities building chambered tombs seem to have located their sites close to safe harbours but with views out over the wider Irish Sea zone. Only one chambered tomb is found on Jura, the site of Cladh Chlainn Iain, located almost on its southern tip. This site is right next to a secluded beach, surrounded on three sides by headlands and Brosdale Island. Positioned next to a stream, the focus of this site is not on the spectacular mountains of Jura itself, but out to sea and back over to the mountainous coastline of eastern Islay.

It is possible to conclude, therefore, that these sites were built by seafaring communities with an intimate knowledge of the coastline in this part of western Scotland. Just like in other parts of the Irish Sea zone, inland and mountainous parts of the landscape were avoided for chambered tomb construction. This means that for both Islay and Jura, the vast majority of these islands did not see chambered tomb construction. On Arran, most of the northern portion of the island is likewise devoid of chambered tombs. Instead, the focus is on sheltered coastlines with views of other parts of the Irish Sea zone.

Summary of the sites
- Perhaps not surprisingly for a group of sites located on islands and a peninsula, there seems to have been a considerable focus on the sea, with chambered tombs being constructed close to safe landing places, usually with a view of the sea
- Chambered tombs in this area were also positioned so that distinctive mountains were also visible on the horizon, most notably the mountains of Arran and the Paps of Jura
- When standing at these chambered tombs there is very much the sense of being part of a bigger world, as distant locales are frequently visible at sites, including Ireland, mainland Scotland and Ailsa Craig
- Some sites were in such significant locations, either in terms of navigation or in terms of belief systems, that later sites were frequently built close by, including standing stones and stone circles. Many sites were also reused in the Bronze Age for burial.

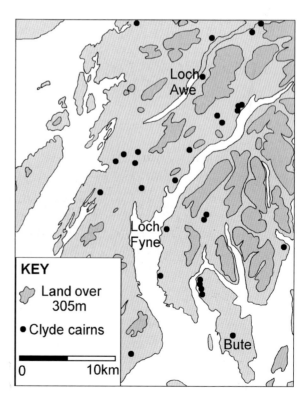

Figure 7.8. The distribution of chambered tombs in the firths, kyles and lochs of western Scotland

Figure 7.9. Port Sonachan, Argyll

Figure 7.10. Auchachenna, Argyll

The firths, kyles and lochs of western Scotland

Staying in western Scotland, there is another distinctive cluster of early Neolithic chambered tombs which are found around the Firth of Clyde, the Kyles of Bute and Loch Fyne and Loch Awe (Fig. 7.8). Here 31 definite chambered tombs are found, but apart from the small series on Bute, very few have been excavated in recent times. Again, it is immediately obvious that we are dealing with communities who had a maritime focus. For example, there are series of sites along both Loch Awe and Loch Fyne, almost lining the edge of these two lochs. For example, at the northern end of Loch Awe there are the three chambered tombs of Cladich, Port Sonachan and Auchachenna. Each site is located a few hundred metres inland from the loch close to modern roads. All three sites command spectacular views of the loch and also of mountains (Figs. 7.9 and 7.10). By foot, these sites are difficult to get to as the landscape is quite steep and rugged. However, by boat, all three sites could quite easily be accessed, and to move between them would also simply be a short boat journey.

I think there is the tendency to think of chambered tombs as isolated monuments, perhaps serving a community who would visit the site occasionally to deal with the dead. These people may have lived locally, or perhaps moved through the landscape, but there is the sense that these were places that were 'set away' from everyday life. I think this idea probably originated with Renfrew's 1973 consideration of monuments and territories. Even though post-processual archaeologists no longer talk explicitly about monuments in this way, nevertheless there must have been some sense of territory or at least the division of land in the Neolithic regardless of whether people were mobile or settled (or a bit of both). This may have been as simple as certain groups moving around specific landscapes as part of a seasonal round or similar (see Whittle 1997), or may relate more to notions of belonging. We know that there was violence in the Neolithic (Schulting and Wysocki 2005) but nowadays we rarely speak in terms of pressure on resources or disputes over land ownership. I am in favour of this: I think we are dealing with dispersed communities, who had notions of tenure to particular landscapes but not formalised senses of ownership. The evidence in western Scotland supports this idea of mobile people.

So how do chambered tombs fit into this? As I said, I think there is a tendency to think of monuments as isolated sites, but actually they may have been interconnected. Certainly there were no formalised links between sites, such as avenues, that are found at later sites. However, the location of sites along well-established routeways, such as the narrow northern section of Loch Awe, may well have meant that chambered tombs were actually designed to be visited not in isolation, but in a series or sequence. People may well have moved from one site to another by boat. This may well also have been the case with the series of four chambered tombs on the north-west tip of the Isle of Bute. Here the four sites are spread along the 2.5km of a protected and sheltered coastline. We could envisage different rituals being conducted at different sites, or perhaps different parts of the community using different sites. Whatever the case, these may not have been isolated monuments, but these clusters may represent connected sites linked by waterways. A series of sites are also found along the shores of Loch Fyne between Inveraray and Lochgilphead, and here again we might imagine people moving between sites in a prescribed order as they moved along the loch by boat.

The final set of monuments I want to consider in this area are found around Kilmartin. Kilmartin is best known for the series of later Neolithic and early Bronze Age monuments in the area, consisting of stone circles, henges, standing stones, cairns, cists and cup and ring marked rocks (Butter 1999). Distributed, for the most part, along the valley bottom and Kilmartin Burn, these sites create an entire monumental landscape. This was obviously a very special landscape, particularly apposite for the large-scale construction of megalithic architecture, akin to Machrie Moor on Arran, and further afield, around Maes Howe on Orkney and Callanish on the Isle of Lewis. Yet this landscape saw the construction of monuments in the early Neolithic. The focus in the early Neolithic, however, was not the area that became elaborated later on. Instead, the seven chambered tombs in this area are set around, and with views of, Mòine Mhòr. This area is now a raised bog and a wildlife reserve, with the River Add running through it. However, back at the start of the Neolithic, the bog would not have been there (Glen 2007). Instead there was a freshwater loch with surrounding saltmarsh with the mouth of the River Add a wider estuary. This may well have been a rich hunting ground as well as a desirable location for habitation. However, the real significance of this area lies with the fact that it is an important routeway (Noble 2007), connecting Loch Fyne with the sound of Jura. We might envisage this as a 'central place' in the landscape where people came together at particular times of the year and met up with other communities, perhaps before dispersing again (for the winter for example). Over time, the area became formalised by the construction of monumental architecture.

Summary of the sites
- These sites are all constructed close to the waterways of the area, which undoubtedly acted as conduits for people to travel along
- Many, but not all, chambered tombs in this area were positioned so that mountains were visible from the site. Amongst this set, the loch-side location was obviously more important than views of mountains
- Points in the landscape that would have acted as short-cuts between different parts of the Irish Sea zone seem to have had a number of chambered tombs constructed around them
- There is the possibility that these chambered tombs were designed to be visited in sequence, but instead of being connected by formalised routeways, as found in the later Neolithic, they were connected by waterways.

Eastern Ireland

The distribution of chambered tombs in Ireland is not quite so clear-cut as with western Scotland, further complicated by the fact that there are different monument types whose distribution overlaps (see chapter 4). However, there are clear clusters of sites in eastern Ireland with notable blanks areas between sites: the biggest blank between sites on the eastern seaboard is between Dundalk in County Louth (the end of the court cairn distribution) and Dublin, where a cluster of dolmens can be found, a distance of 75km. There are also blank areas between the eastern distribution of sites and those in the Midlands of Ireland, and a close look at the map identifies a series of monumental clusters, which I want to consider in more detail here. As with western Scotland, there are some regional variations which may well relate to more localised notions of identity and belonging, while people still felt themselves to be part of a broader Irish Sea zone.

The Mournes and Carlingford Mountain

Many years ago, Carlingford had a staring role in Neolithic studies. Piggott (1954) named the primary Neolithic culture of western Scotland and eastern Ireland the Clyde-Carlingford culture, partly based on similarities between the monuments either side of the Irish Sea. As the two countries (Northern Ireland and Scotland) developed their own national archaeologies, and archaeologists searched for more detailed understandings of regional sequences, the Clyde-Carlingford label was abandoned, although the notion of a Carlingford culture persisted for a time (e.g. Corcoran 1960). Nowadays, monuments are known either as court cairns or portal dolmens (see chapter 4). Quite clearly, though, there is a density of early Neolithic chambered tombs in this area (Fig. 7.11), focussing on Carlingford Mountain (579m OD) and its neighbour, the escarpment with its highest point Black Mountain (508m OD). Monuments are also found around the Mournes, the visually spectacular range rising up from the Irish Sea and culminating with Slieve Donard at 849m OD. To the east, monuments are also found around Slieve Gullion (576m OD). In total, 34 monuments are found in this region, 12 dolmens (including one passage grave) and 23 court cairns.

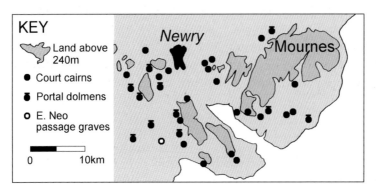

Figure 7.11. The distribution of chambered tombs around the Mournes

Figure 7.12.
Dunnaman,
Co. Down

The general location of these sites is very typical for sites in the Irish Sea zone: these monuments are not positioned in the mountains or on the shores of the Irish Sea itself. Instead, they are located between these two zones on what is now good quality agricultural land. The clustering around the mountains is the most distinctive characteristic of these sites, especially when compared to the areas immediately east, south and north, which are much flatter and devoid of monuments. It is not that people were not living in these areas: indeed, in the middle Neolithic the modern county of Meath, devoid of early Neolithic monuments, saw the construction of the massive passage graves and associated sites at the Bru na Boinne. Those particular landscapes were suited to monumental construction, just not early Neolithic chambered tombs. Clearly, people in the early Neolithic were attracted to the mountains. The Mournes are the largest and highest of the mountains in this area, and over half of the sites in the area have a view of them. While you might think that people in the Neolithic would have orientated their monuments so that they 'point' at these mountains, in fact they seem to have preferred to have a view of mountains to one side (see previous chapter on sidedness). Thus at Dunnaman, Co. Down, for example, the gallery of the monument does not 'point' at the Mournes, instead the mountains are visible to one side of the chamber (Fig. 7.12). This works at other sites too, for example at Goward court cairn in Co. Down.

It is even harder to work out the orientation of the dolmens, since most do not have surviving cairns and the chambers have been mutilated. This is the case at Wateresk in Co. Down, but it is clear that there would have been spectacular views of the Mournes from this site (Fig. 7.13). Not all sites in the area are located with views of the Mournes though, and it is possible to

Figure 7.13.
Wateresk,
Co. Down

avoid a view of this mountain range from much of the surrounding landscape. Goward dolmen is positioned to the north of the Mournes, and there is a wide view out to the north of this monument out towards Slieve Croob. There is a blank in the distribution of chambered tombs north of Goward, but the next monument is found in the foothills of Slieve Croob, and it may be the case that Goward is located here to visually connect one set of monuments (those around the Mournes) with the next grouping of sites, set around Slieve Croob. Yet Goward also has views south to the Mournes, and had this site been located just a few metres downslope, this view would have been lost. Fleming (2005) would argue that a site like Goward is located where it is as people used an *in situ* rock boulder as the capstone for a monument, simply propping it up where it was. I do not disagree with the idea of people lifting up and displaying large impressive stones such as the capstone at Goward, indeed I suggested this elsewhere (Cummings and Whittle 2004, chapter 7). However, people still had a choice as to *which* stone they decided to turn into a monument. Even nowadays when much of the landscape has been improved with major stone clearing activity, many suitable stones can be found in the landscape. I would argue that this stone was converted from a natural place, perhaps already redolent with meaning, into a monument, because it fitted the pattern: it was in the 'right place' for a chambered tomb.

The Mournes are certainly the most impressive mountain range in the area but other mountains are visible from early Neolithic sites. The distinctive domed profile of Slieve Gullion is visible from 42% of sites. At Ballykeel in Co. Armagh, for example, this mountain is visible, and again the monument is

Figure 7.14.
Ballykeel,
Co. Armagh

Figure 7.15.
Ballymacdermot,
Co. Armagh

not 'pointing' at this feature, but visible to one side of the long cairn axis (Fig. 7.14). Slieve Gullion continued to be a significant locale in the middle Neolithic, when a large passage grave was constructed on its summit. 30% of sites have views of Carlingford Mountain, and 24% have views of Black Mountain. Black Mountain again was elaborated in the middle Neolithic with the construction of a passage grave on its summit. One of the most spectacular sites setting-wise is the court cairn at Ballymacdermot in Co. Armagh (Fig. 7.15). This court cairn is orientated north-south, so that when you are standing in the façade looking into the chambers and down the length of the cairn, there are spectacular views. The

*Figure 7.16.
Kilfeaghan,
Co. Down*

site is located on the lowest slope of Ballymacdermot Mountain on the edge of the cultivated land. The view from the west to the east is entirely restricted, but from east to west there are wide views of the Mournes, Carlingford Mountain, Black Mountain and Slieve Gullion. It seems that the arc of the court is echoed in the arc of mountains beyond.

Amongst this group, a view out over the sea occurs at 41% of sites, and as such, does not seem to have been as significant as a view of mountains. Many of the sites in this group are located many kilometres inland and thus a seaview might have been harder to obtain. At Ravenspark court cairn, Co. Louth, however, even though the site is 7km from the coast, there is a view of the sea. Here the monument is carefully set part way up the side of a hill with the long cairn orientated towards down towards the sea. From this site there are also views of Slieve Gullion and the Black Mountain. There are also a number of sites clustered on the shores of Carlingford Lough. A number of early authors identified this as an area of enclosed and calm water, an ideal area for seacraft to land (e.g. Piggott 1954). In particular a number of sites are found on the stretch between Killowen Point and Mill Bay: this type of landscape is favoured by builders of chambered tombs throughout the Irish Sea zone: low-lying land set between the mountains and sea. One of these sites, Kilfeaghan, is a dolmen with an associated long cairn (Fig. 7.16). The cairn is orientated on the local topography, so that on approach to the entrance to the chamber, and following the long axis of the cairn, the sea (Carlingford Lough) is visible behind the monument, with the Mournes to the left (east) and Carlingford Mountain to the right (west).

The chambered tombs of this region are very similar indeed to those of western Scotland in terms of form (see chapter 4), but the landscape is rather different. Western Scotland is a landscape of lochs and firths, but very few exist in this part of Ireland and I would argue that here there was less emphasis on the sea and movement by boat, and more emphasis on terrestrial-based communities. This may explain the presence of mountain views from sites: these would have been key features in the landscape for orientating oneself and moving around the landscape. Interestingly here there is little difference in the setting of court cairns and portal dolmens: in fact in a number of cases, dolmens seem to have been 'paired up' with court cairns, located only a short distance (less than 1km) from each other. Likewise, the court cairns are often found in clusters giving the impression that particular zones in the landscape were considered appropriate for the construction of megalithic architecture. Many of these monuments also seem to have been carefully orientated so that mountains were visible in one direction only, or to mirror the architecture of the monument itself.

Summary of the sites
- The key locational factor with this cluster of sites is their vicinity to, and views out over, mountains
- Monuments are usually carefully positioned in the landscape so that the views of mountains are 'presented' to people in a particular way, either to one side of the cairn, or so that there is a wide arc of mountain vistas present
- Some sites are located so that there were views of the sea, and the potential importance of Carlingford Lough should also be noted.

Glens of Antrim
Antrim is a very different landscape to that of the Mournes and Carlingford. The glens of Antrim are much gentler and rounded than the peaks of the Mournes: under the classification system used in this book many of the Antrim glens count as mountains, and in fact this is reflected in the topographic names (e.g. Cushleake Mountain). The big difference, though, is the nature of the coastline itself. Around the Mournes, there is a strip of land, between the mountains and the sea, which is low-lying and agricultural. There is no comparable strip in Antrim, instead much of the coastline is rocky and steep, with cliffs bordering straight onto the sea and thus often unsuitable for occupation or agriculture. There are a few safe natural landing places that would have been suitable for small craft: Cushendun, Cushendall, Carnlough and Ballycastle all have modern settlements with harbours, but otherwise the coastline is quite rugged.

There are a total of 29 sites in County Antrim as a whole (Fig. 7.17), but

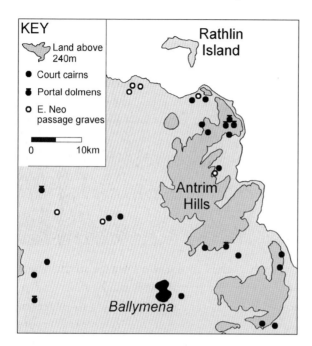

Figure 7.17. The distribution of chambered tombs in the Glens of Antrim

three of these are found close to the River Bann and share similarities not with the Glens of Antrim 'set', but those in neighbouring County Derry, also found along the River Bann. A fourth is an outlier close to Belfast. That leaves us with a discrete set of 25 sites, which comprise 16 court cairns, four dolmens and five early Neolithic passage graves. Just like the monuments around the Mournes and Carlingford, these monuments all have views of mountains. No one single mountain seems to have been visible from all sites, and this is perhaps because these mountains are less visually impressive in the landscape than their counterparts further south. One mountain does have a particularly distinctive profile and that is Slemish, a distinctive volcanic plug with steep cliffs. At Ticloy, the dolmen is set 6.5km away from Slemish to the north, there are clear views of this mountain (Fig. 7.18). Indeed, the profile of Slemish is so distinctive that it is possible to spot it immediately when moving around this part of Antrim. One can only assume people in the Neolithic also used this mountain for navigation.

Two parts of Antrim were also used as a stone axe source in the Neolithic: Tievebulliagh and Rathlin Island produced thousands of stone axes (Cooney 2000, 202–3 and see chapter 3). Tievebulliagh is another very distinctive mountain in Antrim, with a severe steep eastern side where one can still see rivers of scree from Neolithic stone working running down the hillside. There were only two early Neolithic chambered tombs built in the vicinity of this

Figure 7.18. Ticloy,
Co. Antrim

mountain, and one, Ossian's Grave, has been placed in the landscape so that there
are views of Kintyre instead (see below). However, from Cloughs court cairn,
Tievebulliagh is visible on the horizon. I was surprised by this, and expected
that perhaps such a significant mountain in the Neolithic would have been more
visible from a number of sites in the area, but there are a number of factors
to consider here. Much of the general area around Tievebulliagh is not typical
of the type of location chosen for chambered tomb construction (see previous
chapter). We might also envisage only a small number of people utilising the
nearby area (around Cushendall), hence the presence of only two chambered
tombs. Furthermore, stone axe manufacture elsewhere in the Irish Sea zone,
most notably at Langdale, did not commence until after 3600 BC (Bradley and
Edmonds 1993), and we would envisage these early Neolithic chambered tombs
predating that. Thus it may not have been a particularly significant mountain
when these monuments were constructed.

While few sites are located close to Tievebulliagh, seven sites have views out
over Rathlin Island, although no monuments are actually found in the island
itself. Instead, monuments are found in clusters along the northern shores of
Antrim, firstly around Larry Bane Head and also around Benmore Head. These
are not the only sites located so that there are views of islands or distant places.
Ballyvoy court cairn is located with views out to Islay. In fact there are views
out to Scotland from at least six sites. I have already mentioned Ossian's Grave,
located a few kilometres inland from Cushendall. This site is very carefully placed
in the landscape so that there are views out towards Kintyre. When standing at
the site, there are views down Glencorp to the north-east. Beyond this valley
a small part of the Irish Sea can be seen, with Kintyre in the background (Fig.
7.19). Scotland can also be seen to the east, where there are further views of

*Figure 7.19.
Ossian's Grave,
Co. Antrim*

the sea and Mainland Scotland. The reason this view out from the chambered tomb seems so deliberate is that if the site had been positioned just a few metres downslope from its current location, the views out to the sea and Scotland would no longer be visible. In this way, this site, and others with views of Scotland, are making reference to a wider Irish Sea world.

I also want to briefly mention four sites in this area which illustrate a rather different point with regards landscape. There are three dolmen sites and a court cairn, all by the name of Ballyvennaght, found on the plateau between Cushleake Mountain North and Cushleake Mountain South. Two of these sites are within 500m of Loughareema, the Vanishing Lake. Due to the underlying geology, this lough fills with water from the surrounding streams, only to drain away and disappear, hence its name. The reason the lough now forms is that its drainage hole is bunged with peat, and it takes time for the water to drain through this. It is hard to know whether this lough would therefore have been present in the Neolithic: peat typically begins to form in the Bronze Age, although it did form in some places in the Neolithic (Richard Tipping *pers. comm.*). It is the kind of landscape feature, though, that surely would have attracted myths in the Neolithic, and that as archaeologists we sometimes struggle to identify. A lake that appears and disappears may be a rare thing, but ethnography tells us of stones that move around the landscape (Kahn 1990), trees that are connected to the underworld (see Bradley 2000a), and other features which may have appeared magical or special. It often strikes me that trees would have been particularly potent symbols in the Neolithic (Rival 1998; Tilley 2007). There is now a literature which talks about the impermanence of wood as compared

Figure 7.20.
Ballyvennaugh,
Co. Antrim

with stone (e.g. Parker Pearson and Ramilisonina 1998), and this has been related in particular to late Neolithic monumentality (the idea that wood is impermanent and connected to the living, in contrast with stone which is durable and connected to the dead). In terms of people's lives, however, trees would have been very durable places in the landscape, especially mature trees such as oaks that were found throughout most of the British Isles. Would people have actually perceived trees growing in their lifetimes? Perhaps not in the case of large mature trees. Would these large trees really have been thought of as impermanent and temporary? Stone of course could be impermanent: it can be quarried, moved around and ultimately destroyed in the same way as wood: with fire. Outcrops of rock may well have been significant locales in the Neolithic, but I would argue trees would have been as well. Sadly, it is this kind of relationship that we will probably never to be able to get at archaeologically, and one that must remain conjecture only.

The landscape at Ballyvennaugh I dolmen in particular reinforced the point that many of the landscapes I visited have changed radically since the Neolithic. A few sites in the study area as a whole are now surrounded by housing, but much of this is modern, and even photos from 50 years ago show these sites set in the open. But at Ballyvennaugh, two of the dolmens are now rather difficult to find, because since their construction, peat has formed across the entire landscape. These monuments have been, in recent times, cut from the peat (Fig. 7.20), and it is a timely reminder that the peaty moorland within which these sites are now found would have been completely different in the Neolithic. The peat has essentially covered the essence of the land: outcrops,

Figure 7.21.
Ballynamona,
Co. Waterford

gullies, streams, palaeochannels: only the landscape in its barest form exists here now. Views of mountains, of sea, of islands and of distant places may well only be half the story.

Summary of the sites
– Just as with the Mournes and the Carlingford group, these monuments are located close to, and with views out over, mountains and hills
– A number of sites (70%) have views of the sea and also out to Scotland, showing this group was tied to the wider Irish Sea zone
– Eight sites also have views of islands: Rathlin Island and Islay.

The dolmens of south-east Ireland
This group of monuments is quite special for a number of different reasons. Firstly, they are spread out across south-east Ireland (see Fig. 6.13), in contrast to the density of monuments in the north-east and in western Scotland. Secondly, all but one of this group of 27 monuments are portal dolmens, with just one solitary court cairn: this is in direct contrast to the situation in the north-east of Ireland where the majority of sites are court cairns. Thirdly, while these sites are loosely found on the shores of the Irish Sea, they do not command views out to sea. Only two sites have sea views, in remarkable contrast to the rest of the Irish Sea zone group (see previous chapter). Amongst this group the site of Howth has views out to sea: this dolmen is located on the Howth peninsula, attached to Dublin proper by a thin finger of land. The other site with sea views

*Figure 7.22.
Kiltiernan,
Co. Dublin*

is the only court cairn in the area, Ballynamona Lower in County Waterford. This site has spectacular views out over the Irish Sea as it is situated above the cliffs on Mine Head and has commanding views of both mountains and sea (Fig. 7.21). At the remainder of the sites, even though in close proximity to the sea, there are not views out to the sea. Instead, the focus is inland, and like many chambered tombs in the Irish Sea zone, there are views of distant mountains. Indeed, this disparate group of dolmens cluster around the few mountains ranges in the south-east, again with notable blanks in the distribution where there are no mountains. Instead, monuments cluster around the Wicklow Mountains in the north of the area (just south of Dublin), and the Blackstairs Mountains and the Comeragh Mountains further south. Sites seem to have been very carefully positioned so that these mountains are visible on the horizon.

Many of these monuments are massive and impressive structures. Two sites just south of Dublin (Brennanstown and Kiltiernan) are incredibly large dolmens, utilising massive capstones in their construction (Fig. 7.22). In both cases here, and as we shall see at many other sites in this area, this means that the monument is actually located in a fairly secluded location: tucked away on the edge of a hillside just a short distance from a stream. At Brennanstown, the stream can clearly be heard from the dolmen itself, even though it cannot be seen (due to dense overgrown vegetation in this area). Both sites are quite hard to locate in the landscape and neither are now, or would have been, visually prominent sites.

These two sites are located in the landscape in very similar ways to many sites in this group. Firstly, there is the location close to a stream. This relationship has

Figure 7.23.
Ballyquin,
Co. Waterford

been noted before (see O'Nualláin 1983) and is very obvious when visiting a site. Some of these streams are quite small (Fig. 7.23), but others are larger tributaries of Rivers, such as Killonerry, which is close to the River Lingain which joins the major River Suir. We must of course be aware that many of these waterways may have changed their course over time, but even if that is the case, there would still have been a general connection between these sites and streams. By the very nature of being located close to streams, these sites are also frequently tucked away in fairly secluded locations, found at the bottom of hills. Even with a map, these sites are hard to find, and one gets the strong impression that in the past, people would have needed specialist knowledge in order to locate these sites. In a number of instances one could easily pass very close to a site without knowing it was there. This is somewhat in contrast to many other early Neolithic chambered tombs which stand out more prominently in the landscape (i.e. they are visible in the surrounding area). Nevertheless, the builders of these sites found locations where there were views of mountains. At most sites, the location of the site means that there is a wide view of mountains, but these only appear in one direction on the skyline at a distance. These views of mountains are not as striking as the views of mountains amongst the north-east dolmens and court cairns. Only one site seems to have been placed in relation to a visually striking mountain: Glaskenny in County Wicklow has spectacular views of Great Sugar Loaf Mountain which is prominent on the skyline (Fig. 7.24).

A few sites seem to have been located in relation to other landscape features.

Figure 7.24.
Glaskenny,
Co. Wicklow

Figure 7.25.
Knockeen,
Co. Waterford

This is most striking at Knockeen in County Waterford (Fig. 7.25) where the very distinctive double capstone dolmen is positioned in the landscape just a short distance from the distinctive outcrop of Sugar Loaf Rock (Fig. 7.26). The position of chambered tombs in relation to outcrops is found elsewhere in the study area: in west Wales, dolmens are located with striking views of outcrops

Figure 7.26. Sugar Loaf Rock near Knockeen

(see Cummings and Whittle 2004), and similar relationships have been noted elsewhere (Bradley 1998b; Tilley 1996b). There may well be something about portal dolmens in particular which had a particular resonance with outcrops. Elsewhere I have argued that people may not have full understood the difference between what we would call natural places and humanly-made constructions (see Cummings 2002a), and the ambiguity between natural and built places may have meant that outcrops were frequently named and significant places in the landscape (indeed, there is a wealth of ethnographic literature about the potential significance of outcrops: again see Cummings and Whittle 2004, chapter 7). Uniquely to dolmens, with their massive outcrop-like capstones, there may have been a strong connection between these and their unaltered counterparts, part of the set of sites within a single landscape.

Many of the sites in south-east Ireland are now in or on the edge of agricultural land. Indeed, many of these dolmens have actually been incorporated into field boundaries. Some sites now sit in rather sad isolation in the middle of fields (Fig. 7.27), and one gets the sense that we are missing something here. The fact that sites are in agricultural land means that the land has probably been improved: stones may been moved, and knolls potentially ploughed out. I have already mentioned the presence of trees in the past, obviously now long gone, which may well have been a key element in the positioning of sites in the landscape. Another element missing from the puzzle in most areas is the location of settlements. Were any of these monuments built in relation to where people at the time, or had previously, lived? There may well have been connections which we now struggle to identify archaeologically, or where very detailed fieldwork is required to illicit such relationships. We are frustrated further in the case of these dolmens as they very rarely survive with their chamber contents intact,

Figure 7.27.
Glencloughlea,
Co. Kilkenny

so we can say little about the people who built them or broader connections in terms of artefacts or traditions of practice.

What is clear, though, is that the builders of these sites knew their landscape. They positioned sites close to streams and tucked out of easy sight, but still with the broader visual references of mountains, the mountains tying people into a broader world. Unlike the western Scottish set, though, there is no sense of these places being tied to the sea: indeed, these dolmens, even when located close to the coast, seem to avoid a view of the sea. This contrasts with the dolmens of Wales, and indeed the other early Neolithic chambered tombs of the Irish Sea zone in general.

Conclusion

Here I have discussed in detail the landscape setting of five different clusters of early Neolithic chambered tombs in western Scotland and eastern Ireland. These discussions can also be added to the discussion of the settings of sites in Wales (in Cummings and Whittle 2004, chapters 4, 5 and 6). We have seen in the previous chapter how early Neolithic monuments in the Irish Sea zone share many similarities with regards their setting in the landscape, specifically in relation to which parts of the landscape were chosen for monumental construction, and which parts of the landscape were visible from these locales. These overarching themes were then played out slightly differently in specific parts of the Irish Sea zone. At some sites there was an emphasis on waterways, which I have argued were used extensively for transport in the Neolithic, and may potentially have been a critical part of the use of these sites as well. A connection with waterways seems to have been particularly resonant with the western Scottish sites, which are found around the lochs and islands of the area. In north-east Ireland on the other hand, the single most significant landscape feature visible from the sites was mountains. In south-east Ireland, while monuments were still constructed so that there were views of mountains, more localised features such as streams and outcrops seem to have been of particular significance.

That monuments in different parts of the Irish Sea zone emphasise some components of a broader suite of landscape settings more than others is perhaps not surprising if we consider the distances involved here. Communities in western Scotland were a long way from those in south-east Wales. Even within western Scotland, for example, there may well have been a diverse range of communities. In the next and final chapter, I go on to consider what a study of these chambered tombs and their landscape settings can tell us about the nature of the Neolithic, the types of communities that might have lived on the shores of the Irish Sea, and place all of this into a broader British, Irish and European context.

The meaning of megaliths and the Neolithic of the Irish Sea zone: conclusions

Introduction

In this chapter I will return to a number of key issues raised elsewhere in the volume. In particular I want to consider the significance of the settings of chambered tombs across the Irish Sea zone, tying together different elements discussed throughout the volume, specifically the setting of chambered tombs, the architecture of chambered tombs and the material culture found in chambered tombs. Furthermore, these observations then need to be placed into the wider Neolithic context discussed in chapter 3. I also want to consider what this study can tell us about what went before (i.e. the Mesolithic-Neolithic transition) and also what happened afterwards, thinking in particular about the long term trajectory of the Neolithic in the Irish Sea zone. Finally, this study has, in many ways, highlighted how little we actually know about this crucial period of prehistory, so I outline some of the issues we might wish to address in the future.

The Mesolithic background and the transition to the Neolithic

When I started this research over ten years ago I hoped a consideration of the chambered tombs of the Irish Sea zone might be able to further our understanding of the Mesolithic-Neolithic transition. Since then, a number of things have convinced me that studying these chambered tombs may not be as useful as I had hoped in considering the transition. We know that Neolithic things appear everywhere around about 4000 BC in Britain and Ireland, but the very earliest of the chambered tombs in this area are likely to date to 3800 BC. 200 years is not very much time archaeologically, but in terms of people's lives, it is a long period of time indeed. People may well have been keeping domesticated animals, growing new domesticated plant species and making pottery (as well as making and exchanging polished stone axes) for 12 generations or more before they even began building chambered tombs. Furthermore, 3800 BC is the earliest date for the construction of these sites (made by analogy with the sites in southern Britain: Bayliss and Whittle 2007): the reality is that many of the chambered tombs in the Irish Sea zone may well have been built between 3700–3600 BC. When I originally thought about the transition, a few hundred years did not seem that long, but the more I think about it, I am increasingly convinced that this is too long a period of time for any meaningful insights to be made from this evidence alone.

While a study of the chambered tombs of the Irish Sea zone may not be able to directly inform discussions on the nature of the Mesolithic-Neolithic transition, I do think that we can look at these issues in terms of long term sets of ideas or practices. In chapter 2 I outlined the evidence from the late Mesolithic. In particular, I wanted to see if there were any hints of a worldview or mindset in the late Mesolithic which may have had an impact on the subsequent introduction and development of the Neolithic. Was there anything present in the late Mesolithic which might explain why and how people adopted the Neolithic, and why some people eventually ended up constructing chambered tomb architecture? A study of the late Mesolithic highlights a few key issues. Firstly, people were developing, and in some cases had developed, very strong connections to place (and see Cobb 2008). This was not just in terms of which parts of the landscape were used for settlement, but also which types of landscape people utilised. In western Scotland that was clearly the coastal zone, the islands and the lochs. In Ireland there seems to have been a closer link with mountains and rivers. As we saw in chapter 6, these are a crucial component of the setting of subsequent chambered tombs. The late Mesolithic also saw a practice which clearly continued into the early Neolithic and through to the construction and use of the chambered tombs. This relates to the fragmentation and deposition of material substances. Although by the time that chambered tombs were constructed the medium had changed (i.e. which materials were manipulated, fragmented and then deposited), the processes seem to have remained the same. People were essentially citing other events, other people and other places in their use and deposition of material objects.

In a previous volume I argued for continuity between the late Mesolithic and the early Neolithic, suggesting that in western Britain at least, there was no major influx of people at the start of the Neolithic (Cummings and Whittle 2004, chapter 7). Instead it was argued that the native Mesolithic populations were those who 'went over' to the Neolithic (cf. Whittle and Cummings 2007). I would still argue that this was the case throughout western Britain and also in Ireland, although I would now suggest that there was some small-scale movement of people from the Continent. I wonder if one of the mechanisms for the introduction of Neolithic things into Britain was the reforging of exchange networks between western

Britain, Ireland and the Continent? Throughout the volume I have highlighted the idea that these were mobile maritime-based communities (in both the late Mesolithic and early Neolithic), for whom moving considerable differences across water was almost certainly not a problem. The Mesolithic-Neolithic transition may have come about quite simply through the creation, recreation or slight alteration of social networks between different communities in this area. I have argued before, and I maintain here, that the initial introduction of Neolithic things did not suddenly change these communities from hunting and gathering communities to 'farmers', certainly in terms of how people thought about the world. Instead, domesticated plants and animals were simply fitted into ways of engaging with the environment which already existed (cf. Kent 1989). Pottery and polished stone tools were simply more objects fitted into the suite of objects which already existed and which were understood within pre-existing frameworks. It was only long term that these things started to have an impact on the way in which people understood their world. The start of the change seems to have come a few hundred years later with the sudden, but widespread, construction of chambered tombs, which I will now go on to discuss in more detail. I just want to stress here that the evidence from the very late Mesolithic and very earliest Neolithic remains frustratingly sparse, and so at present we are restricted in what we can say about this crucial period of time. Ideally, we want fine-grained detail from sites covering the date 4200–3800 BC which would enable us to have a much better context against which to place the initial construction of the chambered tombs of the Irish Sea zone around 3800 BC. This must be one of the goals of future research in this area.

The settings of the chambered tombs in their wider context

I want to move on now to consider the chambered tombs themselves. We have considered different aspects of these monuments throughout this volume: their architectural form, their landscape setting and the material substances used to construct them and deposited in them. I now want to consider all of these things together. One of the most surprising elements of this research has been how similar these sites are, not just in terms of their architecture, but in terms of how they were used and where they were located. Early Neolithic chambered tombs across wide areas of Britain share many key features. Firstly, as we have seen they share many *architectural similarities*. Throughout this study area there are only three dominant architectural traditions: dolmens (west Wales, eastern Ireland), the old Clyde-Carlingford culture (the court cairns of eastern Ireland and the Clyde cairns of western Scotland), and the small early passage graves, the latter, I have argued, to be included with the dolmen group. These monuments do exhibit some small regional differences in architectural form, however considering the distances involved, they remain remarkably similar across such a wide area. Similarities in monument form across the Irish Sea zone are particularly noticeable if you engage with the site instead of looking at plans. One wonders whether Neolithic people were concerned with precise architectural detail, or whether they were more concerned with the overall effect. The *experience* of encountering and engaging with a court cairn in Ireland or a Clyde monument in Scotland is actually very similar, where people would encounter a stone-built and defined forecourt leading to divided chambers. It is also significant that the *finds* from these sites are also very similar. Chambered tombs more or less ubiquitously seem to have been used for the deposition of human bone and other artefacts including burnt material. In many cases it is also notable that objects deposited in the megaliths have come from distant places. On top of this, as I outlined in chapter 6, the *settings of these monuments* are also remarkably similar across massive areas. Sites repeatedly have views of mountains, of water, the sea, rivers and lochs, and are set on the side of hills. Monuments are also carefully orientated and positioned in the landscape. The *experience* of the landscape at these sites is therefore very similar throughout the Irish Sea zone. Using and engaging with these megaliths, then, in terms of both architecture and the surrounding landscape may well have created remarkably similar engagements with place, whether in western Scotland, west Wales or north-east Ireland.

The fact that these monuments are architecturally very similar is interesting, but perhaps not exceptional. After all, as we saw in chapter 3, other forms of early Neolithic material culture such as carinated bowls are found across wide areas of Britain. It is perhaps also not surprising that monuments seem to have been used in similar ways, hence their broader name of burial chambers or chambered tombs. However, it is unlikely that these sites were used exclusively for the burial of the dead, with other aspects of their use being equally, if not more important. These were places for the meeting and gathering of people, for feasting, for rites perhaps connected with transformations in the lifecycle and for the manipulation of material culture and personal identity. I think it is more unexpected, however, that megaliths are found in virtually identical parts of the landscape, and I have argued here that the precise location of sites was both an intrinsic part of monument itself and that these particular places in the landscape were fundamentally connected to the identity and use of the sites. It seems that these places and these places alone were appropriate for megalithic construction. So what we have are people across these massive swathes of western Britain and eastern Ireland, *deliberately* and *knowingly* building monuments in

Figure 8.1. Craig, Co. Antrim, with views out over the Irish Sea

very similar ways and in similar parts of the landscape. They were creating places that enabled people to have very similar encounters with these monuments even though they were in quite different parts of the Neolithic world. So what does all this tell us about the early Neolithic in this area?

It is possible to suggest that megaliths share so many similarities in use, form *and* location that they were constructed by people who were in contact and aiming to produce similar monuments. Another observation which adds currency to this argument is that many sites are positioned so that there are views of this wider Irish Sea zone itself. A number of sites have views of distant landmasses, so for example sites in south-west Scotland have views of the Isle of Man, chambered tombs in western Scotland have views of Ireland, and sites in Ireland have views of Scotland. Many sites seem to have been deliberately positioned so these views were present. At Ossian's Grave in County Antrim, for example, the monument is built so that Kintyre is visible on the horizon (Fig. 7.19). A few metres downslope and this view would be gone. Another example, Blasthill on Kintyre, is carefully positioned so that Arran is visible in one direction and northern Ireland in the other (Fig. 7.2). Elsewhere I have also argued that the views of mountains from the megaliths also creates wider connections across the wider Irish Sea world (Cummings 2004). From the mountains which are visible from the megaliths, it is possible to see other parts of the Irish Sea world which themselves have concentrations of megaliths. The intervisibility of the mountains of the Irish Sea zone, which are the focus for megalithic construction, means people could literally see other parts of the Irish Sea world (Fig. 8.1). And as we have already seen, many monuments have views over the Irish Sea itself.

Could this mean that these monuments represent a broader sense of identity created and shared across this entire area? Could it be that the beginning of the

Neolithic saw the emergence of a new identity which was focussed on the Irish Sea zone? Could it suggest that the beginning of the Neolithic was something that happened around the whole of the Irish Sea area in a very similar way? Are these megaliths representative perhaps of an incoming population, with a common origin point, which explains why people from western Scotland to south-west Wales to eastern Ireland knew how and where to build their megaliths?

One argument might be that these monuments represent, if you like, an ideological reaction to the change from a Mesolithic way of life to a Neolithic life, simplistically, a change from hunting and gathering, to keeping domesticates and having pottery. As we have already seen, this is not a reaction to the transition itself, which happened a few hundred years prior to the construction of chambered tombs, but a reaction to a process which had already happened. The construction of chambered tombs, then, may well have been the delayed result of something which had already happened, what we now call the Mesolithic-Neolithic transition. In the few hundred years since this transition, which involved all the elements of the Neolithic *except* monument construction, communities may well have been involved in quite critical reconsiderations of themselves, their communities and their place in the world. Around about 3800 BC it suddenly became important to construct chambered tombs, bury the dead and compose and deposit suites of material culture at these places.

It may be slightly problematic, however, to suggest that we are looking at a single Irish Sea wide community building these monuments. Firstly, the similarity of setting and form over a massive area does not mean that these people were part of the same cultural group with a shared cultural identity. Firstly, it has been shown that the presence of shared material culture does not delineate cultural groups (Hodder 1986). Secondly, megalithic construction does not happen everywhere within the study area. It was not ubiquitous and all embracing. As already noted there are blanks in the distribution and as already suggested it may be that it was only appropriate to build megaliths in very specific places within the landscape which these blank areas do not have. This suggests a few hundred years *after* the introduction of domesticates and new material culture there was a *reaction* which was widespread and dramatic. People around specific parts of the Irish Sea seem to have deliberately constructed monuments in very similar ways and in similar parts of the landscape. One argument might be that whatever the nature of the original *transition*, the *reaction* was shared and repeated across a wide area. Perhaps megaliths were the result of realising that the world had changed and moved on. Perhaps megaliths were part of a process of creating a new sense of identity, the desire to feel part of a broader Neolithic community. Perhaps this was particularly resonant in areas which had a very rich, yet very specific, landscape mythology.

An Irish Sea community?

Is it really possible that the people who built the chambered tombs of the Irish Sea zone were aware of what was going on within this wider area? A first consideration of this seems that this is unlikely: how could small-scale communities tied to particular parts of the country have a detailed knowledge of the Irish Sea zone? However, there are different stands of evidence which suggests that this may well have been possible. Firstly, I have argued throughout this book that we are dealing with maritime communities who were focussed on the sea, rivers and lochs, especially in western Britain. While they may not have been eating much, if any, fish (cf. Schulting and Richards 2002b), I have argued that people were moving around by boat and that the sea played an important role in their lives. This is demonstrated by the movement of materials across the Irish Sea throughout the Neolithic as well as from the location of the chambered tombs. Maritime communities would not have found it difficult to move around quite broad areas, especially those bordering the Irish Sea. There may well have been very strong connections between groups of people either side of the Irish Sea, especially in the northern part of this area (i.e. western Scotland and eastern Ireland).

Secondly, the Irish Sea zone is rather unique in the sense that the entire area is intervisible from certain points in the landscape (see above and Cummings 2004). It is the mountains of the Irish Sea zone which are intervisible across the water, so that it is possible to see distant landmasses across the sea. Snowdon is the one mountain from which you can see the most distant mountains around the Irish Sea zone, and from its summit on a clear day you can see south Wales, south-east Ireland, north-east Ireland, the Isle of Man, Cumbria and south-west Scotland (Fig. 8.2). Other parts of the Irish Sea zone are intervisible, and in many areas one does not need to even be on a mountain to see out across this area, such as on the Isle of Man or in Kintyre. Quite simply, the Irish Sea zone is visible to people standing on its shores. This indicates knowledge of that wider area.

Moreover, the movement of materials across the Irish Sea is clearly evidenced in stone (axes, Antrim flint, Arran pitchstone: Fig. 8.3), but may well have also involved the movement of perishable goods too, including everything from food to animals to organic material culture. What is intriguing about the exchange or movement of lithics is that the sources of stone which were transported across the Irish Sea were often visually very distinctive stones, and it has been suggested that people may well have known about the origin of these stones (cf. Bradley 2000a). If people understood that Langdale stone came from Cumbria and

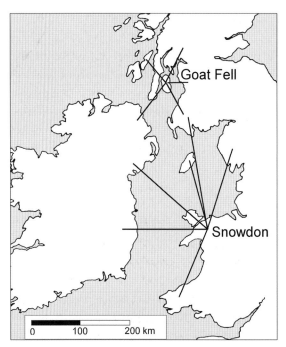

Figure 8.2. The intervisibility of the Irish Sea zone, from Snowdon and Goat Fell

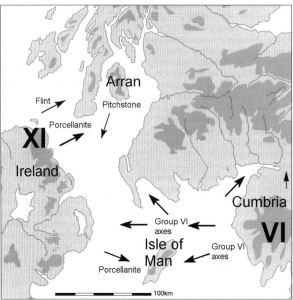

Figure 8.3. The movement of materials in the northern Irish Sea zone (after Cooney 2000)

Arran pitchstone from Arran, particular objects may well have been understood as pieces of distant places, as well as being tied up with object and individual's biographies. Knowledge of the wider Irish Sea zone, therefore, may also have been widely understood and accessible through material culture. We can see this with stone objects, but another intriguing possibility involves animals. We know that domesticated animals were introduced into Britain and Ireland at the start of the Neolithic, and that some wild animals were also introduced into Ireland at the beginning of the Neolithic. Clearly people had to ability to move animals around by sea. There is the possibility that animals were exchanged along with stone, meaning that herds (along with meat and milk and other animal products) may well have also represented different places. This would add a further resonance in Ireland in relation to the wild species introduced in the Neolithic. We must also consider people moving around the Irish Sea zone as marriage partners, so that entire communities were composed of different people and places.

In fact, we must consider the possibility that entire communities were mobile in the Neolithic. Although there are examples of houses in the Neolithic (see chapter 3), these remain fairly exceptional and frequently short-lived and I think we can envisage people moving around quite a bit at this time, probably moving with their herds. Of course, people would have had a choice concerning their mobility patterns, and it is as likely that people moved for trade, exchange, social reasons or spiritual reasons as for purely 'practical' reasons. There may well have been a 'mobility ethos', which has been documented with hunter-gatherer groups (cf. Kelly 1995, chapter 4) and this may well still have been relevant to these early farming groups. There may well have been a strong desire to travel around and to have knowledge of the wider area and the peoples in it. Some members of the community may have moved around more than others, and we should be careful not to assume that everyone in the Neolithic had the same mobility patterns as others throughout space and time. Nevertheless, I think we could argue that people actually had an extensive knowledge of quite a wide area. In some cases, individuals or whole communities may have moved around this area.

If this were the case, it is also interesting and relevant to discuss broad trends across this area. Very generally, the Irish Sea zone seems to be split into three zones, where people did similar things across a wide area over time. As we have seen, in north-east Ireland and western Scotland there is excellent evidence in the early Neolithic for widespread and extensive construction of chambered tomb architecture. From an early stage, there also seems to have been the exchange of lithics, especially fragmentary and small (token) pieces such as Arran pitchstone. Here then, people either side of the Irish Sea zone shared the desire to construct large numbers of chambered tombs. This is in stark contrast to the middle Irish Sea zone area, Cumbria and Lancashire to the east and central-eastern Ireland to the west. In the early Neolithic in these areas people did not build chambered tombs and I have argued that this was because there were not the 'correct' sets of landscape features in these areas. It may also have been the case that chambered tomb architecture did not resonant here as it did in other parts of Britain and Ireland. What is interesting is that these two areas of the Irish Sea zone see an explosion of activity in the middle Neolithic: in Cumbria the intensification of the Langdale axe factory and in County Meath, the construction of the Bru na Boinne complex. The bottom third of the Irish Sea zone was a different sequence again. Here in south-east Ireland and west Wales people did build monuments in the early Neolithic, but these were dolmens dispersed thinly in the landscape. In south-east Ireland as well, people seem to have been very actively ignoring the sea. These very broad zones across this wide area may indicate primary zones of contact between communities, or simply areas which shared a common response to the start and subsequent development of the Neolithic.

The Irish Sea: east or west? Sequences and affinities beyond the Irish Sea zone

This very broad-brush patterning within the Irish Sea zone contrasts again with the area beyond the shores of the Irish Sea and it is worth just very briefly mentioning these. Starting in west Wales, if we look to the east of this area (central and east Wales), the most striking thing is the absence of chambered tomb architecture in central Wales. However, there are chambered tombs in east Wales, where the Cotswold-Severn tradition is found (see Cummings and Whittle 2004). The people who built this set of monuments were clearly much more closely connected with eastern Britain, which may well have had a rather different origin and subsequent development than western Britain (see Cummings and Whittle 2004, chapter 7). This may relate, in part, to the landscape, but also the native people and how (and from where) the Neolithic was adopted. If we move up to west Scotland, we can see a similar situation: again there is a blank area to the east of this area where there are no chambered tombs (see Henshall 1972, 28–9). Taking one section of this wider area, south-west Scotland, you can see a similar picture to that in Wales: in western Galloway there are Clyde chambered tombs in the early Neolithic which share similarities with counterparts found in north-east Ireland. However, further east into eastern Dumfries and Galloway there are unchambered long cairns, a couple of wooden structures mortuary structures (Lochhill and Slewcairn) and also wooden 'houses' (Locherbie), all of which are more typically 'eastern' than 'western' (and see Cummings 2002b). Again, we seem to have a situation where there were different traditions between east and west.

Figure 8.4.
Creevykeel,
Co. Sligo

If there were very broadly different traditions in eastern and western Britain, perhaps representative of the different origins of the Neolithic, or perhaps the adoption of the Neolithic by native populations, the situation in Ireland seems rather different. There is a small gap in the distribution of chambered tombs in northern Ireland beyond the Irish Sea, but more widely, chambered tombs were built throughout the northern part of Ireland in the early Neolithic. There are large numbers of court cairns beyond the Irish Sea zone, which immediately contrasts with the situation across the water in western Britain. If it was only appropriate to build Clyde cairns and dolmens on the shores of the Irish Sea in western Britain, this was not the case in the north of Ireland. However, there were differences between the east and west of this area. A number of court cairns in north-west Ireland vary in form, comprising essentially of two court cairns 'stuck' together at the horns to create an central enclosed forecourt area (see de Valera 1960; Fig. 8.4). None of these central court cairns are found in eastern Ireland and they are quite different in form from the single court cairn. This led to considerable debate in the 1950s and 1960s as to the origins of the court cairn in Ireland, with some scholars seeing the first monuments constructed in the east of Ireland and spreading west (e.g. Corcoran 1960; Piggott 1954), and others claiming the first monuments were those built in the west which subsequently spread east (e.g. de Valera 1960). There is now no reason to see either style as derivative of the other, and we are likely looking at the two different styles being constructed simultaneously. Nevertheless, it does demonstrate that there were perhaps two different traditions of construction in Ireland, one in the east and one in the west. This may relate to differences between east and west, of the beginning of the Neolithic, or of native peoples adopting the Neolithic. The difference between Britain and Ireland, however, was that in Ireland, the two 'traditions' were not isolated from one another. Instead, court cairns are found throughout northern

Ireland. Whatever chambered tombs represented here (perhaps again a delayed reaction to the change from the Mesolithic to the Neolithic, or a desire to turn specific places into more permanent locales, or a combination of these and other reasons), they were resonant across a wide area.

The dolmens of south-east Ireland sit somewhat in isolation, in terms of their overall setting as outlined in the previous chapter, but also in terms of megalithic construction in the early Neolithic in southern Ireland more generally. In the north the west coast sees very intensive early Neolithic megalithic construction, even more so than in the east, particularly in the counties of Mayo, Sligo and Leitrim. But in south-west Ireland, especially in counties Kerry, Cork and Limerick, there are very few known early Neolithic chambered tombs. Clearly, then, not everyone in Ireland constructed chambered tombs in the early Neolithic, just as in Britain. It is interesting to note that while the south-east of Ireland saw the construction of chambered tombs in the early Neolithic, the focus of construction shifted to the south-west at a later time, as there are large numbers of wedge tombs known from this area (O'Brien 1993).

From the start of the sequence in Ireland there were small passage graves, a few found in the Irish Sea zone, with others found in other parts of Ireland. Intriguingly, a little later on in the early Neolithic, there was a major shift in focus, away from the construction and use of court cairns and towards the construction of passage graves. Many of these middle Neolithic passage graves in Ireland are fundamentally different from the early Neolithic chambered tombs of the Irish Sea zone: they are constructed in cemeteries. These passage grave clusters essentially converted entire areas into monumental landscapes. Virtually all of the monuments in this study are essentially isolated sites, which in terms of other chambered tombs, means they sit in isolation in the landscape (although how they relate to settlement areas is unknown at this stage). A very small number of sites in the Irish Sea zone were constructed in pairs (a total of 9 in the whole Irish Sea zone), but these are exceptional. Passage grave cemeteries, however, saw the construction of large numbers of monuments in the same landscape (for example, 29 were constructed at Loughcrew, and 60+ at Carrowmore passage grave cemetery). This is a radical departure from the isolated early Neolithic sites in this study, and suggests a fundamental shift in the way that people wanted to build and engage with monumental architecture. Interestingly, as far as our discussion goes here, these passage grave cemeteries are found in most parts of Ireland, although again there are very few in south-west Ireland. As discussed in previous chapters, they were also constructed in parts of the landscape that did not see early Neolithic chambered tomb construction.

All of this suggests that we must not view the Irish Sea zone in isolation.

Although there may well have been strong connections between people and communities across this area, there would almost certainly have been connections with other areas too (with central and eastern Britain, and with central and western Ireland). Furthermore, there seems to have been shifts in focus and intensity across this broad area. This meant that some areas saw early Neolithic chambered tomb construction. Other areas seem to have become appropriate for middle and later Neolithic architecture. It is clear that as the Neolithic progresses, different people came into contact with different ideas and sets of communities. Connections and alliances may well have shifted and changed.

It is interesting to think, not only about chambered tomb construction, but also about other elements of the Neolithic. We know that from about 3600 BC axe production at Langdale seems to have increased considerably (see Bradley and Edmonds 1993). How did this have an impact on communities bordering the Irish Sea zone? Causewayed enclosures and cursus monuments are rarely found in the Irish Sea zone (see chapter 3), perhaps because the sets of ideas bound up with these places were not as relevant to these communities. However, at a later date, stone circles and henge monuments *were* constructed in the Irish Sea zone. Again, these monuments are not found everywhere in the area, but only in specific parts of the landscape. Notable examples and concentrations of these sites are found at Llandegai in north Wales, around Penrith in Cumbria and at Kilmartin in western Scotland. It is also interesting to note that there are notable differences between Britain and Ireland in the long term development of the Neolithic. After the early Neolithic and the mass construction of chambered tombs, western Britain and eastern Ireland seem to follow different trajectories. This may relate to the fact that western Britain had different hunter-gatherer lifeways prior to the start of the Neolithic. The resultant Neolithic was therefore slightly different to that of eastern Ireland.

All of this discussion may seem only relevant to archaeologists looking at the long term picture of the Neolithic over time. However, I would argue that people in the Neolithic would also have had a sense of where they came from, where they fitted in with the broader scheme of things, and a sense of how they wanted to live their lives. This brings me onto another crucial point: how we understand patterning and scale across broad areas.

A note on similarity and difference
For several decades then, post-processual archaeologies have emphasised regional and contextual archaeologies. This is an understandable backlash against the all-embracing and homogenising nature of processual archaeology and earlier culture-historical approaches. On one hand, the search for regional Neolithics

remains theoretically in vogue, while on the other hand it is also inherently practical, as it would be difficult for archaeologists to undertake the kind of detailed contextual studies which are currently popular across anything but small regional areas. As such, scholars are now used to exploring differences in the archaeological record with different regions of Britain and Ireland having different sequences. This must be one of the strengths of a post-processual approach: understanding the nuances of different areas, and what this might have meant for both the beginning and subsequent development of the Neolithic.

However, I would argue that post-processual approaches are less comfortable with understanding *similarity* in the archaeological record. The recent debates on the form of long barrows and stone circles is a good example of this. There is has been some wonderful detailed contextual work on individual long barrows, which draws out the long and complex histories of these sites (Benson and Whittle 2005; McFadyen 2006). Similar work has also been done on stone circles (Richards 2004). While almost all would agree that local biographies, landscapes and mythologies played a crucial role in the creation and use of these sites, there is less agreement about how these sites fit into a broader pattern of monument construction. The final form of the vast majority of Cotswold-Severn long barrows is remarkably similar, an issue discussed in detail in culture-historical and processual archaeological discourse. Likewise, stone circles also share many similarities across wide areas of Britain. Yet there is currently debate about these similarities. Some authors argue that the construction process was ongoing, with the builders having no preconceived plan of the final form of each monument (Barrett 1994; McFadyen 2006; Richards 2004). This is an attractive idea, and works well with regards the earliest phases of long barrows. Furthermore, the importance of the construction process itself should not be underestimated, and the significances assigned to building a monument are critical in gaining a better understanding of these sites. Yet, people were knowingly working towards creating very similar constructions in very similar parts of the landscape. People *did* have a preconceived finished form in mind when constructing long barrows (certainly the later phases of these sites) and stone circles. To deny the similarities between sites across broad areas of the country restricts our understanding of concepts of monumentality.

This is not a return to earlier theoretical paradigms, but is perhaps more to do with issues of scale. I advocate that archaeologists should work at a whole range of different scales. The detailed contextual analysis of individual sites is critical in gaining a better understanding of the lives of people in the Neolithic, and yet that must be combined with patterns observed in wider local, regional and national contexts. Stone circles are roughly circular and made of stone across wide areas of Britain for a reason. Those reasons may be inherently tied to local knowledges, processes, histories and identities, yet drawing on a 'common template' if you like shows knowledge of a wider world as well as the desire to somehow be involved in that wider context. This book, therefore, has attempted not only to explore differences in the Irish Sea zone, but all similarities, and most critically, what those similarities may have represented.

The essence of landscape and substance

We may never really be able to say with any certainty how people in the Neolithic thought about the landscape forms that were visible to them at the chambered tombs. I have suggested throughout this book that people had a particular affinity with particular places in the landscape and these locales may well have played an important role in the world views and belief systems of people in these areas. In particular, I have emphasised the potential role of stories and myths embedded within these landscape features and suggested that they were potent places in terms of mythology and history. I have also argued that the setting of a chambered tomb was as important a part of the site as the stones that made up the chamber. It is tempting to think that similar views from the chambered tombs around the Irish Sea zone meant similar things to people across that area, but it is likely that these features were bound up with localised understandings of landscape. We must not forget that people would have had very particular engagements with these places which would have been an integral part of their lifeways and mobility strategies. What we can suggest, however, is that these places seem to have had an agency which made people do things in very specific ways.

Although I have done this here in order to highlight particular elements in the location of early Neolithic chambered tombs, we should not separate out the landscape from people's engagement with other things. In the same way that landscape structured and was structured by people's engagement with it, the material substances used by people everyday were also cited and recomposed at these specific places in the landscape. Again, then, there seems to have been particular essences within materials or objects which resonated with people in particular ways. I have demonstrated that materials were used in very specific ways in the chambered tombs of the Irish Sea zone. These substances should not be seen as 'offerings ' or 'deposits' created solely for being placed in a chambered tomb. Instead, these things articulated with all other parts of life, just as the landscape was both the medium and outcome of praxis.

Figure 8.5.
Ballybriest, Co.
Derry

   In the early Neolithic of the Irish Sea zone, people seem to have been particularly concerned (or motivated) to turn specific places into tangible things. The process of doing this, I have argued, was all about citing other events, other people and other places. People turned clay into pots, stones into axes, places into monuments and big stones in megaliths. In doing so, people were involved in a dynamic relationship with material substances, substances that were part and parcel of the landscape, not outside or separated from that landscape. Megaliths became places where specific parts of the landscape were cited, fragmented and recomposed. At the same time, a whole range of other substances, places and people were cited, fragmented and recomposed. This was a continual engagement of people, place, substance and form. Essences and identities, notions of belonging and tenure, life and death: these were the things being negotiated and reworked at these places. Landscapes became substances which became things, which were recomposed and deposited at places in the landscape (Fig. 8.5).

   As I outlined above, we are missing here an essential component of this picture: if we had access to all aspects of people's daily lives we would surely be able to further our understanding of how these places fitted into broader cosmological schemes. I go on now to suggest some ways in which we could pursue further research into this area.

The future of studies of the Irish Sea zone

The Irish Sea zone benefits from the large number of well-preserved chambered tombs which have made this study possible. However, while a study of the chambered tombs of the Irish Sea zone in their landscape setting inform us about elements of the Neolithic, there are also shortcomings in looking at this type of evidence only. While I have attempted to locate these monuments within a broader context, it becomes obvious that there are considerable areas of the Irish Sea zone which could benefit from more detailed archaeological investigation. Furthermore, we need to look for specific types of evidence if we are to gain more insights into the beginning and development of the Neolithic in this area.

First, we need some up-to-date excavations of some of the chambered tombs covered in this study. The vast majority of excavations conducted at these sites were done many decades ago, and there have not been many recent explorations utilising the latest techniques. We are also restricted in what we can ascertain from these older excavations: often, material that would have been suitable for radiocarbon dating has not been retained, and artefacts have been conserved so that we are restricted with regards which scientific methods we can use. If we are to conduct modern excavations at these monuments we also need to change our focus on which parts of the monument we explore. In the past there has been the tendency to look at the 'business end', usually involving the excavation of the chambers. This has, of course, produced quantities of material culture which have been very useful in understanding these monuments, but we lack good and detailed understandings of the construction of the cairns themselves and a sense of the broader context in which these monuments sit. This is not to say that the excavation of chambers is not fruitful; in particular, a suite of radiocarbon dates to precisely pinpoint the use of these monuments would be very welcome, to be compared ideally with the recent work on the Cotswold-Severn monuments in southern Britain (Bayliss and Whittle 2007). A high priority, then, is to locate well-preserved but unexcavated chambered tombs in the Irish Sea zone and conduct thorough excavations of the monument and its immediate environs.

Secondly, these monuments also need to be placed in a broader landscape context. I have mentioned throughout this book that we really have no idea how these monuments articulated with settlement activity. Did people live around these monuments or were they isolated in the landscape? Do they relate to earlier settlement activity (i.e. ancestral occupation or previous hunter-gatherer occupations or are they located in relatively virgin parts of the landscape?). How did people occupy the landscape once these sites had been constructed? Is there a similar pattern across the study area or were there different patterns of occupation in different parts of Britain and Ireland? This question is potentially very hard to answer, because of the nature of occupation in the early Neolithic. We are probably looking at being able to obtain lithic scatters only from much of this area, and lithic scatters, while useful in some ways, restrict the types of information that can be gained about settlement activity. The primary problem with lithic scatters is the lack of secure and precise dating of each scatter, and we are therefore restricted to discussing settlement in very broad terms (early or late Neolithic occupation, for example). Unploughed landscapes therefore need to be targeted to look for sites with *in situ* material. This is obviously a difficult and time-consuming task, but one which can potentially provide us with a much more nuanced understanding of these different landscapes and the ways in which people were using them in the Neolithic. Such a project is currently underway with these research questions in mind, in Kintyre, western Scotland (Cummings and Robinson in prep). It would be desirable to see similar detailed landscape projects elsewhere in western Scotland, in Cumbria, in north and south Wales and in north-east and south-east Ireland. With more detailed contextual information we would be able to make more insights into the differences and similarities in these areas in the early Neolithic and place the chambered tombs into a much firmer local, regional and national context.

Thirdly, another area worthy of investigation is a thorough geological investigation of various elements of the Neolithic record of the Irish Sea zone. Geological assessment can almost certainly offer us further insights into the chambered tombs themselves. There are hints that people right from the early Neolithic were moving large stones around (a couple of examples are documented in Wales: see Cummings and Whittle 2004), but a large scale assessment needs to be made of sites across the area. We need to know precisely where the stones came from that were being used to construct the chambered tombs. We also need a geological assessment of various different strands of evidence from both late Mesolithic and early Neolithic contexts, especially relating to lithic sources. We have a good indication of the movement of materials such as Arran pitchstone but a much poorer understanding of the movement of flint. Techniques are now available to enable us to start sourcing flint (Chris Greenwell *pers. comm.*). This work could potentially enable us to see the extent of exchange networks present amongst both late Mesolithic and Neolithic communities, and this may assist us in modelling the connections between groups of people across this time frame. Another project to consider is a detailed consideration of the pottery of the Irish Sea zone. This has been done successfully in Wales (Peterson 2003) but now needs to be done in the wider Irish Sea zone. An important element of this would be an assessment of the inclusions in pottery to ascertain further links and connections across the Irish Sea zone. Ultimately, this will enable us to really get to grips with different scales of interaction between people and enable us to articulate local meanings into the bigger picture.

Bibliography

Aldhouse Green, S. 2000. Palaeolithic and Mesolithic Wales. In F. Lynch, S. Aldhouse-Green and J. Davies, *Prehistoric Wales*, 1–41. Stroud: Sutton.

Armit, I., Murphy, E., Nelis, E. and Simpson, D. (eds) 2003. *Neolithic settlement in Ireland and western Britain*. Oxford: Oxbow.

Ashmore, W. and Knapp, B. 1999. Archaeological landscapes: constructed, conceptualized, ideational. In W. Ashmore and B. Knapp (eds), *Archaeologies of landscape: contemporary perspectives*, 1–30. Oxford: Blackwell.

Bahn, P. 1996. *Cambridge illustrated guide: archaeology*. Cambridge: Cambridge University Press.

Barclay, G., Brophy, K. and MacGregor, G. 2002. Claish, Stirling: a major Neolithic building in context. *Proceedings of the Society of Antiquaries of Scotland* 132, 65–132.

Barker, C. 1992. *The chambered tombs of south-west Wales: a reassessment of the Neolithic burial monuments of Carmarthenshire and Pembrokeshire*. Oxford: Oxbow.

Barrett, J. 1994. *Fragments from antiquity: an archaeology of social life in Britain 2900–1200 BC*. Oxford: Blackwell.

Barton, R., Berridge, P., Walker, M. and Bevins, R. 1995. Persistent places in the Mesolithic landscape: an example from the Black Mountain uplands of south Wales. *Proceedings of the Prehistoric Society* 61, 81–116.

Basso, K. 1984. "Stalking with stories": names, places, and moral narratives among the Western Apache. In E. M. Bruner (ed.), *Text, play and the story: the construction and reconstruction of self and society*, 19–55. Washington DC: Washington DC American Ethnological Society.

Basso, K. 1996. Wisdom sits in places: notes on a Western Apache landscape. In S. Feld and K. Basso (eds), *Senses of places*, 53–90. Santa Fe: School of American Research Press.

Bayliss, A. and Whittle, A. (eds) 2007. Histories of the dead: building chronologies for five southern British long barrows. *Cambridge Archaeological Journal* 17 (S1).

Baynes, N. 1909. The excavation of Lligwy cromlech, in the county of Anglesey. *Archaeologia Cambrensis* 9, 217–31.

Bender, B. (ed.) 1993. *Landscape: politics and perspectives*. Oxford: Berg.

Bender, B. and Winer, M. (eds) 2001. *Contested landscapes: movement, exile and place*. Oxford: Berg.

Benson, D. and Whittle, A. (eds) 2005. *Building memories: the Neolithic Cotswold long barrow at Ascott-under-Wychwood, Oxfordshire*. Oxford: Oxbow.

Bergh, S. 1995. *Landscape of the monuments. A study of the passage tombs in the Cúil Irra region, Co. Sligo, Ireland*. Stockholm: Riksantikvarieämbetet Arkeologiska Undersökningar.

Bird-David, N. 1992. Beyond 'the hunting and gathering mode of subsistence': culture-sensitive observations on the Nayaka and other modern hunter-gatherers. *Man* 27, 19–44.

Bloch, M. 1995. The resurrection of the house amongst the Zafimaniry of Madagascar. In J.

Carsten and S. Hugh-Jones (eds), *About the house; Levi-Strauss and beyond*, 52–71. Cambridge: Cambridge University Press.

Bogaard, A. and Jones, G. 2007. Neolithic farming in Britain and central Europe: contrast or continuity? In A. Whittle and V. Cummings (eds), *Going over: the Mesolithic-Neolithic transition in north-west Europe,* 357–76. London: British Academy.

Bonsall, C. 1997. Coastal adaption in the Mesolithic of Argyll. In G. Ritchie (ed.), *The archaeology of Argyll,* 25–37. Edinburgh: Edinburgh University Press.

Bonsall, C., Sutherland, D.G., Tipping, R.M. and Cherry, J. 1990. The Eskmeals Project: late Mesolithic settlement and environment in north-west England. In C. Bonsall (ed.), *The Mesolithic in Europe,* 175–205. Edinburgh: John Donald.

Bowen, E. 1970. Britain and the British Seas. In D. Moore (ed.), *The Irish Sea province in archaeology and history,* 13–28. Cardiff: Cambrian Archaeological Association.

Bradley, R. 1998a. *The significance of monuments.* London: Routledge.

Bradley, R. 1998b. Ruined buildings, ruined stones: enclosures, tombs and natural places in the Neolithic of south-west England. *World Archaeology* 30:1, 13–22.

Bradley, R. 2000a. *The archaeology of natural places.* London: Routledge.

Bradley, R. 2000b. *The good stones: a new investigation of the Clava cairns.* Edinburgh: Society of Antiquaries of Scotland.

Bradley, R. 2004. *The moon and the bonfire. An investigation of three stone circles in north-east Scotland.* Edinburgh: Society of Antiquaries of Scotland.

Bradley, R. 2005. *Ritual and domestic life in prehistoric Europe.* London: Routledge.

Bradley, R. 2007a. Burning down the house. In A. Whittle and V. Cummings (eds), *Going over: the Mesolithic-Neolithic transition in north-west Europe,* 347–56. London: British Academy.

Bradley, R. 2007b. *The prehistory of Britain and Ireland.* Cambridge: Cambridge University Press.

Bradley, R. and Edmonds, M. 1993. *Interpreting the axe trade: production and exchange in Neolithic Britain.* Cambridge: Cambridge University Press.

Brindley, A. 1999. Irish Grooved Ware. In R. Cleal and A. MacSween (eds), *Grooved Ware in Britain and Ireland,* 23–35. Oxford: Oxbow.

British Archaeology. 2007. *News March/April.* York: Council for British Archaeology.

Brück, J. 1998. In the footsteps of the ancestors. A review of Tilley's *A Phenomenology of Landscape. Archaeological Review from Cambridge* 15, 23–36.

Brück, J. 2004. Material metaphors: the relational construction of identity in Early Bronze Age burials in Ireland and Britain. *Journal of Social Archaeology,* 4, 7–33.

Bryce, T. 1902. On the cairns of Arran – a record of further explorations during the season of 1902. *Proceedings of the Society of Antiquaries of Scotland* 1902, 36–67.

Burenhult, G. 1984. *The archaeology of Carrowmore: environmental archaeology and the megalithic tradition at Carrowmore, Co. Sligo, Ireland.* Stockholm: Institute of Archaeology at the University of Stockholm.

Burl, A. 1995. *A guide to the stone circles of Britain, Ireland and Brittany.* Yale: Yale University Press.

Burrow, S. 1997. *The Neolithic culture of the Isle of Man.* Oxford: British Archaeological Reports.

Burrow, S. 2003. *Catalogue of the Mesolithic and Neolithic collections in the National Museums and Galleries of Wales.* Cardiff: National Museums and Galleries of Wales.

Butter, R. 1999. *Kilmartin: a guide to Scotland's richest prehistoric landscape.* Kilmartin: Kilmartin House Trust.

Carmichael, J., Hubert, J., Reeves, B. and Schande, A. (eds) 1994. *Sacred sites, sacred places.* London: Routledge.

Caseldine, A. 1990. *Environmental archaeology in Wales.* Lampeter: Cambrian Printers.

Chambers, F. 1983. The palaeoecological setting of Cefn Gwernffrwd – a prehistoric complex in mid-Wales. *Proceedings of the Prehistoric Society* 49, 303–16.

Chapman, J. 2000. *Fragmentation in archaeology: people, places and broken objects in the prehistory of south-eastern Europe.* London: Routledge.

Chapman, J. and Gaydarska, B. 2006. *Parts and wholes: fragmentation in prehistoric context.* Oxford: Oxbow.

Chatterton, R. 2006. Ritual. In C. Conneller and G. Warren (eds), *Mesolithic Britain and Ireland. New approaches,* 101–20. Stroud: Tempus.

Childe, V.G. 1930. The origin of the bell-beaker. *Man* 30, 200–1.

Childe, V.G. 1934. Neolithic settlement in the west of Scotland. *Scottish Geographical Magazine* 50, 18–28.

Childe, V.G. 1940. *Prehistoric communities of the British Isles.* Edinburgh: Edinburgh University Press.

Clark, J.G.D. 1952. *Prehistoric Europe: the economic basis.* London: Methuen.

Clark, J.G.D. 1954. *Excavations at Star Carr.* Cambridge: Cambridge University Press.

Cleal, R. and MacSween, A. (eds) 1999. *Grooved Ware in Britain and Ireland.* Oxford: Oxbow.

Clough, T. and Cummins, W. (eds) 1988. *Stone axe studies: volume two.* London: Council for British Archaeology.

Cobb, H. 2007. Mutable materials and the production of persons: reconfiguring understandings of identity in the Mesolithic of the northern Irish Sea basin. *Journal of Iberian Archaeology* 9/10, 123–36.

Cobb, H. 2008. *Media for movement and making the world: An examination of the Mesolithic experience of the world and the Mesolithic to Neolithic transition in the northern Irish Sea basin.* Manchester: Unpublished PhD Thesis.

Cochrane, A. 2006. The simulacra and simulations of Irish Neolithic passage tombs. In I. Russell (ed.), *Images, representations and heritage: moving beyond a modern approach to archaeology,* 251–82. New York: Springer-Kluwer.

Coles, J. 1971. The early settlement of Scotland: excavations at Morton, Fife. *Proceedings of the Prehistoric Society* 37, 284–366.

Collins, A.E.P. 1954. The excavation of a double horned cairn at Audleystown, Co. Down. *Ulster Journal of Archaeology* 17, 7–56.

Collins, A.E.P. 1956. A horned cairn at Ballynichol, Co. Down. *Ulster Journal of Archaeology* 19, 115–20.

Collins, A.E.P. 1976. Dooey's Cairn, Ballymacaldrack, County Antrim. *Ulster Journal of Archaeology* 39, 1–7.

Collins, A.E.P. and Wilson, B.C.S. 1964. The excavation of a court cairn at Ballymacdermot, Co. Armagh. *Ulster Journal of Archaeology* 27, 3–22.

Conneller, C. 2006. Death. In C. Conneller and G. Warren (eds), *Mesolithic Britain and Ireland. New approaches,* 139–64. Stroud: Tempus.

Conneller, C. and Warren, G. (eds) 2006. *Mesolithic Britain and Ireland. New approaches.* Stroud: Tempus.

Cooney, G. 2000. *Landscapes of Neolithic Ireland.* London: Routledge.

Cooney, G. and Grogan, E. 1991. *Irish prehistory: a social perspective*. Dublin: Woodwell.

Cooney, G. and Mandal, S. 1998. *The Irish stone axe project*. Bray: Wordwell.

Cooney, G., Mandal, S. and Byrnes, E. 1999. An Irish stone axe project report: non-porcellanite stone axes in Ulster. *Ulster Journal of Archaeology* 58, 17–31.

Corcoran, J.X.W.P. 1960. The Carlingford culture. *Proceedings of the Prehistoric Society* 7, 98–148.

Corcoran, J.X.W.P. 1969. Excavation of two chambered tombs at Mid Gleniron Farm, Glenluce. *Transactions of the Dumfries and Galloway Natural History and Antiquarian Society* 46, 29–90.

Cormack, W. 1970. A Mesolithic site at Barsalloch, Wigtownshire. *Transactions of the Dumfries and Galloway Natural History and Antiquarian Society* 47, 63–80.

Cormack, W. and Coles, J. 1968. A Mesolithic site at Low Clone, Wigtownshire. *Transactions of the Dumfries and Galloway Natural History and Antiquarian Society* 45, 44–72.

Counihan, C. (ed.) 1999. *Anthropology of food and gender*. London: Routledge.

Cowie, T. and MacSween, A. 1999. Grooved Ware from Scotland: a review. In R. Cleal and A. MacSween (eds), *Grooved Ware in Britain and Ireland*, 48–56. Oxford: Oxbow.

Crawford, O.G.S. 1912. The distribution of early Bronze Age settlements in Britain. *Geographical Journal* 40, 299–303.

Crawford, O.G.S. and Keiller, A. 1928. *Wessex from the air*. Oxford: Clarendon Press.

Cross, S. 2003. Irish Neolithic settlement architecture – a reappraisal. In I. Armit, E. Murphy, E. Nelis and D. Simpson (eds), *Neolithic settlement in Ireland and western Britain*, 195–203. Oxford: Oxbow.

Crown, P. and Wills, W. 1995. Economic intensification and the origins of ceramic containers in the American southwest. In W. Barnett and J. Hoopes (eds), *The emergence of pottery*, 241–54. Washington: Smithsonian.

Cummings, V. 2002a. All cultural things: actual and conceptual monuments in the Neolithic of Western Britain. In C. Scarre (ed.), *Monumentality and landscape in Atlantic Europe*, 107–21. London: Routledge.

Cummings, V. 2002b. Between mountains and sea: a reconsideration of the monuments of south-west Scotland. *Proceedings of the Prehistoric Society* 68, 125–46.

Cummings, V. 2002c. Experiencing texture and touch in the British Neolithic. *Oxford Journal of Archaeology* 21:3, 249–61.

Cummings, V. 2003. Mesolithic world-views of the landscape in western Britain. In L. Larsson, H. Kindgren, K. Knutsson, D. Leoffler and A. Åkerlund (eds), *Mesolithic on the move: papers presented at the Sixth International Conference on the Mesolithic in Europe, Stockholm 2000*, 74–81. Oxford: Oxbow.

Cummings, V. 2004. Connecting the mountains and the sea: the monuments of the eastern Irish Sea zone. In V. Cummings and C. Fowler (eds), *The Neolithic of the Irish Sea: materiality and traditions of practice*, 29–36. Oxford: Oxbow.

Cummings, V. 2007a. From midden to megalith? The Mesolithic/Neolithic transition in western Britain. In A. Whittle and V. Cummings (eds), *Going over: the Mesolithic-Neolithic transition in NW Europe*, 493–510. London: British Academy.

Cummings, V. 2007b. Megalithic journeys: moving around the megalithic landscapes of Neolithic western Britain. In V. Cummings and R. Johnston (eds), *Prehistoric journeys*, 54–63. Oxford: Oxbow.

Cummings, V. 2008. Virtual reality, visual envelopes and characterising landscape. In B. David and J. Thomas (eds), *Handbook of landscape archaeology,* 285–90. Walnut Creek: Left Coast Press.

Cummings, V. and Fowler, C. 2004a. Interpreting the landscape settings of the Manx chambered cairns. In V. Cummings and C. Fowler (eds), *The Neolithic of the Irish Sea: materiality and traditions of practice,* 113–122. Oxford: Oxbow.

Cummings, V. and Fowler, C. 2004b. Introduction: locating *The Neolithic of the Irish Sea: materiality and traditions of practice.* In V. Cummings and C. Fowler (eds), *The Neolithic of the Irish Sea: materiality and traditions of practice,* 1–8. Oxford: Oxbow.

Cummings, V. and Fowler, C. (eds) 2004c. *The Neolithic of the Irish Sea: materiality and traditions of practice.* Oxford: Oxbow.

Cummings V. and Fowler, C. 2007. *From cairn to cemetery: an archaeological investigation of the chambered cairns and early Bronze Age mortuary deposits at Cairnderry and Bargrennan White Cairn, south-west Scotland.* Oxford: British Archaeological Reports.

Cummings, V., Jones, A. and Watson, A. 2002. In between places: axial symmetry and divided space in the monuments of the Black Mountains, south-east Wales. *Cambridge Archaeological Journal* 12:1, 57–70.

Cummings, V. and Robinson, G. 2006. *The Southern Kintyre Project: Interactions across the Irish Sea. Interim Report.* Preston: University of Central Lancashire Interim Reports.

Cummings, V. and Robinson, G. in prep. *The Southern Kintyre Project: the investigation of a prehistoric landscape.*

Cummings, V. and Whittle, A. 2003. Tombs with a view: landscape, monuments and trees. *Antiquity* 77, 255–66.

Cummings, V. and Whittle, A. 2004. *Places of special virtue: megaliths in the Neolithic landscapes of Wales.* Oxford: Oxbow.

Daniel, G. E. 1950. *The prehistoric chamber tombs of England and Wales.* Cambridge: Cambridge University Press.

Darvill, T. 1996. Billown and the Neolithic of the Isle of Man. In T. Darvill and J. Thomas (eds), *Neolithic houses in northwest Europe and beyond,* 112–119. Oxford: Oxbow.

Darvill, T. 2002. White on blonde: quartz pebbles and the use of quartz at Neolithic monuments in the Isle of Man and beyond. In A. Jones and G. MacGregor (eds), *Colouring the past,* 73–91. Oxford: Berg.

Darvill, T. 2003. Billown and the Neolithic of the Isle of Man. In I. Armit, E. Murphy, E. Nelis, and D. Simpson (eds), *Neolithic settlement in Ireland and western Britain,* 112–9. Oxford. Oxbow.

David, A. 1990. Some aspects of the human presence in west Wales during the Mesolithic. In C. Bonsall (ed.), *The Mesolithic in Europe,* 241–53. Edinburgh: John Donald.

David, A. and Walker, E. 2004. Wales during the Mesolithic period. In A. Saville (ed.), *Mesolithic Scotland and its neighbours,* 299–337. Edinburgh: Society of Antiquaries of Scotland.

David, A. and Williams, G. 1995. Stone axe-head manufacture in the Preseli Hills, Wales. *Proceedings of the Prehistoric Society* 61, 433–60.

Davies, O. 1938. Excavations at Mourne Park. *Proceedings of the Belfast Natural History and Antiquarian Society* 1938, 18–26.

Davies, O. 1949. Excavations at the horned cairn of Ballymarlagh, Co. Antrim. *Ulster Journal of Archaeology* 12, 26–42.

Davies, O. and Evans, E. 1933. Excavations at Goward, near Hilltown, County Down. *Proceedings of the Belfast Natural History and Antiquarian Society* 1933, 90–105.

Davies, O. and Paterson, T.G.F. 1937. Excavations at Clontygora large cairn, County Armagh. *Proceedings of the Belfast Natural History and Antiquarian Society* 1937, 19–42.

Davis, M. 1945. Types of megalithic monuments of the Irish Sea and north Channel coastlands: a study in distributions. *Antiquaries Journal* 25, 125–44.

DeMarrais, E., Gosden, C. and Renfrew C. (eds). 2004. *Rethinking materiality: the engagement of mind with the material world*. Cambridge: McDonald Institute for Archaeological Research.

De Valera, D. 1960. The court cairns of Ireland. *Proceedings of the Royal Irish Academy* 60, 1–139.

De Valera, D. and Ó Nualláin, S. 1961. *Survey of the megalithic tombs of Ireland. Volume 1, County Clare*. Dublin: Stationery Office.

De Valera, D. and Ó Nualláin, S. 1964. *Survey of the megalithic tombs of Ireland. Volume 2, County Mayo*. Dublin: Stationery Office.

De Valera, D. and Ó Nualláin, S. 1972. *Survey of the megalithic tombs of Ireland. Volume 3, Counties Galway, Roscommon, Leitrim, Langford, Westmeath, Laoighis, Offaly, Kildare and Cavan*. Dublin: Stationery Office.

Dineley, M. and Dineley, G. 2000. Neolithic ale: barley as a source of malt sugars for fermentation. In A. Fairbairn (ed.), *Plants in Neolithic Britain and beyond*, 137–53. Oxford: Oxbow.

Edmonds, M. 1995. *Stone tools and society*. London: Batsford.

Edmonds, M. 1999. *Ancestral geographies of the Neolithic: landscape, monuments and memory*. London: Routledge.

Edwards, K. 1996. The contribution of Tom Affleck to the study of the Mesolithic of southwest Scotland. In T. Pollard and A. Morrison (eds), *The early prehistory of Scotland*, 108–22. Edinburgh: Edinburgh University Press.

Edwards, K. and Whittington, G. 1997. Vegetation change. In K. Edwards and I. Ralston (eds), *Scotland: environment and archaeology, 8000 BC – AD 1000*, 62–82. Chichester: John Wiley.

Eogan, G. 1986. *Knowth and the passage graves of Ireland*. London: Thames and Hudson.

Eogan, G. and Roche, H. 1999. Grooved Ware from Brugh na Bóinne and its wider context. In R. Cleal and A. MacSween (eds), *Grooved Ware in Britain and Ireland*, 98–111. Oxford: Oxbow.

Evans, C., Pollard, J. and Knight, M. 1999. Life in woods: tree-throws, 'settlement' and forest cognition. *Oxford Journal of Archaeology* 18, 241–54.

Evans, E.E. 1938a. A chambered cairn in Ballyedmond Park, County Down. *Ulster Journal of Archaeology* 1, 49–58.

Evans, E. E. 1938b. Dooey's cairn, Dunloy, County Antrim. *Ulster Journal of Archaeology* 1, 59–78.

Evans, E.E. 1953. *Lyles Hill: a late Neolithic site in county Antrim*. Belfast: Her Majesty's Stationary Office.

Evans, E.E. and Davies, O. 1934. Excavation of a chambered horned cairn at Ballyalton, Co. Down. *Proceedings of the Belfast Natural History and Antiquarian Society* 1934, 79–104.

Evans, E.E. and Davies, O. 1935. Excavation of a chambered horned cairn, Browndod, Co. Antrim. *Proceedings of the Belfast Natural History and Antiquarian Society* 1935, 70–87.

Evans, H. 2004. Where is the Cumbrian Neolithic? In V. Cummings and C. Fowler (eds), *The Neolithic of the Irish Sea: materiality and traditions of practice*, 123–8. Oxford: Oxbow.

Evans, J.G., Limbrey, S. and Cleere, H. (eds) 1975. *The effect of man on the landscape: the highland zone.* London: Council for British Archaeology.

Fairweather, A. and Ralston, I. 1993. The Neolithic timber hall at Balbridie, Grampian region, Scotland: the building, the date, the plant macrofossils. *Antiquity* 67, 313–23.

Fenton, J. 1848. Cromlech at Llanwnda, Pembrokeshire. *Archaeologia Cambrensis* 3, 283–4.

Finlay, N. 2000. Microliths in the making. In R. Young (ed.), *Mesolithic lifeways: current research in Britain and Ireland*, 23–31. Leicester: Leicester University Press.

Finlay, N. 2003. Cache and carry: defining moments in the Irish later Mesolithic. In L. Bevan and J. Moore (eds), *Peopling the Mesolithic in a northern environment*, 87–94. Oxford: British Archaeological Reports.

Finlay, N. 2006. Gender and personhood. In C. Conneller and G. Warren (eds), *Mesolithic Britain and Ireland. New Approaches*, 35–60. Stroud: Tempus.

Fleming, A. 1999. Phenomenology and the megaliths of Wales: a dreaming too far? *Oxford Journal of Archaeology* 18, 119–25.

Fleming, A. 2005. Megaliths and post-modernism: the case of Wales. *Antiquity* 79, 921–32.

Fleure, H. J. 1915. Archaeological problems of the west coast of Britain. *Archaeologia Cambrensis* 15, 405–20.

Fowler, C. 2004. *The archaeology of personhood.* London: Routledge.

Fowler, C. and Cummings, V. 2003. Places of transformation: building monuments from water and stone in the Neolithic of the Irish Sea. *Journal of the Royal Anthropological Institute* 9, 1–20.

Fox, C. 1932. *The personality of Britain.* Cardiff: National Museum of Wales.

Fraser, S. 1998. The public forum and the space between: the materiality of social strategy in the Irish Neolithic. *Proceedings of the Prehistoric Society* 64, 203–24.

Gell, A. 1995. The language of the forest: landscape and phonological iconism in Umeda. In E. Hirsch and M. O'Hanlon (eds), *The anthropology of landscape: perspectives on place and space*, 232–54. Oxford: Oxford University Press.

Gell, A. 1998. *Art and agency: an anthropological theory.* Oxford: Clarendon Press.

Gibson, A. 1999. *The Walton Basin project: excavation and survey in a prehistoric landscape 1993–7.* York: Council for British Archaeology.

Gibson, A. 2002. *Prehistoric pottery in Britain and Ireland.* Stroud: Tempus.

Gibson, A. 2005. *Stonehenge and timber circles.* Stroud: Tempus

Gibson, A. and Woods, A. 1990. *Prehistoric pottery for the archaeologist.* Leicester: Leicester University Press.

Glen, M. 2007. *Mòine Mhòr, the Great Moss.* Lochgilphead: Scottish Natural Heritage.

Green, S. and Zvelebil, M. 1990. The Mesolithic colonization and agricultural transition of south-east Ireland. *Proceedings of the Prehistoric Society* 56, 57–88.

Grimes, W. 1936. The megalithic monuments of Wales. *Proceedings of the Prehistoric Society* 2, 106–39.

Grimes, W. 1948. Pentre Ifan burial chamber, Pembrokeshire. *Archaeologia Cambrensis* 100, 3–23.

Grogan, E. 1996. Neolithic houses in Ireland. In T. Darvill and J. Thomas (eds), *Neolithic houses in northwest Europe and beyond*, 41–60. Oxford: Oxbow.

Harrington and Pierpoint. 1980. Port Charlotte chambered cairn, Islay: an interim note. *Glasgow Archaeological Journal* 1980, 113–5.

Hartwell, B. 1998. The Ballynahatty complex. In A. Gibson and D.D.A. Simpson (eds), *Prehistoric ritual and religion. Essays in Honour of Aubrey Burl*, 32–44. Stroud: Sutton.

Hawkes, J. 1946. *Early Britain*. London: Collins.

Hemp, W. 1926. The Bachwen "cromlech". *Archaeologia Cambrensis* 81, 429–31.

Hemp, W. 1935. The chambered cairn known as Bryn yr Hen Bobl near Plas Newydd, Anglesey. *Archaeologia* 85, 253–92.

Henshall, A. 1963. *The chambered tombs of Scotland volume one*. Edinburgh: Edinburgh University Press.

Henshall, A. 1972. *The chambered tombs of Scotland volume two*. Edinburgh: Edinburgh University Press.

Herity, M. 1974. *Irish passage graves: a study of Neolithic tombs and their builders, 2500–2000 BC*. Dublin: Irish University Press.

Herity, M. 1987. The finds from Irish court tombs. *Proceedings of the Royal Irish Academy* 87c, 103–281.

Herring, I. 1941. The Tamnyrankin cairn: west structure. *Journal of the Royal Society of Antiquaries of Ireland* 71, 31–52.

Heyworth, A. and Kidson, C. 1982. Sea-level changes in southwest England and Wales. *Proceedings of the Geological Association* 93, 91–111.

Hodder, I. (ed.) 1982. *Symbolic and structural archaeology*. Cambridge: Cambridge University Press.

Hodder, I. 1986. *Reading the past*. Cambridge: Cambridge University Press.

Houlder, C. 1968. The henge monuments at Llandegai. *Antiquity*. 42, 216–21.

Ingold, T. 1996. Hunting and gathering as ways of perceiving the environment. In R. Ellen and K. Fukui (eds), *Redefining nature*, 117–55. Oxford: Berg.

Ingold, T. 2000. *The perception of the environment: essays on livelihood, dwelling and skill*. London: Routledge.

Isbister, A. 2000. Burnished haematite and pigment production. In A. Ritchie (ed.), *Neolithic Orkney in its European context*, 191–5. Cambridge: McDonald Institute.

Jardine, W. 1964. Landscape evolution in Galloway. *Transactions of the Dumfries and Galloway Natural History and Antiquarian Society* 20, 1–13.

Jardine, W. 1975. Chronology of the Holocene marine transgression and regression in south-west Scotland. *Boreas* 4, 173–96.

Jones, A. 1999. Local colour: megalithic architecture and colour symbolism in Neolithic Arran. *Oxford Journal of Archaeology* 18, 339–50.

Jones, A. 2002. *Archaeological theory and scientific practice*. Cambridge: Cambridge University Press.

Jones, A. 2003. Technologies of remembrance: memory, materiality and identity in early Bronze Age Scotland. In H. Williams (ed.), *Archaeologies of remembrance: death and memory in past societies*, 65–88. New York: Kluwer Academic/Plenum Publishers.

Jones, G. 2000. Evaluating the importance of cultivation and collecting in Neolithic Britain. In A. Fairbairn (ed.), *Plants in Neolithic Britain and beyond*, 79–90. Oxford: Oxbow.

Jordan, P. 2003. Peopling the Mesolithic: insights from ethnographies of landscape and material culture. In L. Bevan and J. Moore (eds), *Peopling the Mesolithic in a northern environment*, 27–34.

Kador, T. 2007. Stone age motion pictures: an object's perspective. In V. Cummings and R. Johnston (eds), *Prehistoric journeys*, 32–44. Oxford: Oxbow.

Kahn, M. 1990. Stone-faced ancestors: the spatial anchoring of myth in Wamira, Papua New Guinea. *Ethnology* 29, 51–66.

Kan, S. 1989. *Symbolic immortality: the Tlingit potlatch of the nineteenth century.* Washington: Smithsonian.

Karlsson, H. 1997. *Being and post-processual archaeological thinking.* Goteborg: Gotarc Serie C, Arkeologiska Skrifter no. 15.

Kelly, R. 1995. *The foraging spectrum.* Washington: Smithsonian.

Kent, S. 1989. Cross-cultural perceptions of farmers as hunters and the value of meat. In S. Kent (ed.), *The implications of sedentism,* 3–32. Cambridge: Cambridge University Press.

Kimball, M. 2000. Variation and context: ecology and social evolution in Ireland's later Mesolithic. In A. Desmond, G. Johnson, M. McCarthy, J. Sheehan and E. Shee Twohig (eds), *New agendas in Irish prehistory,* 31–47. Bray: Wordwell.

Kinnes, I. 1992. Balnagowan and after: the context of non-megalithic mortuary sites in Scotland. In N. Sharples and A. Sheridan (eds), *Vessels for the ancestors,* 83–103. Edinburgh: Edinburgh University Press.

Kinnes, I. 1995. An innovation backed by great prestige: the instance of the spiral and twenty centuries of stony sleep. In I. Kinnes and G. Varndell (eds), *'Unbaked urns of rudely shape': essays on British and Irish pottery,* 49–54. Oxford: Oxbow.

Leivers, M. 1999. *The architecture and context of mortuary practice in the Neolithic period in north Wales.* Unpublished Ph.D. Thesis: University of Southampton.

Leivers, M., Roberts, J. and Peterson, R. 2002. Bryn yr Hen Bobl, Anglesey: recent fieldwork and a reassessment of excavations in 1935. *Archaeology in Wales* 41, 3–9.

Linnard, W. 2000. *Welsh woods and forests: a history.* Llandysul: Gomer Press.

Lynch, F. 1969a. The contents of excavated tombs in north Wales. In T.G.E. Powell, J.X.W.P. Corcoran, F. Lynch and J.G. Scott, *Megalithic enquiries in the west of Britain,* 149–74. Liverpool: Liverpool University Press.

Lynch, F. 1969b. The megalithic tombs of north Wales. In T.G.E. Powell, J.X.W.P. Corcoran, F. Lynch and J.G. Scott, *Megalithic enquiries in the west of Britain,* 107–48. Liverpool: Liverpool University Press.

Lynch, F. 1972. Portal dolmens in the Nevern Valley, Pembrokeshire. In F. Lynch and C. Burgess (eds), *Prehistoric man in Wales and the west,* 67–84. Bath: Adams and Dart.

Lynch, F. 1975. The impact of the landscape on prehistoric man. In J. Evans, S. Limbrey, and H. Cleere (eds), *The effect of man on the landscape: the highland zone,* 124–27. York: The Council for British Archaeology.

Lynch, F. 1989. Wales and Ireland in prehistory: a fluctuating relationship. *Archaeologia Cambrensis* 138, 1–19.

Lynch, F. 1995. *Gwynydd: a guide to ancient and historic Wales.* Cardiff: CADW.

Lynch, F. 1998. Colour in prehistoric architecture. In A. Gibson and D. Simpson (eds), *Prehistoric ritual and religion,* 62–7. Stroud: Sutton.

Lysaght, P. (ed.) 2002. *Food and celebration: from fasting to feasting.* Ljubljana: ZRC.

MacKie, E. 1963. New excavations on the Monamore Neolithic chambered cairn, Lamlash, Isle of Arran in 1961. *Proceedings of the Society of Antiquaries of Scotland* 97, 1–27.

Marshall, D. and Taylor, I. 1976. The excavation of the chambered cairn at Glenvoidean, Isle of Bute. *Proceedings of the Society of Antiquaries of Scotland* 108, 1–39.

Masters, L. 1973. The Lochhill long cairn. *Antiquity* 47, 96–100.

Masters, L. 1981. Chambered tombs and non-megalithic barrows in Britain. In J. Evans, B. Cunliffe and C. Renfrew (eds), *Antiquity and man,* 161–76. London: Thames and Hudson.

Maynard, D. 1993. Neolithic pit at Carzield, Kirkton, Dumfriesshire. *Transactions of the Dumfries and Galloway Natural History and Antiquarian Society* 68, 25–32.

Mays, S. 1998. *The archaeology of human bones*. London: Routledge.

McCartan, S. 2000. The utilisation of island environments in the Irish Mesolithic: agendas for Rathlin Island. In A. Desmond, G. Johnston, M. McCarthy, J. Sheehan and E. Shee-Twohig (eds), *New agendas in Irish prehistory*, 15–30. Bray: Wordwell.

McCartan, S. 2004. The Mesolithic of the Isle of Man: an island perspective. In A. Saville (ed.), *Mesolithic Scotland and its neighbours*, 271–83. Edinburgh: Society of Antiquaries of Scotland.

McCullagh, R. 1988–9. Excavation at Newton, Islay. *Glasgow Archaeological Journal* 15, 23–51.

McFadyen, L. 2006. Building technologies, quick and slow architectures and early Neolithic long barrow sites in southern Britain. *Archaeological Review from Cambridge* 21, 70–81.

Mellars, P. 1976. Fire ecology, animal populations and man: a study of some ecological relationships in prehistory. *Proceedings of the Prehistoric Society* 42, 15–46.

Mellars, P. 1987. *Excavations on Oronsay*. Edinburgh: Edinburgh University Press.

Mellars, P. and Wilkinson, M. 1980 Fish otoliths as indicators of seasonality in prehistoric shell middens. *Proceedings of the Prehistoric Society* 46, 19–44.

Merleau-Ponty, M. 1962. *Phenomenology of perception*. London: Routledge.

Meskell, L. (ed.) 2005a. *Archaeologies of materiality*. Oxford: Blackwell.

Meskell, L. 2005b. Introduction: object orientations. In L. Meskell (ed.), *Archaeologies of materiality*, 1–17. Oxford: Blackwell.

Milles, A., Gardner N. and Williams, D. (eds) 1989. *The beginnings of agriculture*. Oxford: British Archaeological Reports.

Milner, N., Craig, O., Bailey, G., Pedersen, K. and Andersen, S. 2004. Something fishy in the Neolithic? A re-evaluation of stable isotope analysis of Mesolithic and Neolithic coastal populations. *Antiquity* 78, 9–22.

Mithen, S. 1994. The Mesolithic age. In B. Cunliffe (ed.), *Prehistoric Europe: an illustrated history*, 79–135. Oxford: Oxford University Press.

Mithen, S. 2000a. *Hunter-gatherer landscape archaeology: the Southern Hebrides Mesolithic project*. Oxford: Oxbow.

Mithen, S. 2000b. Mesolithic sedentism on Oronsay: chronological evidence from adjacent islands in the southern Hebrides. *Antiquity* 74, 289–304.

Mithen, S., Pirie, A., Smith, S. and Wicks, K. 2007. The Mesolithic-Neolithic transition in western Scotland: a review and new evidence from Tiree. In A. Whittle and V. Cummings (eds), *Going over: the Mesolithic-Neolithic transition in north-west Europe*, 511–42. London: British Academy.

Mogey, J.M. 1941. The 'Druid Stone', Ballintoy, Co. Antrim. *Ulster Journal of Archaeology* 4, 49–56.

Moore, D. (ed.) 1970. *The Irish Sea province in archaeology and history*. Cardiff: Cambrian Archaeological Association.

Moore, D. 2004. Hostilities in early Neolithic Ireland: trouble with new neighbours – the evidence from Ballyharry, County Antrim. In A. Gibson and A. Sheridan (eds), *From sickles to circles: Britain and Ireland at the time of Stonehenge*, 142–54. Stroud: Tempus.

Morphy, H. 1995. Landscape and the reproduction of the ancestral past. In E. Hirsch and M.

O'Hanlon (eds), *The anthropology of landscape: perspectives on place and space*, 184–209. Oxford: Oxford University Press.

Murray, J. 1992. The Bargrennan group of chambered cairns: circumstance and context. In N. Sharples and A. Sheridan (eds), *Vessels for the ancestors*, 33–48. Edinburgh: Edinburgh University Press.

Nelis, E. 2004. Neolithic flint-work from the north of Ireland: some thoughts on prominent tool types and their production. In A. Gibson and A. Sheridan (eds), *From sickles to circles: Britain and Ireland at the time of Stonehenge*, 155–75. Stroud: Tempus.

Noble, G. 2005. Ancestry, farming and the changing architecture of the Clyde cairns of south-west Scotland. In V. Cummings and M. Pannett (eds), *Set in stone*, 25–36. Oxford: Oxbow.

Noble, G. 2007. Monumental journeys: Neolithic monument complexes and routeways across Scotland. In V. Cummings and R. Johnston (eds), *Prehistoric journeys*, 64–74. Oxford: Oxbow.

O'Brien, W. 1993. Aspects of wedge tomb chronology. In E. Shee Twohig and M. Ronayne (eds), *Past perceptions: the prehistoric archaeology of south-west Ireland*, 63–74. Cork: Cork University Press.

O'Kelly, M. 1982. *Newgrange*. London: Thames and Hudson.

O'Kelly, M. 1989. *Early Ireland*. Cambridge: Cambridge University Press.

Ó Nualláin, S. 1972. A Neolithic house at Ballyglass near Ballycastle, Co. Mayo. *Journal of the Royal Society of Antiquaries of Ireland* 102, 49–57.

Ó Nualláin, S. 1983. Irish portal tombs: topography, siting and distribution. *Journal of the Royal Society of Antiquaries of Ireland* 113, 75–105.

Oswald, A., Dyer, C. and Barber, M. 2001. *The creation of monuments: Neolithic causewayed enclosures in the British Isles*. London: English Heritage.

Parker Pearson, M. (ed.) 2003. *Food, culture and identity in the Neolithic and early Bronze Age*. Oxford: British Archaeological Reports.

Parker Pearson, M. and Ramilisonina 1998. Stonehenge for the ancestors: the stones pass on the message. *Antiquity* 72, 308–26.

Pearce, M., Garton, D. and Howard, A. 1997. *Dumping the dead in the late Neolithic*. Unpublished paper presented at TAG Bournemouth, December 1997.

Peterson, R. 2003. *Neolithic pottery from Wales: traditions of construction and use*. Oxford: British Archaeological Reports.

Peterson, R. 2004. Away from the numbers: diversity and invisibility in late Neolithic Wales. In V. Cummings and C. Fowler (eds), *The Neolithic of the Irish Sea: materiality and traditions of practice*, 191–201. Oxford: Oxbow.

Phillips, C. W. 1936. An examination of the Ty Newydd chambered tomb, Llanfaelog, Anglesey. *Archaeologia Cambrensis* 91, 93–99.

Piggott, S. 1931. The Neolithic pottery of the British Isles. *Archaeological Journal* 88, 67–158.

Piggott, S. 1932. The Mull Hill circle, Isle of Man, and its pottery. *Antiquaries Journal* 12, 146–57.

Piggott, S. 1954. *The Neolithic cultures of the British Isles*. Cambridge: Cambridge University Press.

Piggott, S. and Powell, T.G.E. 1949. The excavation of three Neolithic chambered tombs in Galloway. *Proceedings of the Society of Antiquaries of Scotland* 83, 103–61.

Pollard, J. 2000a. Ancestral places in the Mesolithic landscape. *Archaeological Review from Cambridge* 17, 123–38.

Pollard, J. 2000b. Neolithic occupation practices and social ecologies from Rinyo to Clacton. In A. Ritchie (ed.), *Neolithic Orkney in its European context*, 363–69. Cambridge: McDonald Institute for Archaeological Research.

Pollard, J. and Gillings, M. 1998. Romancing the stones. Towards a virtual and elemental Avebury. *Archaeological Dialogues* 2, 143–64.

Powell, T.G.E. 1973. Excavations at the megalithic chambered cairn at Dyffryn Ardudwy, Merioneth, Wales. *Archaeologia* 104, 1–50.

Powell, T.G.E., Corcoran, J.X.W.P., Lynch, F. and Scott, J.G. 1969. *Megalithic enquiries in the west of Britain*. Liverpool: Liverpool University Press.

Price, B. 2007. Journeying into different realms. Travel, pilgrimage and rites of passage at Graig Lwyd. In V. Cummings and R. Johnston (eds), *Prehistoric journeys*, 85–101. Oxford: Oxbow.

Ray, K. 2004. Axes, kula and things that were 'good to think' in the Neolithic of the Irish Sea. In V. Cummings and C. Fowler (eds), *The Neolithic of the Irish Sea: materiality and traditions of practice*, 160–173. Oxford: Oxbow.

Renfrew, C. 1973. Monuments, mobilisation and social organisation in Neolithic Wessex. In C. Renfrew (ed.), *The explanation of culture change*, 539–58.

Renfrew, C. 1979. *Investigations in Orkney*. London: Society of Antiquaries.

Richards, C. 1996. Henges and water: towards an elemental understanding of monumentality and landscape in late Neolithic Britain. *Journal of Material Culture* 1, 313–36.

Richards, C. 2004. Labouring with monuments: constructing the dolmen at Carreg Samson, south-west Wales. In V. Cummings and C. Fowler (eds), *The Neolithic of the Irish Sea: materiality and traditions of practice*, 72–80. Oxford: Oxbow.

Richards, C. and Thomas, J. 1984. Ritual activity and structured deposition in later Neolithic Wessex. In R. Bradley and J. Gardiner (eds), *Neolithic studies*, 189–218. Oxford: British Archaeological Reports.

Richards, M. 2003. Explaining the dietary isotope evidence for the rapid adoption of the Neolithic in Britain. In M Parker Pearson (ed.), *Food, culture and identity in the Neolithic and Early Bronze Age*, 31–36. Oxford: BAR.

Richards, M. and Hedges, R. 1999. A Neolithic revolution? New evidence of diet in the British Neolithic. *Antiquity* 73, 891–7.

Richards, M. and Mellars, P. 1998. Stable isotopes and the seasonality of the Oronsay middens. *Antiquity* 72, 178–84.

Ritchie, G. 1997. Early settlement in Argyll. In G. Ritchie (ed.), *The archaeology of Argyll*, 38–66. Edinburgh: Edinburgh University Press.

Robinson, G. 2007. *The prehistoric island landscape of Scilly*. Oxford: British Archaeological Reports.

Robinson, M. 2000. Coleopteran evidence for the elm decline, Neolithic activity in woodland, clearance and the use of the landscape. In A. Fairbairn (ed.), *Plants in Neolithic Britain and beyond*, 27–36. Oxford: Oxbow.

Robb, J. 2004 The extended artefact and the monumental economy: a methodology for material agency. In E. DeMarrais, C. Gosden, and C. Renfrew (eds), *Rethinking materiality: the*

engagement of mind with the material world, 131–39. Cambridge: McDonald Institute for
   Archaeological Research.

Rowley Conwy, P. 2004. How the west was lost. A reconsideration of the agricultural origins
   in Britain, Ireland and southern Scandinavia. *Current Anthropology* 45, 83–113.

Ruggles, C. 1999. *Astronomy in Prehistoric Britain and Ireland*. Yale: Yale University Press.

Saville, A. 1999. A cache of flint axeheads and other flint artefacts from Auchenhoan, near
   Campbeltown, Kintyre, Scotland. *Proceedings of the Prehistoric Society* 65, 83–123.

Saville, A. 2004. The material culture of Mesolithic Scotland. In A. Saville (ed.), *Mesolithic Scotland
   and its neighbours*, 185–219. Edinburgh: Society of Antiquaries of Scotland.

Scarre, C. 2004. Displaying the stones: the materiality of 'megalithic' monuments. In E.
   DeMarrais, C. Gosden, and C. Renfrew (eds), *Rethinking materiality: the engagement of mind with
   the material world*, 141–52. Cambridge: McDonald Institute for Archaeological Research.

Schulting, R. 2000. New AMS dates from the Lambourn long barrow and the question of the
   earliest Neolithic in southern England: repacking the Neolithic package? *Oxford Journal
   of Archaeology* 19, 25–35.

Schulting, R. 2004. An Irish Sea change: some implications for the Mesolithic-Neolithic
   transition. In V. Cummings and C. Fowler (eds), *The Neolithic of the Irish Sea: materiality
   and traditions of practice*, 22–28. Oxford: Oxbow.

Schulting, R. and Richards, M. 2002a. Finding the coastal Mesolithic in southwest Britain: AMS
   dates and stable isotope results on human remains from Caldey Island, south Wales.
   Antiquity 76, 1011–25.

Schulting, R. and Richards, M. 2002b. The wet, the wild and the domesticated: the Mesolithic-
   Neolithic transition on the west coast of Scotland. *European Journal of Archaeology* 5,
   147–89.

Schulting, R. and Richards, M. 2006. Against the grain? A response to Milner *et al* (2004).
   Antiquity 80, 444–58.

Schulting, R. and Wysocki, M. 2005. "In this chambered tumulus were found cleft skulls...":
   an assessment of the evidence for cranial trauma in the British Neolithic. *Proceedings of
   the Prehistoric Society* 71, 107–38.

Scott, J. 1954. The chambered cairn at Beacharra, Kintyre, Argyll. *Proceedings of the Prehistoric
   Society* 9, 134–58.

Scott, J. 1955. The excavation of the chambered cairn at Brackley, Kintyre. *Proceedings of the
   Society of Antiquaries of Scotland* 89, 22–59.

Scott, J. 1960. The excavation of the chambered cairn at Crarae, Loch Fyneside, mid Argyll.
   Proceedings of the Society of Antiquaries of Scotland 94, 1–27.

Scott, J. 1969. The Clyde cairns of Scotland. In T.G.E. Powell, J.X.W.P. Corcoran, F. Lynch
   and J.G. Scott, *Megalithic enquiries in the west of Britain*, 175–222. Liverpool: Liverpool
   University Press.

Scott, J. 1973. The Clyde cairns of Scotland. In G. Daniel and P. Kjærum (eds), *Megalithic graves
   and ritual*, 117–28. Copenhagen: Jutland Archaeological Society.

Scott, J. 1992. Mortuary structures and megaliths. In N. Sharples and A. Sheridan (eds), *Vessels
   for the ancestors*, 104–19. Edinburgh: Edinburgh University Press.

Scott, W. 1933. The chambered tomb of Pant y Saer, Anglesey. *Archaeologia Cambrensis* 38,
   185–228.

Shanks, M. and Tilley, C. 1982. Ideology, symbolic power and ritual communication: a reinterpretation of Neolithic mortuary practices. In I. Hodder (ed), *Symbolic and structural archaeology*, 129–54.

Shee Twohig, E. 1981. *The megalithic art of western Europe*. Oxford: Clarendon Press.

Shee Twohig, E. 1990. *Irish megalithic tombs*. Princes Risborough: Shire.

Sheridan, A. 1986. Porcellanite artefacts: a new survey. *Ulster Journal of Archaeology* 49, 19–32.

Sheridan, A. 1992. Scottish stone axeheads: some new work and recent discoveries. In N. Sharples and A. Sheridan (eds), *Vessels for the Ancestors: essays on the Neolithic of Britain and Ireland in honour of Audrey Henshall*, 194–212. Edinburgh: Edinburgh University Press.

Sheridan, A. 1995. Irish Neolithic pottery: the story in 1995. In I. Kinnes and G. Varndell (eds), *'Unbaked urns of rudely shape': essays on British and Irish pottery*, 3–22. Oxford: Oxbow.

Sheridan, A. 2000. Achnacreebeag and its French connections: vive the 'auld alliance'. In J. C. Henderson (ed.),*The prehistory and early history of Atlantic Europe*, 1–16. Oxford: British Archaeological Reports.

Sheridan, A. 2004. Neolithic connections along and across the Irish Sea. In V. Cummings and C. Fowler (eds), *The Neolithic of the Irish Sea: materiality and traditions of practice*, 9–21. Oxford: Oxbow.

Sheridan, A. 2007a. Green treasures from the magic mountains. *British Archaeology* 96.

Sheridan, A. 2007b. The pottery. In In V. Cummings and C. Fowler, *Cairnderry and Bargrennan*, 97–107. Oxford: British Archaeological Reports.

Sheridan, A., Cooney, G. and Grogan, E. 1992. Stone axe studies in Ireland. *Proceedings of the Prehistoric Society* 58, 389–416.

Shepherd, A. 2000. Skara Brae: expressing identity in a Neolithic community. In A. Ritchie (ed.), *Neolithic Orkney in its European context*, 139–58. Cambridge: McDonald Institute.

Simpson, D. 1995. The Neolithic settlement site at Ballygalley, Co. Antrim. In E. Grogan and C. Mount (eds), *Annus Archaeologiae*, 37–44. Dublin: Office of Public Works.

Simpson, D. 1996. The Ballygalley houses, Co. Antrim, Ireland. In T. Darvill and J. Thomas (eds), *Neolithic houses in northwest Europe and beyond*, 123–32. Oxford: Oxbow.

Smith, C. and Lynch, F. 1987. *Trefignath and Din Dryfol: the excavation of two megalithic tombs in Anglesey*. Bangor: Cambrian Archaeological Association.

Sturt, F. 2004. Fishing for memory: lived space and the early Neolithic of Orkney. In V. Cummings and A. Pannett (eds), *Set in stone*, 68–80. Oxford: Oxbow.

Sutherland, D. 1997. The environment of Argyll. In G. Ritchie (ed.), *The archaeology of Argyll*, 10–24. Edinburgh: Edinburgh University Press.

Taçon, P. 1991. The power of stone: symbolic aspects of stone use and tool development in Western Arnhem Land, Australia. *Antiquity* 65, 192–207.

Taylor, K. 1996. The rough and the smooth: axe polishers of the middle Neolithic. In T. Pollard and A. Morrison (eds), *The early prehistory of Scotland*, 225–36. Edinburgh: Edinburgh University Press.

Thomas, J. 1988. Neolithic explanations revisited: the Mesolithic-Neolithic transition in Britain and south Scandinavia. *Proceedings of the Prehistoric Society* 54, 59–66.

Thomas, J. 1996. *Time, culture and identity: an interpretive archaeology*. London: Routledge.

Thomas, J. 1999. *Understanding the Neolithic*. London: Routledge.

Thomas, J. 2003. Thoughts on the 'repacked' Neolithic revolution. *Antiquity* 77, 67–74.

Thomas, J. 2006a. On the origins and development of cursus monuments in Britain. *Proceedings of the Prehistoric Society* 72, 229–42.

Thomas, J. 2006b. *Place and memory: excavations at the Pict's Knowe, Holywood and Holm.* Oxford: Oxbow.

Thomas, J. forthcoming. *Excavations at Dunragit, Dumfries and Galloway.*

Thomas, J. and Whittle, A. 1986. Anatomy of a tomb – West Kennet revisited. *Oxford Journal of Archaeology* 5, 129–56.

Tilley, C. 1994. *A phenomenology of landscape.* Oxford: Berg.

Tilley, C. 1996a. *Ethnography of the Neolithic.* Cambridge: Cambridge University Press.

Tilley, C. 1996b. The powers of rocks: topography and monument construction on Bodmin Moor. *World Archaeology* 28, 161–76.

Tilley, C. 2007. The Neolithic sensory revolution: monumentality and the experience of landscape. In A. Whittle and V. Cummings (eds), *Going over: the Mesolithic-Neolithic transition in north-west Europe.* London: British Academy.

Tipping, R. 2004. Interpretive issues concerning the driving forces of vegetation change in the Early Holocene of the British Isles. In A. Saville (ed.), *Mesolithic Scotland and its neighbours,* 45–54. Edinburgh: Society of Antiquaries of Scotland.

Tolan-Smith, C. 2001. *The caves of Mid Argyll.* Edinburgh: Society of Antiquaries of Scotland.

Tringham, R. 2005. Weaving house life and death into places: a blueprint for a hypermedia narrative. In D. Bailey, A. Whittle and V. Cummings (eds), *(Un)settling the Neolithic,* 98–111. Oxford: Oxbow

Vyner, B. 2001. Clegyr Boia: a potential Neolithic enclosure and associated monuments on the St David's peninsula, southwest Wales. In T. Darvill and J. Thomas (eds), *Neolithic enclosures in Atlantic northwest Europe,* 78–90. Oxford: Oxbow.

Waddell, J. 1991. The Irish Sea in prehistory. *The Journal of Irish Archaeology* 6, 29–40.

Warren, G. 2005. *Mesolithic lives in Scotland.* Stroud: Tempus.

Warren, G. 2006. Technology. In C. Conneller and G. Warren (eds), *Mesolithic Britain and Ireland: new approaches,* 13–34. Stroud: Tempus.

Warren, G. 2007. Mesolithic myths. In A. Whittle and V. Cummings (eds), *Going over: the Mesolithic-Neolithic transition in north-west Europe,* 311–28. London: British Academy.

Waterman, D. 1965. The court cairn at Annaghmare, Co. Armagh. *Ulster Journal of Archaeology* 28, 3–46.

Wheatley, D. and Gillings, M. 2002. *Spatial technology and archaeology: archaeological applications of GIS.* London: Taylor and Francis.

Whitley, J. 2002. Too Many Ancestors. *Antiquity* 76, 119–26.

Whittle, A. 1995. Gifts from the earth: symbolic dimensions of the use and production of Neolithic flint and stone axes. *Archaeologia Polona* 33, 247–59.

Whittle, A. 1990. A model for the Mesolithic-Neolithic transition in the upper Kennet valley, north Wiltshire. *Proceedings of the Prehistoric Society* 56, 101–10.

Whittle, A. 1996. *Europe in the Neolithic: the creation of new worlds.* Cambridge: Cambridge University Press.

Whittle, A. 1997. Moving on and moving around: Neolithic settlement mobility. In P. Topping (ed.), *Neolithic landscapes,* 15–22. Oxford: Oxbow.

Whittle, A. 2003. *The archaeology of people.* London: Routledge.

Whittle, A. 2004. Stones that float to the sky: portal dolmens and their landscapes of memory and myth. In V. Cummings and C. Fowler (eds), *The Neolithic of the Irish Sea: materiality and traditions of practice*, 81–90. Oxford: Oxbow.

Whittle, A. and Cummings, V. (eds) 2007. *Going over: the Mesolithic-Neolithic transition in north-west Europe*. London: British Academy.

Whittle, A., Pollard, J. and Grigson, C. 1999. *Harmony of symbols: the Windmill Hill causewayed enclosure, Wiltshire*. Oxford: Oxbow.

Wickham-Jones, C. 1986. The procurement and use of stone for flaked tools in prehistoric Scotland. *Proceedings of the Society of Antiquaries of Scotland* 116, 1–10.

Wickham-Jones, C. 2004. Structural evidence in the Scottish Mesolithic. In A. Saville (ed.), *Mesolithic Scotland and its neighbours*, 229–43. Edinburgh: Society of Antiquaries of Scotland.

Wickham-Jones, C. and Collins, G. 1978. The sources of flint and chert in northern Britain. *Proceedings of the Society of Antiquaries of Scotland* 109, 7–21.

Williams, A. 1953. Clegyr Boia, St. David's (Pemb.): excavation in 1943. *Archaeologia Cambrensis* 102, 20–47.

Williams, J. 1970. Neolithic axes in Dumfries and Galloway. *Transactions of the Dumfries and Galloway Natural History and Antiquarian Society* 47, 111–22.

Williams, E. 1989. Dating the introduction of food production into Britain and Ireland. *Antiquity* 63, 510–21.

Williams Thorpe, O. and Thorpe, R. 1984. The distribution and sources of archaeological pitchstone in Britain. *Journal of Archaeological Science* 11, 1–34.

Woodcock, J. 2004. The early Bronze age on the Isle of Man: back into the mainstream? In V. Cummings and C. Fowler (eds), *The Neolithic of the Irish Sea: materiality and traditions of practice,* 214–23. Oxford: Oxbow.

Woodman, P. 1977. Recent excavations at Newferry, Co. Amtrim. *Proceedings of the Prehistoric Society* 43, 155–99.

Woodman, P. 1986. Problems of the colonisation of Ireland. *Ulster Journal of Archaeology* 49, 7–17.

Woodman, P. 2004. Some problems and perspectives: reviewing aspects of the Mesolithic period in Ireland. In A. Saville (ed.), *Mesolithic Scotland and its neighbours*, 285–98. Edinburgh: Society of Antiquaries of Scotland.

Woodman, P. C., Anderson, E. and Finley, N. 1999. *Excavations at Ferriter's Cove 1983–95: last foragers, first farmers in the Dingle Peninsula*. Bray: Wordwell.

Woodman, P. and McCarthy, M. 2003. Contemplating some awful(ly interesting) vistas: importing cattle and red deer into prehistoric Ireland. In I. Armit, E. Murphy, E. Nelis and D. Simpson (eds), *Neolithic settlement in Ireland and western Britain,* 31–39. Oxford: Oxbow.

Zvelebil, M. and Rowley Conwy, P. 1986. Foragers and farmers in Atlantic Europe. In M. Zvelebil (ed.), *Hunters in transition*, 67–96. Cambridge: Cambridge University Press.

Index